D1389941

ROALD DAHL

ROALD DAHL

A Biography

JEREMY TREGLOWN

faber and faber

LONDON · BOSTON

First published in 1994
by Faber and Faber Limited
3 Queen Square London WC1N 3AU

Phototypeset by Intype Ltd, London
Printed in England by Clays Ltd, St Ives Plc

All rights reserved

© Jeremy Treglown, 1994

Jeremy Treglown is hereby identified as the author of this work
in accordance with Section 77 of the Copyright, Designs and
Patents Act 1988

A CIP record for this book is available from the British
Library

ISBN 0-571-16573-7

2 4 6 8 10 9 7 5 3 1

To Fleur, Grace and Sam

Contents

Illustrations

Preface and Acknowledgements

In the mid-1980s, Roald Dahl published two autobiographical books for children: *Boy*, about his childhood, and *Going Solo*, which takes the story up to his departure for Washington at the end of 1941. He was helped with them by his most recent US editor, Stephen Roxburgh, whom he subsequently authorized to write a full biography. Later, Dahl fell out with Roxburgh over his editing of *Matilda*,[1] and the project was abandoned.

After Dahl's death in November 1990, responsibility for choosing a new biographer fell to the third of his four surviving children, Ophelia.[2] She decided that she would in due course write the book herself, and her stepmother Felicity Dahl (the author's widow by his second marriage) asked close relatives not to co-operate in any similar project. They are a tightly-knit family, centred on Dahl's old home, Gipsy House, in Great Missenden, Buckinghamshire, where Mrs Dahl still lives and from which she runs both her husband's literary estate and a charitable foundation named after him. Readers may ask the question I often put to myself when I began researching the book: should I have given up and gone away?

Morally, I reckoned that quite apart from his interest as a hugely successful writer, Dahl was so active in encouraging his own, often controversial, public myth that it would not be wrong for an outsider to look into it. I have tried to be tactful in various ways, while assuming that the family and friends of so quarrelsome a man are used to the fact that not all that is said about him is admiring. And I have respected the stipulations of those I have interviewed. Most of the people who spoke to me did so unconditionally, but some asked me to leave certain of their remarks unattributed, and a few – not the most critical of Dahl – wanted to remain anonymous.

In practical terms, the fact that the book was 'unauthorized' wasn't as much of an obstacle to research as I feared it might be when I started. Most of Dahl's acquaintances whom I approached agreed to talk to me, from people who were at school with him to those who edited his last books. One interview led to another and, as time went by, some members of the family decided to meet me after all. I had, of course, read the autobiography of Dahl's wife of thirty years, Patricia Neal, *As I Am* (1988), and the moving fictionalized memoir, *Working for Love*, published in the same year by their eldest surviving daughter, Tessa Dahl. Early in 1992, Patricia Neal allowed me to interview her at her Manhattan apartment, and about a year later we spent time together in London and Great Missenden. Soon afterwards, I talked at some length to both Tessa Dahl and her younger sister Lucy. I also interviewed, among the many other people listed below, the actress Annabella (Suzanne Charpentier), whom Dahl met in 1944 and to whom he remained close for the rest of his life, and Dennis Pearl, a friend for even longer, and eventually a relative by marriage.

There was another route to Roald Dahl, or set of routes: his letters. He was a voluble correspondent, and because he lived and worked in both the USA and Britain, his friendships, as well as his dealings with his publishers, were often carried on by mail. In the 1940s and 1950s he was one of the protégés of a US newspaper owner and philanthropist, Charles Marsh, whose secretary, now his widow, Claudia, kept both sides of their substantial correspondence and gave me access to it. And for thirty years from the day when the publisher Alfred Knopf first read Dahl's *New Yorker* story 'Taste' and signed him up for a book, Knopf's staff kept their letters, memos, readers' reports, legal agreements and other files, which are now at the Harry Ransom Humanities Research Center at the University of Texas, Austin. I read Dahl's exchanges with some other publishers too (particularly Farrar Straus Giroux), and those with Walt Disney and the BBC. I was fortunate in being able to discuss some of this correspondence with people who were involved: especially Claudia Marsh, and Dahl's most important editors: Virginie Fowler Elbert, Robert Gottlieb and Stephen Roxburgh.

On pages 258–60 I make other acknowledgements both to individuals and to institutions: people who had met Dahl and who wrote to me or spoke to me on the phone, editors of magazines in which his work appeared, libraries which hold materials about him, his foreign publishers, and so on – an alarming number of debts for so small a book. I also acknowledge there the owners of copyrights in materials from which I have quoted. My warmest thanks, however, go to those who knew Dahl or an aspect of his life well, and who agreed to be interviewed – in some cases more than once. Apart from those already mentioned, they are: Liz Attenborough, Sir Isaiah Berlin, Robert and Helen Bernstein, Quentin Blake, Harold Jack Bloom, John Bradburn, Amanda Conquy, Camilla Corbin, Betsy Drake, Creekmore Fath, Colin Fox, Martha Gellhorn, Brough Girling, Edmund and Marian Goodman, Maria Tucci Gottlieb, Valerie Eaton Griffith, Antoinette Haskell, Douglas Highton, Angela Kirwan Hogg, Robin Hogg, Ken Hughes, Alice Keene, Tony Lacey, Tom Maschler, Peter Mayer, David Ogilvy, Antony Pegg, Charles Pick, Ian Rankin, Alastair Reid, Gerald Savory, Sir David Sells, Roger Straus, Mel Stuart, Kenneth Till, Rayner Unwin and Kaye Webb.

Several of these people also gave time to reading and commenting on drafts – of the whole book in the cases of Patricia Neal and Dennis Pearl, and of individual sections in those of Sir Isaiah Berlin, Quentin Blake, Robert Gottlieb, Valerie Eaton Griffith and Alice Keene. I am grateful for their suggestions and factual corrections. Any mistakes which remain are, of course, my own.

One of the book's subjects is the creative role of publishers' editors. So I am even more aware than I anyway would have been of my debt to Susanne McDadd and Julian Loose at Faber & Faber, who suggested that I write it and who, along with Stephen Roxburgh and John Glusman at Farrar Straus Giroux and my agent Deborah Rogers, made useful criticisms of successive drafts. My friend and former *TLS* colleague, Alan Hollinghurst, also read and commented helpfully on the typescript.

Among the best editors I know is my wife, Holly, but that is the least I have to thank her for.

1

Almost Anything You Could Say about Him Would Be True

Diplomats often receive odd propositions, so on the face of it there was nothing unusually unusual about the contents of a letter sent to the British Embassy in Washington DC in the spring of 1944, with the request that it should be passed to the Ambassador, the then Lord Halifax. The correspondent said he thought that Halifax might like to help him write a school textbook. Its aim would be 'to improve the sex stance of American male juvenility which grows in the dense New England area called the Preparatory School district'.[1] Its model was to be the mores of the English public school. This was where the fourth Viscount Halifax (Eton and Christ Church) came in. The correspondent claimed to regard him as a perfect example of English virility.

A reply came a week later under the thick wax Embassy seal, with a covering note from a junior Embassy official, who said he had passed the letter to Lord Halifax that morning. The Ambassador had read it more than once, the official claimed, and the correspondent would doubtless find his answer very satisfactory.

The enclosure was long and enthusiastic. It could have been written by a schoolboy. It spoke of Halifax's excitement at this opportunity of communicating to others his deep experience of the subject. Halifax was widely travelled, the letter said, and had even been accused of libertinism. Admittedly, that was in his younger

I

days, 'when I was in the habit of pleasuring others (not to mention myself) at least once every fourteen days.' Even so, he had maintained what he regarded as an unusually vigorous sex-life, and would be delighted to communicate the secrets of his success to the young. 'As you say, I would improve their stance. I would teach them to slice and to hook, to play a low ball into wind and a backspin onto the green right beside the hole.'

April 1944 might not have seemed the best time for such a project. The Allied invasion of France was only six weeks away. Day and night, the US Air Force and the RAF were bombing German cities and Italian ports. In the Pacific, there were many more islands to fight over before the atom bomb would bring Japan to surrender in August 1945. And while human beings were killing each other in tens of thousands, there was the question of what would happen once they stopped. The Allies were by now confident of victory, and in Washington, London and Moscow, politicians were drawing provisional maps of the post-war world. It was also election year in the USA. Roosevelt, already in his unprecedented third term of office, was standing for a fourth that autumn. But his policies, and particularly his support for Britain, were far from universally popular with voters. In the Wisconsin primary early in April, the internationalist presidential candidate Wendell Willkie, whose support of military loans to Britain had earned him the nickname 'the American Beaverbrook', was sensationally defeated.

These were among the matters which the British Ambassador, Lord Halifax, formerly Foreign Secretary and before that Viceroy of India, was occupied in analysing, together with his staff, and reporting on to London.[2] Yet meanwhile, the correspondence about sex education went in and out of the Embassy. So, for example, on 16 April Halifax told Whitehall that Willkie's downfall was widely seen in the USA as a victory for isolationism, and also sent news of other matters: US opinion about the imminent betrayal of Poland, and the Vice-President's forthcoming trip to China.[3] The following day, a long-suffering secretary turned to the matter of 'male juvenility'.

Except of course that Halifax's correspondence wasn't entirely, or even at all, his own. His official dispatches, like those of any senior diplomat, were for the most part put together by his staff: the 'weekly summaries', for example, by the young Oxford political philosopher Isaiah Berlin, who had been seconded from the Ministry of Information. The ambassador added some finishing touches and sent them on. As for the enquiry about English public-school sexuality, it was part of an extended joke of which Halifax was completely unaware, and in which his own part was played by a young member of the Embassy staff. Readers of *My Uncle Oswald* will have recognized him as Roald Dahl.

Dahl had been invalided out of active service as a Royal Air Force fighter pilot after surviving the desperate, lost battle for Greece. He had come to Washington as Assistant Air Attaché two years previously at the beginning of 1942, when he was twenty-five. Real live six foot six, handsome, articulate and battle-hardened heroes were rare at the time in the USA, which had only recently entered the war. Later, they were in plentiful supply – so much so that by 1944, Dahl's practical joking may have been prompted by a sense both that he was excluded from the main action, and that he was no longer as special as he had once seemed (a feeling he disliked even more than most people). But there was anyway something in him which made him continually look for ways of regressing to the carefree childhood he had enjoyed until he was four, when both his elder sister and his father had suddenly died.[4]

His partner in the joke, as in many other exploits frivolous and otherwise, was a man who had become his surrogate father – one of several such figures in his life, but the most important of them. Charles Marsh was in his mid-fifties when Dahl met him in Washington: a self-made multi-millionaire oil tycoon, newspaper owner, art collector and power broker. Almost as tall as Dahl, he was – according to the observer's standpoint – a man of deep charm or a philandering chancer, an idealist or a fantasist, a fascinating talker or a self-regarding bore. Dahl had been told by the Embassy to cultivate him, partly because Marsh was powerful, and partly because he was a friend of the radical – and therefore to many eyes, suspect – US Vice-President Henry Wallace. They took an instant liking to each other, and Marsh became a lasting role model to the younger man.

Another protégé of Marsh's was the future President, Lyndon Johnson. In his biography of Johnson, Robert Caro describes how Marsh, who was 'addicted to the grandiose gesture',[5] had offered to bankroll the young politician by selling him a million-dollar share in his oil business, to be paid for by an interest-free loan on which there was to be no down payment, and which could easily be repaid out of the profits. (Johnson refused, knowing that if the public learned about the arrangement, his chances of becoming President would be damaged.) On an earlier occasion, Marsh had rewarded a reporter he liked by giving him a newspaper. 'The dividends [Marsh] wanted from his munificence,' Caro harshly continues, 'were gratitude and deference: he wanted to be not only the patron, but the seer.'[6] Someone who knew him well said that 'he always had to be the pontificator, the center of attention. He was the most arrogant man I ever met.'

In this respect Dahl, like L. B. J., was close to being his match. To Marsh this was part of his attraction. As the war progressed, they saw each other continually, both in Washington and at Longlea, the country house in Virginia where Marsh entertained at weekends with his beautiful mistress Alice Glass. Sometimes alone together, sometimes with other friends such as Creekmore Fath, a young Roosevelt aide, the men would sit up late two or three nights a week, arguing, joking, plotting and gossiping about the recently-departed guests: politicians, journalists, businessmen. 'Washington was a sieve,' Fath says now. 'You could sit at Charles's house and hear more of what was going on than you'd hear in practically any place in town. I'm afraid that we weren't brought up properly as to how to keep secrets.'

It was a heady time for the provincial but ambitious young RAF officer, and as Dahl and Marsh came to know each other better, they fed one another's involvement in a fiction of power increasingly removed from real people and situations. In June 1943, for example, Marsh wrote to Dahl:

You have weight on your spirit. Your duty to your country . . . is one weight. The demands of superiors and colleagues which do not coincide with your judgment or your spirit is another.

But these weights will lessen if the inside of your spirit, which has nothing to do with the particular, slowly becomes serene. This illusive [sic] quality can never be possessed in immaturity. But the embryo is there at birth. You have it in the potential . . .

You have had the wisdom already to refuse to tie yourself to a personal ambition such as becoming a Member of Parliament. Another side of you tells you that you are twenty-seven; that the future is uncertain; that you have certain responsibilities of family and country.[7]

Soon, Marsh continued, the spirit would show Dahl what it was that he had to do. Then, 'I may be of service to you.'

Dahl was quick to imitate Marsh's semi-mystical brand of personal encouragement, with its high gibberish quotient ('the embryo is there at birth'). Soon he was urging the older man to go to Roosevelt and impress his world-view on him.[8] It requires a little courage, Dahl dramatically concluded: 'I do not know whether you have it; you might like to find out.'

Not all of this was impracticable. Marsh would have had little difficulty in getting to see Roosevelt, and Dahl gave him the sensible, if uncharacteristic, advice that in conjuring up a picture before the eyes of the man he called 'the big white chief', he should remember that 'sometimes your colours are too bright and vivid, and the picture which you paint, although at first fantastic and alive, becomes upon second thoughts merely fantastic.' But observers of the relationship were generally unimpressed. Marsh's two sons, John and Charles, who were about Dahl's age, were particularly cool about it. And a later acquaintance recalls, 'Roald and Charles both did a job on each other. It was very extraordinary. I used to wonder what was the purpose of it all. The *bullshit* that washed across the table!'[9]

Part of the purpose was sheer fun, the boyish anti-authoritarianism that led to the joke correspondence about Lord Halifax. In one of Dahl's more straightforwardly young-serviceman-hits-town pranks, as Marsh's step-daughter relates, 'he painted the balls of the bison on the Q Street bridge.'[10] Yet there was a serious side to the relationship. Dahl was among other things trying to resolve an intractable personal conflict. How could he satisfy his ambition to be like Marsh – rich, dominant, a public figure – while appeasing his equally strong desire to return to childhood?

The answer – by becoming one of the world's most successful writers of children's books – may seem clear to readers now, but it certainly wasn't to Dahl at the time. True, he was drawn to children, and one of his first professional pieces of writing was a children's story he produced in wartime Washington.[11] But it wasn't until he was in his forties that he properly – although even then, as we shall see, reluctantly – began the career which made him famous and wealthy.

Powerful, too. What children read helps to form them as adults, and Dahl's readers number many millions. His work is a common point of reference all over the world, popular not only throughout Europe and the United States, but in Brazil, Thailand, Japan and even – despite what is politely called his anti-Zionism – in Israel. Famously, the initial Chinese print-run for *Charlie and the Chocolate Factory* was two million copies. In Britain alone, between 1980 and 1990, over eleven million of his children's books were sold in paperback form – considerably more than the total number of children born there in the same period. By the end of Dahl's life, every third British child on average bought or was given a book by him each year.[12]

Although he became known as an author in the late 1940s, it was during the last twenty-eight years of his life, from 1962 onwards, that he did much of his best, as well as best-selling, work – *James and the Giant Peach, Charlie and the Chocolate Factory, George's Marvellous Medicine, The Twits, Revolting Rhymes, The BFG, Dirty Beasts, The Witches, Matilda* and the two vivid memoirs *Boy* and *Going Solo*. How did his career develop? Could he have been a better writer? Why did so ambitious, so macho a man end up devoting so much of his life to children? The answers are to some extent practical and social: they concern the literary market-place, the power of editors, the growing cultural independence of children. But they are also, of course, personal to Dahl. Quite outside his writing, yet in ways which inevitably affected it, he was an intriguing, contradictory figure. He was famously a war hero, a connoisseur, a philanthropist and a devoted family man who had to confront an appalling succession of tragedies. He was also, as will be seen, a fantasist, an anti-Semite, a bully and a self-publicizing trouble-maker. Although he had a voice of his own as a writer, he was not above taking credit for others' ideas. Many people loved him and had reason to be grateful to him; many – some of them the same people – frankly detested him.

The only common view about Dahl, in fact, is that opinions of him are divided. His early patroness Eleanor Roosevelt said, 'Practically no one in the world is entirely bad or entirely good',[13] but if you were to believe everyone who knew Dahl, you would have to conclude that he was both. Although in some ways his apparent inconsistencies were of a piece, there are points at which he simply cannot be reconciled with himself. More than most people, he was divided between the things he was and the things he wanted to be. His intense, self-dissatisfied perfectionism often produced the worst in him as well as the best.

An old friend of the family told me, 'Almost anything you could say about him would be true. It depended on which side he decided to show you.' Perhaps his inconsistencies seemed to him just part of the act – a way of keeping the audience guessing. Towering half a foot over most people he met, with his shambling gait, keen eyes and scratchy, smoker's voice, he was a performer. Although he said he hated Hollywood, he behaved like an actor, a ring-master, a spell-binder: Mr Willy Wonka in *Charlie and the Chocolate Factory*. But not all of the performance was fun, either for him or for others in the cast. He was once described as looking like Henry Fonda after several hours on the rack.[14]

Some of his sufferings were external, but others sprang from the contradictions in his own mind. For example, he was a tory anarchist. His children's stories are subversive and hedonistic (hence in part their popularity in the 1960s, when they began to appear) and yet conservative, nostalgic, authoritarian (hence some of their appeal to parents). In the ways he brought up his own children, this division caused problems and pain. It was a part of his dividedness that he relished trouble. He enjoyed stirring people up, whether with a book or at a dinner party or in a letter to *The Times*. Yet he was also at his best when there was a genuine tragedy to rise to.

In some respects, his character makes better sense if he is thought of less as a writer than as a capricious tycoon.[15] He pursued money ruthlessly and single-mindedly, using other people as accessories to his various enterprises – 'the Business' as they are collectively called in his will. He came from a commercial family, and was proud of the fact that both his father and his uncle made fortunes. Dahl's own royalties now bring in millions of pounds a year. Like many successful businessmen, he had little interest in abstract thought and was impatient of intellectualism. 'Genius', on the other hand, he revered. Next came courage, practicality, and what he called sparkiness. These were his own qualities, and those which his children's books encourage readers to admire.

Arguably, he never grew up. Much of his behaviour seems like that of someone who had been forced into a premature but permanent, and rather unconvincing, show of adulthood. A handful of his stories for adults are among the most memorable written by a British author since the beginning of the Second World War. But in much of his adult fiction, he is over-anxious to prove his virility to the reader. Noël Coward wrote in his diary, after reading the newly-published *Someone Like You*: 'The stories are brilliant and his imagination is fabulous. Unfortunately there is, in all of them, an underlying streak of cruelty and macabre unpleasantness, and a curiously adolescent emphasis on sex.'[16] So it is heartening to see how a new audience of children (the first of them his own) helped Dahl to turn what were often very similar fictional ingredients – modern folk-tales of oppression and revenge, cunning and sorcery – into something warmer, much funnier, more fanciful and better written.[17] One of the rare things about Roald Dahl is that his books, on the whole and with help from outside, continued to improve. Not all of them will last. But the best – especially *The BFG* – surely will. Like folk-tales, they draw on deep, widespread longings and fears. They bind characters, readers and writer into a private fantasy. They make you laugh and cry. They do all this with well-tried technical expertise, and in a way that is often a cryptogram of the life which produced them.

2

The Apple

Dahl's parents were both Norwegian. When his mother, Sofie Hes-selberg, married his father, Harald Dahl, in 1911, she was in her mid-twenties, Harald in his forties. He was a prosperous widower with two children, co-owner of a ship-broking business in Cardiff. He had settled there in the 1880s, in the boom years of the South Wales coalfields and the port of Cardiff, at the time among the biggest cargo shipping centres in the world.

Harald came from a lower middle-class mercantile family. His own father – whom Roald, himself very tall, later remembered as a seven-foot giant – kept a general store in a small town near Oslo. Grandfather Dahl had three daughters and two sons, both of whom emigrated and flourished, the younger, Roald's uncle, with a fleet of trawlers in La Rochelle. Harald lost his left forearm in a boyhood accident, but he didn't allow the disability to prevent him from making a similarly successful career. By 1905, at the age of forty, he had built a comfortable home for his wife Marie and their two-year-old daughter Ellen in Llandaff. The medieval town was by then rapidly becoming a suburb of Cardiff, but even today, with its ancient cathedral and its green scattered with low, white cottages, Llandaff retains some of its old rural seclusion. Five minutes' walk from the cathedral close, the Dahls' steeply gabled house still stands in Fairwater Road. It is now called Ty Gwyn, but Harald named it Villa Marie after his wife.

Two years after they moved in, Marie died, aged twenty-nine. Harald was left with Ellen, now aged four, and a one-year-old son, Louis. He managed alone for four years until in 1911 he married

Sofie (her name has three syllables), whom he had met on holiday in Norway, travelling on the Oslofjord.

Sofie's background was more bourgeois than Harald's. Her father, Karl Hesselberg, came from a long line of clergymen and was a naturalist: for a time, he edited the Norwegian magazine *Nature*.[1] Her formidable, possessive mother was born Ellen Wallace, of a Norwegian family which claims descent from the Scottish national hero Sir William Wallace. Sofie was Karl and Ellen's first child. Shortly before her birth in 1885, her father took a job with the Norwegian state pension fund, eventually rising to become its senior manager – although not, to his disappointment, its chief. A family picture taken around the time of Sofie's marriage shows him, trim-bearded and sharp-eyed, with his wife and three of their daughters: Sofie, Astrid and Ellen (again). A fourth had died in 1907. The girls are all good-looking, but Sofie is the most striking.[2] She has her father's slender nose and watchful eyes, but the full lower lip and strong chin are her mother's.

As it turned out, Sofie was the only daughter who married. She sailed to Cardiff and moved into Villa Marie, taking charge of her step-children and soon beginning her own family. A daughter, Astri, was born in 1912. Another, Alfhild, followed two years later. Two years after that, on 13 September 1916, her only son was born. They gave him just the one name, Roald, which Norwegians pronounce 'Roo-ahl' without sounding the final d. The family were still living in Fairwater Road when another daughter, Else, arrived, but the first house Roald remembered was on the hill near Radyr, a few miles further out from Cardiff, where they moved in 1918 at the end of the First World War.

Even by the opulent standards of the past half-century, that was a time of fabulous prosperity in Cardiff. Until the slump of the early 1920s, shipping, according to one historian, 'developed from a business to a craze. The Port became the centre of a great . . . boom which attracted millions of pounds from investors and speculators.'[3] Now, when Harald returned home each day from his office beside the hectic West Dock Basin, it was to Ty Mynydd, a Victorian country mansion with its own farm. On the other side of the valley stood a castle so impressive to a small boy that, in his old age, Roald Dahl thought he remembered its turrets as belonging to his father's own house.[4] It was the Disneyish but genuinely medieval Castell Coch, restored to neo-gothic extravagance by the Victorian architect William Burges for a South Wales magnate at around the time of Harald's arrival in Cardiff.

Harald was a domineering man, both a romantic and a perfectionist.[5] At the end of 1919 Sofie became pregnant once more, and began to prepare for the regime which her husband had devised for the benefit of his future children. In *Boy* their son described how, after six months of her pregnancy, Harald would declare that 'the glorious walks' should begin. On these glorious walks they visited beautiful places in the countryside for about an hour each day, with the idea that Sofie would pass on her aesthetic response to the unborn child:

> His theory was that if the eye of a pregnant woman was constantly observing the beauty of nature, this beauty would somehow become transmitted to the mind of the unborn baby within her womb and that baby would grow up to be a lover of beautiful things.[6]

But there were to be no more glorious walks together. In February 1920 Astri died of appendicitis aged seven. Two months later Harald too was dead of pneumonia – or, as many people thought, of a broken heart.

Sofie had no immediate financial anxieties. Harald left over £150,000 (nearly three million pounds in today's terms).[7] Not all of this survived the 1920s slump, but there was enough for the family to live on very comfortably, and for all of the children eventually to go to boarding school. Harald also provided for each of them to buy a house when they grew up. Meanwhile, the family stayed on at Ty Mynydd until the baby – another girl, Asta – was born that autumn. But it now seemed most practical to sell up and move back into Llandaff. Sofie was thirty-five. Her husband and eldest child were both dead. She was solely responsible, in a foreign country, for two orphaned step-children now in their teens and for four small offspring of her own. She was to live for a further forty-seven years, never remarrying, and for the greater part of that time within an hour's journey of each of her children.

Almost seventy years after the deaths of Astri and Harald, one of Roald Dahl's daughters, Tessa, wrote about her state of mind when in her own childhood comparable tragedies struck the family yet again. She described the conflict between on the one hand, feeling required to give unobtrusive support and on the other, wanting to do something extraordinary so as to be noticed amidst all the emotional drama. Above all, she longed to restore everyone's happiness.[8] Dahl rarely talked about his own feelings, but he must have had to cope with all this when he was only four years old – this, and the additional pride and burden of being his mother's only son. Only child was what it seems to have felt like, despite – or perhaps partly because of – the size of the family. His nickname at home was 'the Apple' because he was the apple of his mother's eye. It was an ambiguous role – privileged but demanding. Much was expected of him and although he never lacked either encouragement or material rewards, his mother showed him little physical warmth. The bereaved boy was both the centre of attention and very lonely.

It is as lone operators that children were to figure in his stories. Matilda, in the book named after her, has a negligible brother, but otherwise all Dahl's main child characters are without siblings. Many of the stories are centred on orphans: 'Katina', 'Pig', *James and the Giant Peach, The BFG, The Witches*. Others, such as *Danny the Champion of the World*, involve an intense relationship between a single child and a single parent or surrogate parent. It is, of course, a classic situation in children's literature – partly because writers are often people who have felt isolated as children. But when, late in his life, Dahl was asked by a television interviewer about this emphasis in his work, he seemed surprised and at first denied that it existed.[9]

Sofie, Dahl was to write, 'was undoubtedly the absolute primary influence on my own life. She had a crystal-clear intellect and a deep interest in almost everything under the sun . . . She was the matriarch, the materfamilias, and her children radiated round her like planets round a sun.'[10] He explored the relationship in 'Only This', a story about a bomber pilot and his mother which he wrote in Washington in the 1940s. The emotional centre is not the man's feelings, but the woman's for him. She is seen through the bedroom window of a moonlit English cottage. Awakened by bombers flying overhead to Germany, she sits up thinking about her only son, who is flying in one of them. In her thoughts she flies with him. He hears her speak to him and touches her shoulder before the aircraft is hit by flak and crashes. Son and mother both die, he in the cockpit, she at her bedroom window. The title refers to a passage early in the story where Dahl describes both the mother's feelings for her child and, by implication, his for her: 'the deep conscious knowing that there was nothing else to live for except this.'

In its intensity, 'Only This' may have been touched not only by Dahl's direct feelings as a son and a pilot, but by something he had read when he was still at prep school and which, he later said, 'profoundly fascinated and probably influenced' him.[11] *Can Such Things Be*, a collection by the *fin-de-siècle* US writer Ambrose Bierce, begins with a sinister, psychologically turbulent episode, 'The Death of Halpin Frayser'. A young man, neglected by his powerful father, spoilt by his mother, 'of a dreamy, indolent and rather romantic turn, somewhat . . . addicted to literature', decides to leave home for California. His mother does all she can to stop him, but even when she describes a dream of her own death, he is unpersuaded. Having gone, he is prevented from returning. Shanghaied in San Francisco and shipwrecked in the South Pacific, he is kept away for six years. On his way back at last, Frayser dreams that his mother has been murdered. His guilty fantasy – with which the intricately-structured narrative opens – turns out to be true. Widowed, and unsuccessful in her search for her lost son, his mother remarried. The new husband killed her.

These are the bare outlines of a fiction which, as Dahl's own work was to be, is myth-like in its suggestiveness and extremism. Bierce is explicit about its psychological well-springs. 'Between

[Halpin] and his mother was the most perfect sympathy', he writes. She had hidden its real nature:[12]

> She had always taken care to conceal her weakness from all eyes but those of him who shared it. Their common guilt in respect of that was an added tie between them. If in Halpin's youth his mother had 'spoiled' him he had assuredly done his part toward being spoiled. As he grew to ... manhood ... the attachment between him and his beautiful mother ... became yearly stronger and more tender. In these two romantic natures was manifest in a signal way that neglected phenomenon, the domi-nance of the sexual element in all the relations of life, strengthen-ing, softening, and beautifying even those of consanguinity.

The young Roald was so taken with Bierce's book that he gave it to his best friend at prep school, Douglas Highton, whose parents lived apart and whose own home was also with his mother.[13] Many years later Dahl asked for it back, and Highton exchanged it for signed copies of Dahl's own books.

The two boys were boarders at St Peter's School, Weston-super-Mare. However, it was not until 1925 that Sofie sent her son there. Her first action after Harald's death was to buy a double-fronted, red-brick Victorian house in Cardiff Road, Llandaff, close to where Harald's business partner lived, and close, too, to a new school for girls and small boys. Alfhild, Else, Roald and Asta all in turn went to Elm Tree House, which was then in Ely Road, near the fields, with a well-stocked garden behind.[14] In the summer, les-sons were held among the much-raided fruit bushes. Miss Tucker, one of the two sisters who ran the school, taught nature study.

Dahl often referred to his childhood fascination with birds, moles, butterflies, gnats. He vividly recalled experiments such as eating the bulb of a buttercup ('frighteningly hot') or putting an ear of barley under his sleeve and feeling it climb to his shoulder.[15] Some of this fascination came, he liked to think, from Sofie's pre-natal 'glorious walks', but it may also have been influenced by her father. Certainly, it was nourished on the family's annual Norweg-ian holidays. Although none of them would ever live in Norway,

Harald and Sofie's children were brought up with a strong sense of belonging there. They were christened in the Norwegian church in Cardiff docks. They learned to speak Norwegian. Every summer, Sofie took them home to join her overwhelmingly female tribe, where they ate fresh fish and burnt toffee, and heard stories of trolls and witches. The family included both good cooks and good story-tellers.

It would be hard to miss the influence of northern European folk-tales on Dahl's stories. Witches, and 'hags' in general, took a particular hold. Not that in the 1920s you had to be Scandinavian, or a boy brought up in a matriarchy, to be scared of witches – particularly in druidical Wales. The small boy was especially horrified by an old woman who ran a sweet shop in Llandaff, 'a small skinny old hag with a moustache on her upper lip and a mouth as sour as a green gooseberry.'[16] Four chapters of *Boy* are given over to an episode in which Roald and his friends put a dead mouse in one of her jars and are repaid with a caning. In its comic extravagance, much of *Boy* reads like fiction, but Dahl wasn't the only Llandaff child to have kept such memories. His contemporary, Mrs Ferris, who went to the local primary school which then stood opposite the sweet shop, vividly recalls its proprietors. 'Two sisters, weren't they? Very old, oh, very decrepit. We didn't like going in there, you see . . . We used to be a bit frightened, because they were like witches, weren't they?'[17]

One's mother apart, any woman might be a witch in the subculture in which Dahl was soon to be enrolled. It had always been Harald Dahl's intention to send his children to English 'public' schools, and his widow was sure that Roald needed the influence of men. If he was to get into public school, he would have to be prepared for the Common Entrance exam. He was moved briefly from Elm Tree House to the Cathedral School on the green in Llandaff. There he was a day-boy, but at the age of nine he arrived with his trunk in the long corridors of St Peter's Preparatory School, Weston-super-Mare. You can just see the town from Cardiff docks, on the muddy far bank of the Severn.

Extinct today, St Peter's had been founded in 1900. It was unusual in having been purpose-built as a prep school: a long building from whose spinal corridor branched six classrooms, above which were six dormitories each housing a dozen boys. At one end of the building, in a part strictly out of bounds to them, lived the headmaster, his wife and their two daughters. These girls were objects of a fascination not much calmed by their father's pedagogical approach to the Facts of Life.

In later life, Roald Dahl would describe his sex education in a comic set piece with which he regaled family parties, booksellers' conferences and publishers' gatherings, and even the Prize Days of schools. According to one who heard it, it went roughly like this.[18] The headmaster told the boys, 'You have about your body a certain organ. I think you know what I'm talking about.' (Dahl would say, 'And I think we did know what he was talking about.') 'Well, I want you to realize that it's like a torch. There's a sort of bulb on the end of it. If you touch it, it will light up. And if it lights up, your batteries will go flat.' That was all. Except that afterwards, according to the story, Roald didn't dare touch his penis. Even drying himself after a bath was a source of anxiety, until one holiday when a sister acquired a hair dryer and his problem was solved.

St Peter's itself, if we are to believe Dahl's description in *Boy*, was a cross between Dotheboys Hall and Llanabba Castle, the gothic prep school in Evelyn Waugh's *Decline and Fall*. Waugh's louche master, Captain Grimes, in particular has his Dahl counterpart in 'Victor' Corrado, in love with the sadistic school matron. Dahl had to concede to his St Peter's friend Highton that *Boy* was 'coloured by my natural love of fantasy'; Highton himself found the school ordinary enough. He now thinks that in its attempt to instil integrity and qualities of leadership in a pack of unregenerate seven-to-thirteen-year-olds, the regime was 'a bit strict', but he remembers most of the staff – including the matron – as having been perfectly normal, capable and kind: 'None of it was as grim as in *Boy*.' But he recalls one Dahl-like streak of waywardness when a master became keen on the mother of a pupil and gave the boy an enviably large model racing car. The man later turned up under a pseudo-

17

nym, seemingly as a spy, at the headquarters of a secret experimental armoured division where Highton was a security officer in the Second World War. Knowing that the background he claimed was false, Highton had him removed by MI5.

Dahl himself, to eyes other than his own, seems to have passed his four years at St Peter's unexceptionally. He was tall, soft-faced, neither especially popular nor unpopular, although very close to the few boys who became his friends. (Douglas Highton still has the presents Dahl brought him back from holidays in Norway: a model seal itself made from seal-skin; a paper-knife carved from part of a reindeer's antler; a sketchy carving of a reindeer pulling a sleigh.) Dahl's letters home, meanwhile, were routinely full of football and stamp collecting, Bonfire Night fireworks and the finer points of conkers.[19] He was good at games, promising well at cricket (the school magazine said 'we expect great things in the future') and winning prizes for swimming.[20] Like everyone else, he marched in crocodile on Sundays to All Saints Church, Weston-super-Mare, and called it All Stinks because of the incense. Like everyone else, he made tobacco out of the Virginia creeper on the school wall and smoked it, sickeningly, in a clay pipe.

Academically he was weak: towards the bottom of his form of thirteen boys in Latin and Maths, and only slightly better at English. This must have been a blow to a child who was the centre of attention at home, and of whom, since his father's death, so much was expected. And however comprehensible, practically speaking, he found his mother's decision to send him away to school, it still bewildered and hurt him. In his first term, in an instinctively well-aimed bid for her attention, he faked the symptoms of the appendicitis from which Astri had died, and won a short reprieve. But as time went by, and as he adapted himself to the inevitable, Dahl found other escape routes. In particular, he absorbed himself in stories. He remembered any narrative he read or was told. In his earliest letters home he relates verbatim a dramatized reading from Dickens and a school lecture on bird legends – he particularly admired the 'fine' story in which the King of the Birds is whichever bird can fly highest, and the wren wins by hiding in the feathers of the eagle.[21] As time went by, he read avidly among the novelists of exploration and military adventure popular among boys at the time: Kipling, Captain Marryatt, H. Rider Haggard, G. A. Henty, writers whose emphasis on heroism and masculinity was to influence his life as well as his books.

He seems sometimes to have believed in stories more than he believed in people. If *Boy* is enjoyable for its violence – macabre episodes involving dentistry, car accidents, school beatings, the lancing of a friend's boil – the main *dramatis personae* are correspondingly worked up into caricatures. In a couple of cases Dahl thought it best to change names. In others, he simply misremembered them: Victor for Valentine, Braithwaite for Blathwayt, Wragg for Ragg. He was sixty-seven when he wrote the book and his spelling was always erratic. But it seems not to have troubled him, as he conjured these people up, that they were real and independent, not simply characters in a world of his own invention. This was to become a controversial issue because of some of the things he wrote in *Boy* about his next school.

St Peter's sent its pupils on to good, sound, middling public schools: Blundell's, Charterhouse, Cheltenham, Radley. Highton won a scholarship to Oakham. Dahl got into Repton.

A Midland village seven miles south of Derby, Repton is a dour little sprawl of blackened stone and red brick overlooking the featureless Trent valley. There is nothing much there except the school. Priory House, where Dahl was to spend the next four and a half years, appears from the outside pleasantly domestic. A tile-hung Victorian villa with a corner turret, bay windows and an enclosed garden, it could have been his old home in Llandaff. Yet inside, day and night, week in, week out, the older boys of the house were licensed to terrorize the younger. Repton was 'a tough place', one Priory contemporary recalls: 'Rules and discipline tight, living really spartan, enforced by boys who did 90 per cent of the beating, of which there was a lot'.[22]

The family had recently moved close to London, to a comfortable eight-bedroomed house in Bexley, Kent, more convenient for trains to the school attended by all of Dahl's sisters, Roedean in Sussex. The new family home was called Oakwood. With its tennis court, its table-tennis table in the conservatory and the huge break-fasts ready in the dining room on little flame heaters,[23] it could not have contrasted more sharply with the rigours of school.

Repton, according to another of Dahl's contemporaries, the philosopher Sir Stuart Hampshire, had 'all the worst features of Marlborough or Eton without any of the sophistication. It was full of heavy plutocratic boys from the North.'[24] Not so full though that it didn't find room at the same time for the future novelist Denton Welch. It is the fate of all schools that some of their liveliest pupils grow up to revile them. Repton has been unluckier in this respect than most. Welch's classic autobiography, *Maiden Voyage*, begins with his attempt not to return to the school in the autumn of 1931 (when Dahl had been there for five terms). Much of what Welch ran away from corresponds with Dahl's account in *Boy*: fagging, beatings, the torture of new boys and other miseries common to many, although not all, boys' boarding schools of the time. There are other, more pleasant memories, including some peculiar to Repton – such as the market research done there by Cadbury's and described in *Boy*. A plain cardboard box full of new types of chocolate was given to every boy, with a check-list on which he had to award marks to each.[25] Dahl's taste for high-street brands of chocolate was already well established. The Cadbury's blind tastings turned it into a lifelong addiction.

If chocolate was one form of consolation, both boys were to find another in art: in Welch's case life-drawing, in Dahl's photography. And since Welch's book, unlike Dahl's, was intended for adults, there was less to discourage him from writing about that other consolation, sex.

Boy is the strip-cartoon version of *Maiden Voyage*, Dahl's lurid episodes ringing with Billy Bunterish yells where Welch scrutinizes his world with a sly, sensual eye: 'The next day the House began to fill up with "old boys" ', Welch writes. 'They were everywhere, standing in the corridors and studies, smoking pipes and cigarettes. Two even followed me down to the lavatory and asked me for a first-hand account of my adventures when I ran away.' Given Dahl's more exaggerated style, some readers will be grateful that when he writes about school lavatories, all that concerns him is keeping them warm for a prefect. But in one respect, although there is no reason to think he was himself actively involved, Dahl's reticence about schoolboy homosexuality adds to, rather than moderates, his distortions. *Boy* caused a minor sensation when it first appeared in 1984, because of its allegation that a former headmaster of Repton, Geoffrey Fisher, who had subsequently become Archbishop of Canterbury, was a sadistic flogger. An episode is related in some detail in which the victim was Dahl's best friend. Fisher is described as eking out the ordeal with lengthy pauses to fill and light his pipe, and to 'lecture the kneeling boy about sin and wrongdoing'. At the end he produces a basin and a sponge and tells him to wash away the blood.

According to Dahl, the episode made him have doubts about the organization of English society, and even about the existence of God. It was Fisher, after all, who twenty years later crowned Queen Elizabeth II in Westminster Abbey. How could his ecclesiastical position be reconciled with the behaviour Dahl described? While Fisher had been at Repton,

> He was an ordinary clergyman . . . as well as being Headmaster, and I would sit in the dim light of the school chapel and listen to him preaching about the Lamb of God and about Mercy and Forgiveness and all the rest of it and my young mind would become totally confused. I knew very well that only the night before this preacher had shown neither Forgiveness nor Mercy in flogging some small boy who had broken the rules . . . [26]

Dahl was right about having been confused. The truth is different and more complicated. The beating he describes did take place, but in May 1933, a year after Fisher had left Repton. The headmaster concerned was his successor, J. T. Christie. As well as getting his sadists mixed up, Dahl also gives the impression that the beating was purely arbitrary – a matter of 'flogging some small boy who had broken the rules'. In fact the offender, who was almost eighteen and a house prefect, had been caught in bed with a younger boy.[27]

However sympathetic modern readers may be to Dahl's views on corporal punishment and – implicitly – on schoolboy homo- sexuality, his combination of instant moral outrage with a more general irresponsibility still gives offence. Lord Fisher had died in 1972, twelve years before *Boy* appeared, so there was no risk of libel action, but the archbishop's family and numerous Reptonians complained. Dahl was absolutely unrepentant, and it is one of the complications of the episode that in one sense he was right to be. Although some of his contemporaries remember Fisher as a great and good man who was 'liked and admired by all the boys, and certainly not sadistic',[28] others say that even by the standards of the day he was a severe head. 'Pretty crisp' was his own version of his regime at Repton.[29] That is also how he is remembered by Stuart Hampshire. Fisher was very strict, Hampshire says, if not abnor- mally so by the standards of the time. 'He was very unfeeling and illiberal' and he certainly beat boys excessively – 'by which I don't mean too often, but too hard.'[30]

So does it matter that it wasn't Geoffrey Fisher who beat Dahl's friend? It mattered to the boy. For the man who actually did beat him was, according to Hampshire, 'much worse. He was famous for saying "Those who live by the flesh will perish by the flesh." ' J. T. Christie carried this fame with him to Westminster, where he moved on, still in his thirties, in 1937. There he is remembered for his learning, his piety and his savagery. Another philosopher, Richard Wollheim, has written a vivid description of him:

> He read with us some of the Lesbia poems, not all. He compared Catullus to Burns, and again he tried to convince us of the tor- ments of unsanctified love. When he spoke of such topics he wriggled in his chair. We used to see him wriggle in much the same way in his pew when he came in early to the school service for private prayer.
>
> In both cases, he wrestled with some part of himself he did not like, and I cannot help feeling that he, and we, and the school as

a whole, would have been happier if he had sometimes emerged the loser.[31]

This is clearly the man whom Dahl misremembered as Fisher. And Wollheim confirms that 'Christie rejoiced in beating boys':

He beat boys for a number of offences. He beat them for cheating, and he beat them for sex. Two boys, whom we all knew he wanted to beat for other reasons, he beat for what was regarded in the school as an act of heroic frivolity – stealing the batteries out of his wireless set . . . Some selected offenders he invited to pray with him before he beat them. One, to my knowledge, refused.

But for all this, as Dahl makes clear, most of the violence at Repton (as at other schools) was administered not by the masters but by the boys. Tall and good at games – especially squash – Dahl wasn't an obvious target of the system. Some who knew him dismiss the sufferings described in *Boy* as having been worked up to attract sales. They say that in his early days at the school, although Dahl had 'difficulty settling in' and made few close friends, he wasn't particularly unpopular, and that he passed some of the more arcane social tests, such as being chosen to act in the house play. One gratefully remembers that he found a patent ointment that cured the impetigo with which everyone was afflicted (they blamed the compulsory outdoor plunge bath with its mantle of green slime).[32] Others were amused when he rigged up a mouse-trap consisting of a collapsible jetty over a basin of water, and was bitten by its victim.[33] He invented a slogan for the device: 'Catch as Cats Can't.'[34]

Even so, he was often miserable. He was growing fast, missing his friend Highton and missing the father he had hardly known. He got into a serious fight with a boy who was rude about Norwegians.[35] He wanted to be at home with his mother, his Meccano and his growing collection of birds' eggs.[36] You cannot calibrate psychological suffering any more than you can physical pain. To say that Dahl exaggerated is at least partly to point to the subjectivity of experience – and to the particular varieties of subjectivity which can turn people into writers of fiction. To Dahl, his experiences seemed real enough, and it is clear that he was lonely and insecure. None of the things which isolated him would have been decisive in themselves: other boys had foreign names, or were very tall or unexpectedly sensitive, or had an arrogant, teasing, domineering manner, or were unsuccessful in the classroom. But all of these were true of Dahl.

His accounts of childhood, both autobiographical and fictional, are dominated by bullies: schoolboy bullies in 'The Swan', the aunts in *James and the Giant Peach*, the hostile giants in *The BFG*, the father and headmistress in *Matilda*, the dragon in *The Minpins*. About a tenth of *Boy* is taken up with beatings and other forms of physical punishment. Just how traumatic were the memories involved is clear from a story for adults, 'Galloping Foxley', which he first published in his thirties.[37] The narrator, an elderly commuter, becomes obsessed by the intrusion of a newcomer who has begun to travel regularly in the same train compartment. Gradually, he remembers the source of his anxiety: the man tormented him at school. (Dahl transferred these passages of the story more or less intact into *Boy*.[38]) After some days of increasingly indignant silence, the former victim introduces himself. He was mistaken. The intruder is much younger and was at a different school.

Perhaps Dahl didn't have to look far to understand a bully. Most of the men who knew him, then or later, seem to find it hard not to use the word to describe him, eventually. A contemporary from a different house, David Atkins, has written that he remembers Dahl physically tormenting the older Denton Welch,[39] but most say that his was a verbal rather than physical sadism. At Repton he was good at inventing, and persisting with, cruel nicknames. He mercilessly teased a boy who developed breasts. It was impossible to predict whom he would pick on or why.

Whether the victim was Dahl himself or someone else, there were few chances of escape, short of taking Welch's course and running away altogether. The boys had very little free time. They took all their meals and recreation in the house. The housemaster allocated them to their dormitories and their shared studies, each occupied by about five boys. The 'studyholder' – a senior boy – ruled. Two or three others awaited their turn in power, while the remainder served the fag-master's whims. Fags, Dahl's contemporary Jim Furse recalls (confirming Dahl's own, more savage, onslaught on the system), 'were the body servants, and for all intents and purposes, the slaves of the studyholder. They were at his beck and call at all times, they kept his shoes, clothes, the buttons on his OTC uniform and his study clean and tidy, they made his toast and ran his errands, and they laid, lit and attended to the fire every night in winter – there was no other heating.' If any too-intensely consoling friendship was formed, it could soon be discouraged; the sharing arrangements were reshuffled every term. Meanwhile, Repton as a whole was run by its prefects, known – in a throwback to their Tudor precursors – as 'beausieurs'. (Dahl spelt the name phonetically as 'boazers'.) Under them and the various sporting commissars, everyone was forced to take part in corporate activities, from organized games and the Officers' Training Corps to the lugubrious Inter-House Singing Competition for Broken Voices.

There was one place to which Dahl eventually found he could get away: a cramped room at the end of a brick outbuilding that was cut off from the rest of the school on a small traffic island in a side street, between the wall of the cricket field and a village pub, the Boot. This secret room was a prototype of the famous garden hut at Great Missenden in which he later wrote. Here in the middle of Repton, surrounded by the school yet as remote from it as could be, he lurked every Sunday; so long as they had attended the early-morning Communion service, everyone was free for the rest of that day. It was an airless, evil-smelling place used as a photographic dark-room, which was Dahl's excuse for being there. Later he was joined by a younger photographer in the same house, David Sells. The door was locked and no one could see into the room, so they could smoke. Sometimes they heard voices in the road outside. If the headmaster went by, Dahl with silent ostentation would light another cigarette.

Photography was a serious hobby. Sells remembers Dahl's skill with the enlarger, and still has some of the pictures they took and developed. There are snapshots too in an album kept at Priory House: fire practice; the annual Cadet Force camp; the portly, moustachioed housemaster in his shiny shoes, best foot forward; Dahl and others in their uniform black jackets, striped trousers and straw hats. Dahl's great friend Michael Arnold is there looking out of a window, bespectacled, wearing a wide silk tie, his hair parted neatly in the centre.

Arnold went on to Oxford and a successful, if chequered, scientific career with ICI.[40] In the sixth form at Repton he stood for the truculent, imaginative heterodoxy to which Dahl aspired and which – despite its critics – the school at its rare best still occasionally encouraged. Not all the staff were subservient to the regime. In his early years as headmaster, Geoffrey Fisher had quarrelled with a brilliant and enthusiastic young socialist called Victor Gollancz, who with another master had started an innovative class on politics and current affairs.[41] Anticipating his later career as a publisher, Gollancz based an unofficial but widely-read magazine on the proceedings of this class: *A Public School Looks at the World*. In due course Fisher got rid of him, but the ideas Gollancz put around continued to be aired at Repton. Two notable left-wing writers of the 1930s, Christopher Isherwood and Edward Upward, had been pupils there; and in Dahl's day, a decade later, visiting speakers included the pacifist Cambridge don, Goldsworthy Lowes Dickinson, a pioneer of the League of Nations.

If the young Dahl himself was at all affected by the political climate of the 1930s, he didn't show it until a good many years later when, immediately after the Second World War, a mood of depressed utopian internationalism briefly overcame him. He was much more lastingly influenced by Michael Arnold's form of rebellion: individualistic, attention-seeking, conservative, anarchic. Arnold was a leading figure in the Debating Society, where, as the school magazine records, he spoke against feminism but defended both Hollywood (except for its 'objectionable women') and 'in an off-hand manner' capital punishment. On one occasion the motion was 'Delenda est Chicago': the boys were showing off their super-ciliousness about the USA as well as their classical education.[42] During the debate Arnold, who was 'largely enveloped in a yellow muffler', dismissed Stuart Hampshire's speech in support of US energy and vividness, but argued that Chicago should nevertheless be left intact, if only as 'a polyglot collection of dregs'. The Ameri-cans 'were foul anyway', he concluded.[43]

Dahl occasionally took part in these performances, but without making much impression. Nor, any more than at St Peter's, was he doing well at his academic subjects. This increased his intense competitiveness in other areas, particularly games. At the age of nine he had already taken up golf, which he could continue to play in the holidays.[44] He became captain of the Repton Fives team, played hockey for the school, and football and cricket for his house, swam and played golf. In his final year, without any special preparation but with the advantage of his long reach (he was by then six feet six tall), he won the boxing competition. And he was becoming hooked on bridge, poker and other forms of gambling: games in which, to those who played with him, he seemed to be pitting himself not only against others but against 'the system' as a whole.[45]

In old age, perhaps in oblique response to being frustrated of the knighthood he longed for, Dahl lamented that he had never become a prefect at Repton. Wasn't he a sergeant in the Corps? Hadn't he won two prizes for photography? Some of his contem-poraries point out that he was young for his year, that he did become a (notably unoppressive) 'studyholder' and that in any case the Captain of Fives was *ex officio* one of the sixteen 'School Officers'; it wasn't necessary to make him a prefect. But one Priory House contemporary takes Dahl's side in this ancient grudge: 'The powers-that-were mistrusted him and he got no promotion at all in a very hierarchical society. Probably a great mistake; no doubt it was feared he would be subversive, but in these cases the poachers generally make the best gamekeepers.'[46]

In his last term the subversive seventeen-year-old drove an old motor-bike, a 500cc Ariel, to Derbyshire and kept it in Wilmington, a few miles from Repton. 'It gave me,' he later wrote with revealing grandiosity, 'an amazing feeling of winged majesty and of independence.'[47] Dahl relished obscuring his face with goggles and scarf, and racing through Repton into the neighbouring countryside. As with much that he did, the pleasure largely depended on the anti-authoritarian fantasies he built around it. On one vengeful occasion, driving past the school and seeing the headmaster on his way to chapel, he roared as close as he dared to that 'terrifying figure' who until the end of his life he wrongly believed was Geoffrey Fisher.

3

Flying

'Sometimes there is a great advantage in travelling to hot countries, where niggers dwell,' the young Roald Dahl wrote in a prep-school essay. 'They will give you many valuable things.'[1] There was even, he continued, the outside chance of discovering a gold mine. It's a fair précis of what many British people believed at the time. It could almost have been the unofficial policy statement of multinational enterprises such as Shell, where on leaving Repton, Dahl was taken on as a trainee.

His mother had wanted him to try for Oxford or Cambridge, but Repton made it clear that, given his academic record, this wasn't an option.[2] In any case, what he most wanted to do was to travel. He spent the summer before his eighteenth birthday with fifty or so other young men on a joint public-school expedition to Newfoundland. There he lived under canvas, supplemented his pemmican diet with wild bilberries and whatever fish could be caught, and undertook various challenges designed to inculcate qualities of leadership and endurance.

One of these was a twenty-day march exploring an unmapped region in the centre of the island, south of Grand Falls. The journey was led by a man who had been medical officer on Captain Scott's tragic expedition to the Antarctic in 1910–12, and who had founded the Public Schools Exploring Society[3] two years earlier: Surgeon-Commander George Murray Levick. His young explorers believed that in the blank space on the relevant part of their map of Newfoundland, 'there might be anything, mountains, forests, rivers, Indians, gold'.[4] Forests there were in plenty, and also bogs.

The party struggled along in the rain collecting specimens of the region's flora and fauna, which they were to take back to the British Museum. According to their meticulously-kept records, birds and lepidoptera were surprisingly uncommon, but they found an abundance of insects, ferns and mosses. The main object of the march, however, as the expedition's historian Dennis Clarke recorded, was to provide an exercise in 'the survival of the fittest'. Someone who developed mumps was forced to carry on despite various protests, Dahl and the others sharing out his load. One of Dahl's boots later disintegrated, but he repaired it by encasing it in a canvas bucket, the rope handle tied around his ankle.

None of this dampened his enthusiasm for travel, and once he had returned home and joined Shell in September 1934, he hoped for an early posting to Africa or the Far East. For the moment, the furthest east the job took him was to his mother's house in Bexley, where he lived while he learnt 'all about fuel oil and diesel oil and gas oil and lubricating oil and kerosene and gasoline'.[6] He spent six months working in a refinery and some enjoyable weeks driving a lorry in the West Country, but for the most part he was based in London, commuting daily to Shell's office in St Helen's Court, Leadenhall Street, near the Bank of England.

When they arrived in the morning, employees signed their name in a book. At nine the office manager drew a red line across the page so that he could tell at a glance who was late.[7] After signing, Dahl and the others went out of the back door to a nearby Italian café for bacon and eggs. There wasn't a lot to do: much of the training seemed to consist of sorting letters and drafting replies. Besides, according to Antony Pegg – a fellow Eastern Staff trainee who spent his whole life in Shell – Dahl was 'a very independent person. He didn't like an awful lot of direction and that kind of thing. That's why I was never surprised when he left Shell. If he was told to do things – bah! he wasn't interested.'

Not that he didn't try to be a good company man. Shell was a world in itself, not unlike a vast school in some ways. There were interesting and likeable people in the office: Douglas Bader, for example, the future Second World War hero, who had joined the company as a clerk a year earlier, after losing his legs in a flying accident. Dahl played golf in the company tournament (he was runner-up in June 1936) and entered his photographs in the annual art exhibition; matters which were reported in the *Shell Magazine*, alongside accounts of a Shell amateur dramatic performance near Calcutta and a Shell cocktail party in Rio, and articles on new directions in petrol station architecture.[8] In the September 1937 issue the magazine's humorous gossip column 'Whips and Scorpions', which was compiled in the St Helen's Court office, parodied a currently-popular *News Chronicle* competition, in which readers could win prizes by recognizing and challenging a representative of the newspaper who toured British seaside resorts under the name Lobby Lud. The spoof was illustrated by a photograph taken by Dahl of a bare-chested man on a beach playing the mouth organ. It all reads as if it could have been dreamed up, and possibly even written, by Dahl himself:

> The idea is that, upon recognizing Mr Dud, you should floor him with a Rugger tackle, sit firmly upon his chest, and shout into his left ear: 'You are Mr Dippy Dud. I claim THE SHELL MAGAZINE prize,' at the same time brandishing a copy of the current issue.

'It will be noticed,' the piece warned, 'that Mr Dud is a keen musician, but do not be misled if he is not playing a mouth-organ when you see him':

> He is an equally adept performer on the ... harmonium, euphonium, pandemonium ... dictaphone, glockenspiel and catarrh ...
>
> Don't be afraid to tackle anyone you think may possibly be Mr Dud, unless he is very much bigger than yourself. People who are mistaken for him enter heartily into the fun of things, especially town councillors, archdeacons and retired colonels.

Mr Dud's next visit would be to 'Whelkington-on-Sea' where his itinerary was planned to include a lunchtime tour of 'places of interest, including The Red Lion, The Where's George, The Bookmakers' Arms, and The Slap and Tickle' followed by a two-minute visit to the municipal museum and art gallery and an hour's 'Demonstration of three-card trick in Municipal Fun Fair' before another pub crawl.

In this light-hearted atmosphere, and with home to escape to, Dahl found it easier than at school to make friends. In the evenings he played poker with people from the office or went greyhound racing with them. He also saw much of a young Cambridge undergraduate, Dennis Pearl, whom he had met on the Newfoundland expedition and who spent many weekends at Bexley. Pearl liked both Dahl and his sisters: 'a very lively, bright lot'. Alfhild was the most attractive and most sought-after – her admirers included the composer William Walton. Else was quieter, with a full figure and sleepy eyes. (Much later, divorced from his first wife, Pearl would marry one of Else's daughters.) Asta, angular and very tall, was still at Roedean, and Pearl was once both startled and flattered when her mother, who hadn't expected him to stay the night, directed him, with a Scandinavian disregard for sexual complexity, to the same room as the sixteen-year-old, where a spare bed happened to be already made up.

Pearl remembers these weekends as idylls. The pattern was usually the same: horse-racing or greyhounds with Roald and other male friends on Saturday; golf on Sunday morning; and then an afternoon spent lazing around, listening to Alfhild and Else playing Beethoven piano duets, or reading aloud the latest Damon Runyon story published in the *Evening Standard*.[9] Pearl was an insatiable reader and often recommended books to his friend: R. H. Mottram's First World War trilogy *The Spanish Farm*; Thornton Wilder's *The Bridge of San Luis Rey*; novels by another American writer, Christopher Morley. Dahl shared many of his friend's enthusiasms, and Damon Runyon in particular gave him a taste for American crime fiction which lasted for the rest of his life. (In 1989, the year before he died, he urged Pearl to read Thomas Harris's newly published *The Silence of the Lambs*.) But he was too active to give much of his time to reading and his tastes were less sophisticated and 'literary' than Pearl's. Besides, he was always busy with a game or hobby of some kind. Sports apart, photography still absorbed him – one of the bedrooms at Bexley had been converted into a dark-room – and he spent hours making model aircraft. He was also developing an increasingly complicated and secretive sex life. He had some single girl-friends of his own age, including for a short time a Belgian-Irish girl named Dorothy O'Hara Livesay, later to become Pearl's first wife. But Dahl was particularly attracted, and attractive, to older women, especially if they were married. In Pearl's words, he 'tended to choose something which created difficulties – he seemed to like mystery', so the details are hazy. But among his affairs was one with a baronet's wife, and another with a local woman in Bexley, whom Dahl kept separate from his friends and only saw on nights when her husband was away on business.

Some of these liaisons were organized by telephone from the office, as also were his dealings with bookmakers. He regularly slipped out in the middle of the afternoon to buy an evening paper for the racing results.[10] Although his salary as a trainee was only £130 a year – about £4,000 today – he had no living expenses. To Antony Pegg, whose wages were entirely used up by the rent for his lodgings and who was dependent upon his parents for spending money, Dahl seemed to have much more to spare for gambling than the rest of them.

Meanwhile, the would-be traveller watched impatiently as other Shell staff went to and from Latin America, Australia, Africa, Eastern Europe. On his desk sat a ball which, when he joined the company, he had begun making from the silver wrappings of his daily post-lunch chocolate bar (and which he kept, along with other relics and fetishes, for the rest of his life).[11] It was already as big as a tennis ball. At his desk Dahl fantasized about Africa, while more realistically planning holidays closer to home: a trip to Norway with his old school friend Michael Arnold, now at Oxford, and Dennis Pearl; or a climbing expedition in Snowdonia where he and Pearl took along another Reptonian called Jimmy Horrocks, who had been on the Newfoundland trip with them and had recently quarrelled with his parents. In the conventionally-minded view of Pearl, then a law student and later a successful colonial administrator, Horrocks was 'a complete and utter dead loss from every point of view – an early version of the druggy drop-out'. Pearl noticed that Dahl was often drawn to outsiders.

Eventually, in the autumn of 1938 his posting came through: to Dar es Salaam in what is now Tanzania, was then Tanganyika, and from 1887 until the First World War had been German East Africa.

European imperialism had brought European technological 'needs' to East Africa. Suddenly the nights had come to seem too dark without kerosene lamps, cooking too laborious without kerosene stoves. The first oil storage tank Shell built in East Africa went up in 1900 in Zanzibar, along with a factory for making tins.[12] Lorries, cars and oil-driven ships soon required more and bigger tanks: in Mombasa, Nairobi, Dar es Salaam. Deep harbours were built, with pipelines to draw oil from the ocean tankers. New offices served these installations and from 1930 there was a club in Nairobi for those who worked in them.

Dahl lived with two other young Englishmen in a company house in Dar es Salaam, on the cliffs above the Indian Ocean.[13] Between them, they ran the business in Tanganyika – a country four times the size of Great Britain, one and a half times that of Texas – sharing their somewhat awed sense of power and freedom with the colonial administrators who accommodated them on their travels. Dahl greatly admired the way the District Officers lived, combining the roles of judge, political adviser and doctor. Their Africa wasn't the aristocratic, twenty-four-hour nightclub of Kenya's 'Happy Valley'. It was a more conscientious society and its excitements were more indigenous: a tarantula in a friend's shoe; a green mamba sliding into the living room of a Customs officer and killing the dog; a lion carrying off the District Officer's cook's wife while the DO and his family sat with Dahl listening to Beethoven on the gramophone.

Much of the life was routine. In Dar es Salaam he spent his days sitting in the office in his white suit at a desk partitioned off from the clerks, who were mostly Indians and whose obsequiousness, he told his mother, made him feel 'like a bloody king'.[14] He did a lot of sport, mainly through the club: sailing, swimming, golf, tennis, squash, hockey and soccer, often in temperatures of ninety degrees. The social highlight was the annual dinner of the Caledonian Society. But he often had to make long circular safaris on business, taking his servant Mdisho with him. They travelled west to Lake Tanganyika, south to the borders of Nyasaland (Malawi) and back towards Mozambique, visiting customers who ran mines and plantations and supplying them with fuel and lubricants for their machinery. In *Going Solo* Dahl colourfully describes the wildlife he saw on these trips and his relations with Africans and white settlers. As a writer, he was no Isak Dinesen – he lacked her experience of African life, her patience and her subtlety. But he had read her book *Out of Africa*,[15] published the year before he left England, and respected her interest in non-European ways of thought and her impatience with the unimaginativeness of many settlers. In old age Dahl confessed to feeling 'mildly ashamed' of his youthful acceptance of British imperialism in Africa, and of the social inequalities on which it was based: 'It was only comfortable because we had masses of servants, which is not right, of course it's not right'.[16] But even while he was still fairly young, he became more critical of colonial attitudes than perhaps he later recalled. The point is worth making because, as we shall see, Dahl was accused of racism in the 1970s, when *Charlie and the Chocolate Factory* was attacked for its somewhat unthinkingly Victorian treatment of the 'Oompa-Loompas': cheerful factory labourers who, until he was persuaded to revise the book, were depicted as Congolese pygmy slaves.[17]

Dahl himself satirized racism in his story 'Poison', a psychological thriller which he first published in 1950. The plot was suggested to him by a friend in Washington,[18] but it fitted some of his own African experiences.

A white settler in India is trapped in bed by a deadly snake, a krait.[19] Harry Pope's friend finds him paralysed with terror and fetches the native local doctor. During a scene drawn out over nine sweat-drenched pages, Dr Ganderbai first injects Pope with serum and then pumps chloroform into his bed to immobilize the krait.

But when at last they pull back the sheet, nothing is there. In the story's fierce final twist, Dr Ganderbai asks whether his patient has been dreaming and Pope turns on him: 'Are you telling me I'm a liar? . . . Why, you dirty little Hindu sewer rat! . . . You dirty black – '. The friend, who is also the narrator, apologetically hurries Ganderbai out:

> 'You did a wonderful job,' I said. 'Thank you so very much for coming.'
> 'All he needs is a good holiday,' he said quietly, without looking at me, then he started the engine and drove off.

Ganderbai's dignity here makes its own quiet point, but in the original version Dahl included a more plainly anti-racist paragraph which was obviously based on his time in Tanganyika. The passage both interrupts the tension and, by anticipating Harry's behaviour at the end, weakens its impact. Presumably that is the reason why, although the passage appeared in the version published by *Collier's* magazine,[20] Dahl later removed it:

> [Dr Ganderbai] was worried about his reputation and I must say I couldn't blame him. It was probable that he had never before been called in to attend a European. None of them bothered with him much, except perhaps the British upon whom, in those days, his job depended, and who noticed him only in order to be politely offensive – as only the British can be. I imagined that even now little Ganderbai could hear the thick fruity voice of Dr James Russell in the lounge at the club, saying, 'Young Pope? Ah, yes, poor fellah. Not a nice way to go. But then if people *will* call in a native witch doctor, what can they expect?'

In the late 1930s racists did not always confine the expression of their views to the club, in Europe any more than in Africa. In Dar es Salaam, Dahl followed the news on his Philips ten-valve radio and mockingly named the lizards in his living-room after the leaders of fascism: Hitler and Musso.[21] The leader whom Dahl himself unfashionably favoured was a British politician whose bellicose arguments against appeasement had left him, for now, in the wilderness: Winston Churchill.[22] Of Mussolini, Dahl wrote to his mother saying that the dictator ought to adopt a harmless pastime, like making a collection of birds' eggs rather than of people's countries – although 'he'd probably say that it was cruel'.[23]

Mussolini's Italy already ruled Libya and had invaded Ethiopia in 1935. For Germany too, Africa was vital, especially in the north where it gave access to the Mediterranean and to the oilfields of the Middle East. National pride was at stake as well as economic interest: Germany had been deprived of its imperial 'possessions' – among them Tanganyika – by the punitive Versailles Treaty at the end of the First World War. Its principal rivals in the region were France in most of the north-west, including Algeria; Belgium in the Congo; and of course Great Britain. The British Empire at the time still included Nigeria and the Gold Coast (now Ghana); much of East Africa including Kenya, Tanganyika and Northern and Southern Rhodesia (now Zambia and Zimbabwe); territories on both sides of the Gulf of Aden at one end of the Red Sea; and at its other end, Palestine. Britain also remained powerful in – and on the outbreak of war quickly occupied – both Egypt and Iraq.

To Dahl at the age of twenty-two the build-up to war came as an exciting change in a routine which, however exotic, had begun to turn stale. He had ordered thirty-five records through the HMV agents in Dar es Salaam: popular classics for the most part (the Hungarian Rhapsodies, *Peer Gynt*, the Brandenburg Concertos) but also Gershwin and Paul Robeson. And his childhood interest in flowers had been reawakened by a septuagenarian colonel who had been to South America in search of orchids. (Dahl nicknamed him 'Iron Discipline' after his favourite nostrum.) But his social circle was extremely small, there were few single European girls around, and on many evenings, he wrote to his mother, there was 'bugger all to do except sweat'.

Throughout 1939, as war became clearly inevitable, Dahl urged his mother and sisters to leave Kent, which he rightly thought was bound to be bombed, and move back to Wales. He was enlisted by the colonial authorities as a special constable with 'batons, belts & all sorts of special instructions'. These last were contingency plans for helping to organize Askari troops in the arrest and internment of German nationals around Dar es Salaam. When the time came, this work exempted him from conscription in the Kenyan army, which took most eligible Englishmen in the region. Emergency restrictions on movement prevented him from leaving East Africa and he toyed with the idea of joining the King's African Rifles. But the Royal Air Force was recruiting in Nairobi and sounded, he wrote, 'fairly exciting and interesting and a bloody sight better than joining the army out here and marching about in the heat from one place to another and doing nothing special.' Besides, the RAF would teach him to fly for nothing; he would normally, he said, have had to pay about £1,000 for the lessons which would get him a licence. He hitched a ride on a Shell coastal tanker to Mombasa, changed to a train from which he saw antelope, ostrich, buffalo and giraffe with their young, and early in November 1939 submitted himself to a medical selection board.

With his school cadet corps training, his individualism and his aptitude for games – particularly, his squash-player's reflexes – Dahl was a stereotypical fighter pilot recruit. He was too tall to fit comfortably into a cockpit (his inventive fellow trainees gave him his RAF nickname of Lofty) but he told his mother that, apart from that and the fact that he missed having servants, he had never enjoyed himself so much as during these weeks of flying Tiger Moths over the Kenyan Highlands. From there he moved to the bleaker surroundings of Habbaniya in the Iraqi desert, where he spent six months learning to shoot, to dive-bomb, to navigate and to fly at night before being passed on to a pilots' pool in Ismailia, Egypt.[24] In mid-September 1940 his orders came through to join 80 Squadron in western Egypt, near the frontier with Libya.

Italy had formally entered the war in June, effectively closing the Mediterranean and cutting off much of the British land forces. Since then the Italians had been building up their strength in eastern Libya.[25] The expected push into Egypt began on 13 September, when a large Italian army began a sixty-mile advance across the border, halting at Sidi Barrani on 18 September.

In all this, 80 Squadron had been kept busy and was forced

frequently to move both its main headquarters and its landing grounds. The nineteenth of September was quiet: the squadron's officers organized a cricket match with the senior NCOs. Three hundred and fifty miles to their east Dahl took off from Abu Suweir in a Gloster Gladiator, a type of aeroplane he had not flown before. He stopped twice to refuel, the second time at Fuka, where he was given directions that may have been confused by events. His squadron was not where he expected to find it, and as dusk gathered over the North African desert and his fuel gauge fell, he decided to try to land.

Dahl described the crash in *Going Solo*[26] as well as in 'Shot Down Over Libya' and its subsequent, less heroic version 'A Piece of Cake'.[27] The squadron's own report the next day was typically low-key:

> Weather – wind N.W. – visibility good. A patrol was carried out over Mersa Matruh with 6 Gladiators from 1645 hours to 1800 hours. No enemy aircraft were sighted. P/O Dahl posted to this squadron from T.U.R.P. for flying duties w.e.f. 20th September. This pilot was ferrying an aircraft from No. 102 M.U. to this unit, but unfortunately not being used to flying aircraft over the Desert he made a forced landing 2 miles west of Mersa Matruh. He made an unsuccessful forced landing and the aircraft burst into flames. The pilot was badly burned and he was conveyed to an Army Field Ambulance Station.[28]

It was seven months before anyone in 80 Squadron saw Dahl again. Anyone, that is, who lived that long.

On landing, the Gladiator had hit a boulder and lurched forward into the sand. In the collision Dahl's skull was fractured by hitting the metal reflector-sight and his nose was driven back into his face. Before the aircraft's petrol tanks caught fire he managed to extricate himself from his seat belt and parachute harness, crawl from the cockpit and roll out of danger, to be picked up, bleeding profusely, by British soldiers patrolling near by.

The squadron report was wrong about his burns, which were only slight,[29] but his face was so swollen with bruises that he was blind for several weeks, and the injuries to his head, nose and back were such that it was almost two months before he was sufficiently recovered to get out of his hospital bed in Alexandria. On 20 November he wrote to his mother, from whom he had just received eight letters. With the bravado he always put on for her, he said that apart from persistent headaches he was feeling fine. The weather was like an English summer. He had been visited by some Norwegian expatriates and would be convalescing with wealthy local volunteers who took in wounded officers. Later, when his nose had been rebuilt, he was offered a berth home on the next convoy; he was afraid that it would mean no more flying, so he declined.

The decision took some courage. While he was in hospital Italy invaded Greece, which Britain, jointly with France, had before the war promised to defend. Since France had by now fallen, Britain could have argued that she was no longer bound by an agreement which, given the reversals of the North African campaign and the dangers of a German invasion at home, she couldn't have been worse placed to fulfil. The British Commander-in-Chief in the Middle East, General Wavell, warned Churchill that his forces were already over-stretched and that if they managed to secure an Italian withdrawal from Greece, the Germans would inevitably be drawn in through the Balkans. With the encouragement of US material aid, and buoyed up by what the historian John Terraine calls the 'strategic fantasies' of Churchill, the pro-Greek arguments prevailed. In November and December 1940, British aircraft badly needed in North Africa were sent to Greece; they included three squadrons of Blenheim bombers and two of Gladiator fighters – Squadrons 80 and 112.

As Terraine observes, 'From bad beginnings, things went from worse to worse.' Aircraft and spares were in short supply in Britain, let alone in the Middle East. Winter brought thick mists and low cloud to the mountains of Greece and earthquakes destroyed two airfields. The Greek High Command vacillated in its strategy and in the demands it made of its allies. As Wavell had predicted, Italian failures brought German reinforcements. By the time the

British army's expeditionary force arrived on 5 March, its air support consisted of 200 aircraft (including reserves) against 800 German aircraft on the eastern front, 160 Italian in Albania and a further 150 based in Italy but within range of Greece. Two days earlier Churchill had told his Foreign Secretary, 'We do not see any reasons for expecting success.'

During this time, while Dahl was still in Alexandria, 80 Squadron took heavy losses both of pilots and aircraft. There were some triumphant days, including one at the beginning of March when members of the squadron – including its most famous pilot, Thomas Pattle, and the Commanding Officer, 'Tap' Jones – claimed over twenty Italian bombers and fighters shot down for no loss: a figure made much of in British and Greek propaganda. But Tap Jones himself, who ended up as an Air Marshal (and whom Dahl later falsely maligned as never having flown in combat[30]), remembers it all as 'a most horrid campaign' in which the RAF were outnumbered, frustrated by bad weather and inadequate equipment, and were losing pilots sometimes at the rate of three or four a day.[31]

On 6 April Germany invaded, and within ten days the 60,000 men of the British army in Greece were in full retreat. This was the situation when Dahl arrived from Egypt, flying another unfamiliar aeroplane: one of the much-needed Hurricanes with which 80 Squadron's Gladiators were being replaced. He would be in Greece for less than two weeks, but it was to be one of the most intense periods of his life, and certainly the most dangerous.

In *Going Solo* Dahl talks of having 'come home to my squadron at last' ready for 'the next round'.[32] He was eager for action, for a chance to make good what he must have felt was an ignominious and wasteful mistake. But even if others had once seen his accident in this way, it was by now long forgotten. To the present members of 80 Squadron he was a complete stranger and one who, far from fighting a 'next round', hadn't even been in the ring yet. People were anyway too busy, too combat-shocked and too scared to take much notice of each other. One of the squadron's engine fitters at the time says he has little memory of any of the pilots because 'we used to see them come and go so quick'.[33] Dahl was found a tent and received some rudimentary advice from the Battle of Britain survivor with whom he shared it – the Earl of Leicester's younger son, David Coke, whose elder brother (although he seems not to have told this to Dahl)[34] was Wavell's ADC. The next morning Dahl went up on patrol.

If the squadron history is to be believed, it was an uneventful outing. In *Going Solo* Dahl makes it more dramatic, saying that he shot down a Junkers 88 both on that day and the next, whereas the official account lists no claim by him for almost a week.[35] But it is impossible accurately to reconstruct this hectic period. Some of the squadron's records were destroyed as a security precaution before the evacuation of Greece, and the surviving pilots' memories – including, as Dahl says in *Going Solo*,[36] his own – are inevitably blurred. His account often differs from that of the official history, particularly over who was killed and when: a confusion which, compounded by Dahl's casualness about names, sometimes produces *Catch* 22-like situations in which dead pilots turn up in later air battles.[37]

Everything was in chaos. The RAF campaign history records that 'Our fighters were only able to perform their task by continually taking to the air in aircraft riddled with bullets and in a condition that would normally have been considered quite unserviceable.'[38] On 19 and 20 April all the available Hurricanes, Dahl's among them, were sent to meet a succession of large raids over Athens. In one dog-fight, nine fighters from 80 Squadron and six from 33 Squadron claimed between them at least fifteen enemy aircraft, and possibly three times as many as that.[39] One or two of them were credited to Dahl, who evidently fought with courage and skill.[40] When he got back he learnt that among the British pilots who had been killed was the legendary Thomas Pattle.

What followed was a rout. The army was evacuated from the Peloponnese: a minor Dunkirk in which many more lives would have been lost but for the Germans' mistake in not closing the narrow road and railway through the Isthmus of Corinth over which everyone had to pass. Such aircraft as remained were sent to

Argos in the eastern Peloponnese to do what they could to cover the retreat, and were joined there by five new Hurricanes from Crete. No sooner had these landed than thirty or forty Messerschmitts appeared and, according to the senior officer, 'after silencing the Bofors guns . . . subjected the north and south landing grounds and the olive tree aircraft park to the most thorough low-flying attack I have ever seen.' The onslaught lasted three-quarters of an hour. At the end of it fourteen Hurricanes had been destroyed. It was the last scene in a tragedy which cost the British 209 aircraft and all that they might have contributed to the long struggle in North Africa.

Dahl fictionalized this episode in one of his first stories, 'Katina', published early in 1944[41] – a propagandist tragedy in which the little orphaned Greek girl of the title, who has been adopted by an RAF squadron, runs amidst blazing Hurricanes shaking her fists at the German aircraft, one of which implacably guns her down. In *Going Solo* he is more factual, but cannot resist claiming to have predicted the raid in every detail, including its timing, only to have had his warnings dismissed by a complacent adjutant.[42] Whatever the prediction, the outcome was that there were now more pilots in Argos than aeroplanes. Some went with the army to Crete, where they faced an even more desperate battle. Others, Dahl among them, were flown back to Egypt in a Lockheed on 24 April.

It was only a couple of weeks since Dahl had left Alexandria, and he was able to introduce David Coke and his other exhausted friends to an English couple, Major and Mrs Peel, with whom he had convalesced and who now gave them the run of their bathrooms and larder.[43] From Alexandria he and another pilot officer were ordered to Haifa on the north-west coast of Palestine, where they were to take temporary command of a detachment preparing for the arrival of half the partially re-equipped 80 Squadron. Having a few days to spare, Dahl decided to explore. While in Iraq in 1940 he had travelled with three friends to the deserted ancient city of Babylon – an experience he never forgot.[44] This time, having made his way to the British air base at Abu Suweir in eastern Egypt, he drove on alone in a Morris Oxford across the Sinai Desert. During the journey he encountered a group of Jewish children and their leader, refugees from Germany. In *Going Solo* Dahl says that they were the first people from whom he had heard anything about the Holocaust or about Zionism.[45]

The reason for the squadron's new posting was that a pro-Axis coup in Iraq had been supported by the Vichy French in Syria, which Wavell in consequence decided to invade. Within four days of Dahl's arrival at Haifa the attack was launched; 80 Squadron strafed Vichy French airfields and patrolled the coast to protect the Royal Navy, which was giving artillery support to the advancing infantry.

Between the lines of the squadron history one can read a mild tussle between official scepticism and the extravagant claims of the now battle-hardened, but far from subdued, Dahl. Most pilots wrote their combat reports in the laconic, understated, passive voice on which the RAF prided itself: an enemy aircraft was seen and engaged, shots were fired, the outcome awaited confirmation by other witnesses. Roald Dahl's entries are egotistical, vivid and enthusiastically speculative: 'I followed for approx. 3 mins. after the two others had broken off,' he writes of an encounter with a German reconnaissance plane on the first day of the campaign, 'and left it with Port engine smoking and probably stopped. Rear gunner ceased fire . . . It is very unlikely that this Potez got home, unless it could have done so on one engine, which I understand is not so. The rear gunner was probably wounded.'[46] The starboard engine of a Junkers 88 'burst into black smoke' before the plane 'pancaked on the sea . . . Having attacked my aircraft, I was chased for at least 4 minutes by 2 more Ju 88's in the most persistent manner. They were faster than me, but missed.'[47]

Dahl had a right to boast, and his having been a war hero was to be important to him for the rest of his life. 'Tap' Jones, despite Dahl's ungenerosity about his performance as the squadron's leader,[48] says 'There is no doubt in my mind that "Lofty" . . . was a very good fighter pilot and very gallant.'[49] Even in the cautious official accounts he is confirmed as having shot down five enemy aeroplanes, although he had many fewer opportunities to do so than some of his fellow pilots. Discounting his period in hospital and the jaunt from Alexandria to Haifa, Dahl was active in the squadron for a total of only five furious weeks before he was grounded because of blackouts and headaches resulting from his earlier injuries. It was no longer considered safe for him to fly and he was invalided home.

If exaggeration wasn't the RAF's style, it was always Dahl's, both in his conversation and in his fiction. One friend sums up his attitude: 'If you lost fifty dollars at poker, say you lost five hundred, it was more dramatic.'[50] 'Roald made a meal of everything,' says another, partly apropos of his stories about his school days. 'The advent of a spider on the table would become a great event. If Roald thought there was somebody gullible enough, he would say, "That is a steptocorus polycorus, which is the only highly poisonous spider in the UK. Don't worry, because it will not ever bite unless it starts to jump . . ." *Total* invention.'[51] The short stories he wrote about the war are a striking exception. The only truly introspective work he ever did (not excluding his autobiographies), they divert his natural extravagance into a glum kind of spirituality. They are sentimental, even Biblical ('what was below me was neither mountains nor rivers nor earth nor sea and I was not afraid') and often repetitious. Despite (but also partly because of) all this, they give as good a sense as anything written at the time of what it was like to be a young English fighter pilot.

'Death of an Old Old Man' begins as the vivid first-person account of a pilot who can scarcely control his terror in the mess just before a sortie. After take-off the narrative switches to the third person for a coolly-controlled drama in which the Englishman fights a German thousands of feet above Holland, only to be drowned by him in a pond after their planes have collided and both have baled out. Returning to the pilot's own thoughts as he dies, the story invests this ignominious ending with romantic desirability: 'I think I'll stay here for a bit. I think I'll go along the hedges and find some primroses, and if I am lucky I may find some white violets. Then I will go to sleep. I will go to sleep in the sun.'⁵²

'They Shall Not Grow Old' (the title is another echo from the Remembrance Day services of Dahl's school-days) is set in Haifa and the first part of the story is closely based on his own experiences in June 1942: the sorties described are ones which he flew. The men are waiting for a pilot called Fin to return from a patrol over Beirut harbour. The Scandinavian-sounding hero is a Hollywood version of Dahl himself: 'tall and full of laughter . . . with black hair and a long straight nose which he used to stroke up and down with the tip of his finger'. He doesn't return – or at least not for forty-eight hours. Mysteriously, he is convinced that his mission has taken only an hour. His friends offer him various ready-made excuses for his absence, but he insists that he is right.

The explanation when it comes is a mixture of science fiction and school-chapel mysticism. Fin is subsequently jolted by the death of another pilot into remembering what had happened. He had suicidally plunged through cloud into what should have been the ground and had seen a vision of a kind of Celestial Fly-past, in which friends and enemies flew in line together to what might have been Bunyan's notion of the Eternal Airfield: a great green plain bathed in a transcendent blue light. Here, however, Fin's own aircraft would not permit itself to be landed. He returns, forty-eight hours delayed, to tell the story before going out to repeat the experience, this time without coming back.

One of Dahl's concerns in the story is with different kinds of credibility. 'There is never any doubting of anything that anyone says when he is talking about his flying', the narrator says. 'There can only be a doubting of one's self.' 'They Shall Not Grow Old' is an attempt to balance the prosaic, fact-bound world of the aerodrome, with its official reports and regulations and timetables, against the other-worldly, hallucinatory aspects of flying (with its multiple horizons and the black-outs to which any pilot, but particularly the injured Dahl, was susceptible) and of living so close to death.

It was inevitable that Dahl's later stories for children would often involve flight. It is by air that James escapes on the expanding peach from his tyrannical aunts (and sees mysterious beings in the clouds). The BFG seems to Sophie to fly as he carries her to London on their life-saving mission against the giants – a mission in which the RAF plays a part. And in Dahl's last story, Billy flies through flames on a swan's back in order to free the dragon-oppressed Minpins, then returns home safely to his mother.

Dahl himself went home in the summer of 1941. Sofie had belatedly left Kent, driven out by the German bombing, and had moved to the village of Grendon Underwood between Aylesbury and Bicester, about fifty miles north-west of London. Dahl knew nothing of his family's movements and found it difficult to trace them when he docked in Liverpool. He had made a hazardous voyage in convoy from Suez, around the Cape and up the west coast of Africa. This was his first sight of England in almost three years. He had sent a telegram from Alexandria saying that he was on his way, in excellent health and that the war in Syria had been 'fun'.[53] The message did not arrive, so no one was expecting him. At last he made contact by telephone and was on his way.

There is an intense intimacy about the description of his homecoming at the end of *Going Solo* which comes partly from its stylistic simplicity and awkwardness, and partly from Dahl's concentration on Sofie's feelings about him, as well as his about her:

> I caught sight of my mother when the bus was still a hundred yards away. She was standing patiently outside the gate of the cottage waiting for the bus to come along, and for all I know she had been standing there when the earlier bus had gone by an hour or two before. But what is one hour or even three hours when you have been waiting for three years?
>
> I signalled the bus-driver and he stopped the bus for me right outside the cottage, and I flew down the steps of the bus straight into the arms of the waiting mother.

As in his story 'Only This', the son imagines the mother imagining him and in the process they merge. Yet what Dahl still needed was a father, or fathers. That autumn he tracked one down.

4

Disney

The only delicate colours in paintings by Matthew Smith are used for flowers. They give away that this pupil of Matisse was English. His nudes, on the other hand, sprawl in a palette of crimson, green and bright blue, their big yellow-cream breasts and thighs luminous against a thundery background. Francis Bacon thought him 'one of the very few English painters since Constable and Turner to be concerned with painting' in the sense that 'the image is the paint and vice versa. Here the brush-stroke creates the form and does not merely fill it in.'[1] Whether or not you find Matthew Smith as original as this makes him sound, there is no question that (like Bacon's own) Smith's work caused a shock.

Some of these erratic, unforgettable canvases looked out from gallery windows into the austerity of wartime London. They ignored the Blitz and rationing; Smith had painted most of them in France between the end of the First World War, in which he was wounded at Ypres, and the new German invasion of 1940.

It was now the autumn of 1941 and Dahl had been back in England since July. He was at a loose end and there was some money in his bank account. In North Africa he had found few opportunities to spend his salary, and since coming home he had been promoted from Pilot Officer to Flying Officer. He had saved four hundred pounds (in today's terms, about £10,000).[2] Wandering around the West End of London that autumn, he had been struck by Matthew Smith's vivid paintings and wanted to see more. But Smith had moved studios and the gallery-owners had lost touch with him.

Dahl's years abroad had fostered an appetite for challenges and a questing, obsessive kind of thoroughness in meeting them. He pursued Matthew Smith through a thicket of forwarding addresses – Fulham Road, Edith Grove, Dawes Road, Redcliffe Gardens – finally reaching a hotel near Hyde Park. From a first-floor room he heard one of the Brandenburg Concertos on a gramophone. A pale, scared old man in his socks answered the door and gazed through thick spectacles at an RAF officer in uniform.

Matthew Smith was hiding because both of his sons had recently been killed: Dermot that same year, soon after winning a DSO; Mark the year before. They had been in the RAF. Dermot, the younger son, was the same age as Dahl. Their father, now in his early sixties, was almost crushed by losing them; Cyril Connolly talks of frequent meals with him and their friend Augustus John at which Smith sat speechless with grief.[3] The artist himself was lucky to be alive. Connolly had recently recommended a hotel to him, but when he went there it had no vacancies; that night, it was almost obliterated by a bomb. Dahl's arrival was one of the pieces of good fortune that came to Smith at this unhappy time. Another was meeting Mary Keene, who was to become his most lasting mistress and later a close friend of Dahl's too.

Since the death of his sons Smith had more or less stopped painting, but these new friends stirred him up and he began work on their portraits. Dahl sat for him in uniform, a heavy orange drape behind his tanned head, the red chair-back giving its colour to his full mouth. He looks away to his left but without focusing, like someone sad or apprehensive – or scheming.

If Dahl's pursuit of Matthew Smith showed his determination, the relationship also revealed another trait over the years, one which he had inherited from his father. He was intensely acquisitive. Helped by what he learnt from the painter, he was to build up over the years a valuable collection of modern art. He bought the less expensive work of already-established modern masters – Matisse drawings, Picasso lithographs, Rouault watercolours – and became one of the earliest collectors of the Russian Constructivists, especially Popova, as well as of British artists such as Henry

Moore, Francis Bacon and Matthew Smith himself. Dahl had a good eye: it was as a lover of pictures, not an incipient collector-dealer, that he tracked Smith down. But he was also greedy and regarded expertise itself as a form of possession. Having missed a university education, he was untouched by the scepticism and intellectual modesty which it might have brought: suspicion of fact-learning, consciousness of unreachable horizons. Art to him, like many other interests, quickly became a matter not only of beauty, not only even of collectibility, but of information: names, places, dates, prices. These were hard assets, chips to stack against other people's. It was the same at other stages in his life with birds' eggs, music, women, wine, orchids, edible fungi. They were all things you could enjoy for themselves, but even more for the part that your knowledge about them might play in a socially competitive game.

Matthew Smith was the first established artist in any medium whom Dahl came to know well. The contact widened his horizons, but was also to be of practical use to him in his next posting. According to his own account, during the winter of 1941–42 a friend took him to dinner at Pratt's, one of the grander London men's clubs, off St James's Street.[4] At the common table he found himself sitting next to either the Under-Secretary of State for Air, Harold Balfour, or in another version, the Secretary of State himself, Sir Archibald Sinclair.[5] Whoever it was, he was taken with this cultivated, forceful young injured pilot who seemed to be able to talk about anything – even modern art – and also played a perfectly good hand of bridge. The USA had just come into the war but the British still needed to press their own cause there. In this, Dahl might have something to offer.

He was ordered to Glasgow, to embark on a Polish ship in a convoy bound for Canada. The crossing lasted two weeks, during which he took his turn on watch for U-boats and made friends with another RAF pilot, Douglas Bisgood, with whom he swapped versions of the air force myth of the gremlins: a race of supernatural elves blamed for everything that went mechanically wrong on flying missions.[6] Bisgood was heading for the east coast of Canada as an instructor in an officer training unit. Dahl went south to Washington to join the British Embassy as Assistant Air Attaché.

As when he first joined Shell, Dahl found himself in some ways back at school. In the view of one of his more important Washington colleagues, Isaiah (now Sir Isaiah) Berlin: 'Everywhere the British go, they impose the pattern of the public school.' The country's representatives in wartime Washington were no exception. Berlin recalls:

> At the top was Halifax, who was a kind of Provost, and had some disdain for the officials of the Embassy and the Missions. Very grand, very viceregal. The Headmaster was Sir Ronald Campbell, who was a very nice man. Then the Head of Chancery, Michael Wright, who was an Old Boy: totally devoted to the school, thought about nothing but the school, came back to it with enthusiasm as a housemaster, a rigid disciplinarian with little humour – charmless, with something fanatical about him . . . Then there were the other Missions. They were looked on rather as a grammar school was looked on by public-school-boys, at least in those days.[7]

The senior boys were sober, industrious, high-flying career diplomats like William Hayter, a future ambassador to Moscow, and Paul Gore-Booth, who would become High Commissioner to India. Young Dahl saw little of them, because his desk was not in the Chancery but at the Air Mission, in an annexe. The missions shared a canteen with the main Embassy and sometimes he and Isaiah Berlin lunched together there. But more of the assistant air attaché's time was spent in the company of the future advertising mogul David Ogilvy, with whom Dahl shared a house in Georgetown, and his friend Ivar Bryce, a handsome Etonian playboy who was in turn friendly with the journalist and future thriller writer Ian Fleming.

All three were members of the British intelligence services, to which Dahl himself soon became loosely attached. As allies, the British and the Americans weren't officially supposed to spy on one another but of course they did. Dahl was encouraged to get close to as many well-placed people as he could and listen. The gossip columnist Drew Pearson was one target. Another was the influential reporter Ralph Ingersoll, who had covered the Battle of Britain in 1940, interviewed Stalin in 1941 and was the author of *Report on England* and *America Is Worth Fighting For*. A third was Vice-President Wallace's newspaper-owning friend Charles Marsh.

To Marsh, as to many people in the social world to which he gave Dahl an entrée, the young pilot was unusually attractive. He had all the spiritedness of the RAF, heightened by his early release from the fighting. He was inquisitive and sure of himself in a way that made him seem exceptionally intelligent. And unlike most of his compatriots, but acceptably enough in Washington – and particularly to Marsh – he was a stupendous boaster.

From the point of view of the British war effort all these characteristics could be made use of, particularly the last. Every diplomat is involved in creating a national fiction, and during the early months of the US involvement in the war the many Allied reverses – in North Africa, in Singapore and at sea – were in need of a coat of gloss. Even among US supporters of Britain (by no means the overwhelming majority), plenty of people thought that the Brits were asking for too much and making a mess of what they were given. Since there was little in the current news that could be used to British advantage, the Embassy decided that propaganda efforts should concentrate on past glories, especially those of the Royal Air Force.

This was the kind of work which the novelist C. S. Forester was in the USA to do. 'Captain Hornblower', as he was inevitably known, was in his forties. Sir Isaiah Berlin remembers him as a 'nice, honest British patriot, who did a lot of work with his American admirers for England.'[8] Forester asked Dahl to tell him his own story so that he could write it up. Dahl thought it easier to put something on paper himself. The result was vivid and plainly written, if not without a literary pretension to plainness that showed he had been reading Hemingway. Forester was impressed and placed the piece in an influential US magazine, the *Saturday Evening Post*, where it appeared anonymously in August 1942 under the title 'Shot Down Over Libya'.

The story was introduced as a 'factual report on Libyan air fighting', by an unnamed RAF pilot 'at present in this country for medical reasons' – a reference to Dahl's troubles with his injured back, which were being treated by a surgeon friend of Charles Marsh's in Texas. The narrator describes himself strafing enemy lorries while being pursued by Italian fighters: 'Hell's bells, what was that? Felt like she was hit somewhere. Blast this stick; it won't come back. They must have got my tail plane and jammed my elevators.' His Hurricane crashes in flames. Much later Dahl remembered that he hadn't been shot down. Well, he said, the story had been edited and misleadingly captioned.[9] But this contradicted another claim, that no one had touched a word. When, soon after the war ended, the piece was collected in a book he tried to cover his tracks by rewriting it more factually – no Italian fighters, no battle. He then pretended that this version was the original one.[10]

The incidents themselves, of course, weren't entirely fictional. After Dahl had recovered from the worst of his accident injuries, he really had flown Hurricanes, shot at lorries and been pursued by enemy aircraft. In dramatizing all this he began his career as an imaginative writer. He also considerably enhanced his status in Washington – that and his already considerable sex appeal. Charles Marsh's daughter, Antoinette, says 'Girls just fell at Roald's feet. He was very arrogant with them, but he got away with it. That uniform didn't hurt one bit – and he was an ace. I think he slept with everybody on the East and West Coasts that had more than fifty thousand dollars a year.' To his awed buddy, Creekmore Fath he was simply 'one of the biggest cocksmen in Washington'.

Women vastly outnumbered men in the wartime capital, but those who knew Dahl there – among them the war correspondent Martha Gellhorn, who had recently married Ernest Hemingway – agree with Antoinette Marsh that he was attractive by the standards of any time and place.[11] Particularly, once again, to older women. The French actress Annabella (Suzanne Charpentier), with whom he was to become very close, was seven years his senior. And

Clare Boothe Luce was thirteen years older than Dahl when she was placed beside him at an Embassy dinner.

Mrs Luce was powerful, enterprising and crucial to British interests. She had been involved with the pro-British group 'Union Now' since 1940. A journalist who had been in Belgium just before Dunkirk and in the Pacific just before Pearl Harbor, she was now a member of Congress. And of course she was married to Henry Luce, the owner of *Time* and *Life*. According to Creekmore Fath, she took instantly to the young Dahl, spent the whole evening talking to him and gave him a lift home. Officials were discreetly encouraging, but after some days more than encouragement was needed. In Fath's words, Dahl told him:

> I am all fucked out. That goddam woman has absolutely screwed me from one end of the room to the other for three goddam nights. I went back to the Ambassador this morning, and I said, 'You know, it's a great assignment, but I just can't go on.' And the Ambassador said, 'Roald, did you ever see the Charles Laughton movie of Henry VIII?' And I said 'Yes'. 'Well,' he said, 'do you remember the scene with Henry going into the bedroom with Anne of Cleves, and he turns and says "The things I've done for England"? Well, that's what you've got to do.'

At this distance what comes across most vividly from the story is the atmosphere of a school dormitory, ringing with boasts of sexual adventures during the past holidays. Sir Isaiah Berlin calls the anecdote 'a wild flight of fancy – not untypical!' and says, 'It is inconceivable that Halifax would have talked like that to anybody,' let alone to someone as unimportant as Dahl. But there was no shortage of supporting evidence for Dahl's tales of sexual conquest. He showed Fath a Tiffany gold key which he had been given to the house of the Standard Oil heiress Millicent Rogers, along with a gold cigarette case and lighter and what Fath describes as 'all this stuff. And Roald loved it, absolutely loved it, and he showed you all this junk, you know.'

Dahl was increasingly drawn to conspicuous wealth. Of course, he particularly liked conspicuous modern paintings and in this respect, as in others, wartime Washington must have seemed to him like El Dorado. Millicent Rogers' house was a small museum of French Impressionism. So too was the Charles Marsh country mansion where Dahl and Creekmore Fath spent many of their weekends.

Longlea stood in eight hundred acres of Virginia. Its châtelaine was Alice Glass, a much-photographed beauty in her late twenties who was fond of music, good causes and powerful men. It was she who had chosen the design of the house (Old English Manorial), found stonemasons capable of building it and furnished it to look as though (Monets and Renoirs apart) it belonged in Renaissance Europe. The eighteen black servants and the champagne breakfasts, on the other hand, were more in the style of the house's owner. Alice Glass was Charles Marsh's mistress, but she was in love with one of his protégés, the callow young Lyndon Johnson, whom she often entertained at Longlea.

Washington and its environs had become more than ever the social as well as the political hub of the USA. For the rich, as the journalist David Brinkley recalls in *Washington Goes to War*, there seemed to be nowhere else to go.[12] Foreign travel was impossible. And the capital's attractions were augmented by an inpouring of rich European refugees and visiting statesmen. ('More kings are expected', assistant secretary of state Adolf Berle wrote wearily in his journal. 'They take so much time.'[13]) President Roosevelt added edge to the amusements by attacking 'parasites' and the 'twenty-room mansions in Massachusetts Avenue' which he thought they should have handed over to people more valuable to the war effort. One of his targets was Cissy Patterson, owner of the conservative *Times-Herald*. Another was the preposterously rich society hostess Evalyn Walsh McLean, a gold-mine heiress who in her last years used to encourage soldiers to pass around her biggest diamond and to photograph their girl-friends wearing it. It was in her house, according to Brinkley, that Dahl had a brush with one of the *Times-Herald*'s hard-line isolationist writers, Frank Waldrop. 'Do you realize,' Dahl asked him when there was a pause in the conversation, 'that if you were to go to England today there are men in your US Eighth Air Force who would tear you limb from limb for the things you write?' Waldrop considered. 'Well,' he said eventually, 'I guess I won't go to England.'[14]

Dahl gradually came to know almost everyone. Creekmore Fath got him invited to the White House, where he first met Martha Gellhorn (who thought him 'very, very attractive and slightly mad, which I attributed to hitting the ground') and, through her, Ernest Hemingway. Ralph Ingersoll introduced him to the dramatist Lillian Hellman.[15] Dahl joined a poker school where one of the regular players was Senator Harry Truman, to whom he lost the whole $1000 he earned for his first story – or so he liked to say.[16] When famous British authors came to town, it was Dahl who was deputed to look after them. Some of these – among them Noël Coward, who thought Dahl very bright[17] – were working for the wartime intelligence agencies.

To anyone, let alone a twenty-five-year-old who a year before was being shot at in the sky above Palestine, it would all have seemed like a fantasy. Dahl's daughter Tessa thinks that it permanently turned his head. But he already had an exuberant imagination, and one which he was unusually keen to share with other people.[18] David Ogilvy remembers some of the yarns he told, half-pretending they were true. One was about a friend of his whose car had broken down in the Sinai Desert. According to the story, a rich man had taken him to his home and introduced him to his beautiful wife and daughter. During the night a woman joined him in bed, but he couldn't see her face because it was dark. The next day, as his host drove him back to the garage, he casually mentioned another daughter in the house who would never emerge in daylight. 'Why?', the guest asked. 'Oh, because she has leprosy.' Dahl later wrote up the story as 'The Visitor'. 'It was fantastic!', the narrator says there. 'It was straight out of Hans Christian Andersen or Grimm.'[19]

Almost inevitably, the much talked-of teller of fairy-tales was soon invited to Hollywood. The project was to make a movie of the RAF legend of the gremlins, which Dahl had been turning into a story. The point of the legend was that anything which went technically wrong on RAF flying missions was caused not by human error but by supernatural malice. It was an innocent way of reducing tension between airmen and ground crews, and seems to have gone back at least as far as the 1920s.[20] It could also be limitlessly elaborated. Dahl's version, originally entitled 'Gremlin Lore' and written within months of his arrival in Washington, involves an imaginary world that would be Tolkien-like but for the vigorous sexuality of its inhabitants. The Gremlins have girl-friends called Fifinellas. Their offspring are Widgets. The pilots also encounter other gremlin mutants, including a high-altitude variety to which they give the name Spandules. Dahl's story concerns the pilots' successful efforts to win all these troublesome creatures over to their own side. It was *The Gremlins* more than 'Shot Down Over Libya' which publicly launched Dahl as an author. Even at the time it must have seemed strange that what had been occupying some of the idle hours of this confident, outgoing, ambitious young bachelor-about-town was a children's story. *The Gremlins* is rooted in a mixture of English landscapes, schoolboy fiction and northern European mythology: in other words, in Dahl's own childhood.

As a serving officer he was required to submit everything he wrote for approval by the British Information Services in New York. His first draft landed on the desk of Sidney Bernstein, who in peacetime was a movie entrepreneur. On 1 July 1942 Bernstein sent the story to his friend Walt Disney.

Disney was having both a bad and a good war.[21] His most successful films had made half their revenues in continental Europe: *Snow White*, released in 1937, was a huge commercial success there and financed the move of the Disney studios to their present site in Burbank. But in the newly contracted market *Pinocchio* and *Fantasia*, both released in 1940, lost money. On the other hand there were plenty of opportunities for government-funded training films and propaganda. Most of these – like most of Disney's output in general – were 'shorts', but the company was now preparing two full-length features: *Saludos Amigos*, designed to encourage good relations between North and South America, and *Victory Through*

Air Power. Neither of course involved fairy-tales, at least in the sense Walt Disney was used to. Dahl's story, by contrast, seemed ideally suited to the studio's gifts and expertise, and Disney immediately cabled both Dahl and Bernstein,[22] saying that the author would be contacted by 'our Mr Feitel in Washington'.

Feitel's business-like account of the meeting arrived at Burbank three days later. 'Dahl is a young fellow,' he reported encouragingly, 'and . . . does not regard himself as a professional writer . . . GREMLIN LORE has not been copyrighted, and is not in the hands of any literary agent.' Payment would have to be shared between Dahl and the RAF, but it was Feitel's impression that he 'would accept any reasonable deal on our usual basis.' There was just one problem. 'The Gremlin characters are not creatures of his imagination as they are "well known" by the entire R.A.F. and as far as I can determine no individual can claim credit. Therefore, I doubt that the name "Gremlin" can be copyrighted.'

The Disney machine now went into motion, acquiring rights in the story (subject to a supervisory clause required by the RAF), arranging rapid provision of illustrations for its appearance in *Cosmopolitan* that winter[23] and hiring Charlotte Clarke, who had made the original Mickey Mouse dolls, to do the same for the Gremlins. To Dahl's surprise these figurines were later rented out for use in a magazine ad for Life Saver peppermints. He protested to Walt Disney[24] about the likely damage to the characters' mystique, but Disney patiently explained that this was all part of the business of establishing copyright.

He wasn't being entirely disingenuous. Various other gremlin projects were in the air. A literary agent wrote to Disney in October[25] offering him a book called *David and the Gremlins* by another British writer, R. Sugden Tilley. Meanwhile, rival studios were working on similar films. The Disney brothers leaned hard on their competitors over this, promising to return the favour when it was needed. Warner Brothers duly removed the word 'gremlins' from the titles of two films, including one originally entitled *The Gremlins from the Kremlin* in which Russian elves sabotage Hitler's plane when he decides to lead a bombing raid against Moscow.

As part of the studio's elaborate preparations, an article was sent under Walt Disney's name to the RAF journal asking for first-hand accounts of gremlin sightings. The film project had been widely reported, so some such accounts were already coming in. Disney didn't quite know what to make of them. His own attitude to the characters veered between leaden jocularity ('Do you suppose it would be possible to find one of the little fellows . . . and have him crated and shipped to California?') and the more solemn credence accorded to the studio's 'creations'. No one in the company seems to have had a clear idea where truth ended and fantasy began. In a memo headed 'Gremlin Research', for example, one of Disney's employees reported on a discussion with Dahl in the spirit of an anthropologist engaged in a particularly complex piece of field-work. Enlisted men in the RAF, he explained, 'naturally come from all sections of England and Scotland' so that 'We could feature a wide variety of dialects'. And 'While only flyers who have been in battle can actually see the Gremlins, the evidence of their handi-work can affect all members of the airfield staff.'[26] Whether he knew it or not, Disney was much teased about this seeming cred-ulity by his correspondents. Hearing of the project the author Rayner Heppenstall, who was serving at the RAF Delegation in Dayton, Ohio, wrote to Disney about his misgivings that the film might hurt gremlin sensitivities, with possible repercussions on the war effort – and even on the studio itself.[27]

Roald Dahl meanwhile was having fun with Walt's anxieties about the exact appearance of the gremlins – the subject of many grave conversations in Burbank. Disney wanted authenticity. But he also believed that whatever his studio drew was automatically so, and not otherwise. Dahl would have none of this. 'I am very glad to see that you had no very definite views about Gremlins not wearing bowler hats', he wrote to him in October 1942, 'but their omission in your drawings did cause a little trouble.' Dahl pointed out that however powerful Disney's artists were, the fact that one of them drew a gremlin in a way that differed from 'what he really looks like' would not cause every gremlin in the world to alter itself to match the artist's impression. 'After all, one may as well say that if you drew an elephant that looked rather like a horse, all elephants in every part of the world will henceforth look like horses, which is of course incorrect.'

Time was passing and on the other side of the world real pilots, British and American, were dropping from the sky in flames. In Britain there were signs of popular irritation with the publicity for the project, and when a story got around that Walt Disney was planning a personal trip to England to 'research' it, the *Observer* commented drily: 'It will seem strange indeed to the future historians who, unravelling the tale of our troubled times, discover that in the critical year 1942, a distinguished American travelled five thousand miles in order to make a film about elves.'[28] Whether or not he was influenced by such criticism, Disney stayed at home and as 1942 drifted into 1943 his enthusiasm began to cool. US opinion polls were showing a marked dip in the popularity of war-related topics. Besides, if *The Gremlins* were to be made as a full-length feature, it might have become out of date by the time it was completed. It was already costing a lot of money: over $50,000 between July 1942 and April 1943. The studio's script-writer alone expected $1,500 a week. Two complete scripts were prepared: one of 150 pages for a full-length feature, and another a third as long. They were picked over by teams of advisers (one script was sent out to forty-five different people, Dahl not among them), all of whom had comments to make. What should the title be? *Gremlin Gambols* was suggested, and *Gay Gremlins* and *We've Got Gremlins*. The company's legal counsel, Gunther Lessing by name, objected to a satirical episode involving Hitler: 'pure propaganda stuff which should not be indulged in here'. Questions were raised about audience appeal. Perce Pearce, who had been a sequence director on *Snow White*, said he had run into marketing problems in New York. He also had difficulty in seeing how the Gremlins could be made attractive without costing the aircrews some loss of sympathy: 'basically, if these little guys are the pilots' alibis for their own stupidity, dereliction of duty, neglect, then you are taking some of the glamour off the RAF, for me.'[29] Then there was the problem of technicality. Could the film be made in such a way as to appeal both to a general audience – 'Aunt Bessy' in studio parlance – and to professional airmen? Perhaps it should be turned into a safety training movie aimed solely at the air forces. And so on.

With his sense of humour and his cocksure enthusiasm, Roald Dahl was popular at Burbank. The Disney brothers both liked him and could see his potential, and the attraction was mutual. All his life Dahl would tell stories of how, when he was only twenty-five, Walt Disney brought him to Hollywood, gave him the use of a car and put him up in the Beverly Hills Hotel. Because he was tall and admired Kipling, Walt affectionately called him 'Stalky'. His replies to Stalky's letters, however, were becoming vague. On 2 July 1943 he wrote, 'Let's try to get together for a cocktail when I'm in New York'; and on December 18, 'I was in Washington a couple of weeks ago and fully intended to see you while there, but was bedded with the grippe which shot my plans all to pieces.' In the beginning, the movie was going to be a full-length feature, part live action, part animation. Then it was going to be a cartoon short. Now Disney said he was having trouble getting his crews interested. If they ever hit upon the right angle, they would get in touch.

So the scheme fizzled out. In the words of Richard Shale, one of the Disney Studio's historians, it was 'by no means the only war-time project which failed to reach the screen, though it was surely the costliest'. Eventually, in 1943, *Walt Disney: The Gremlins (A Royal Air Force Story by Flight Lieutenant Roald Dahl)* was turned into a Disney picture-book published by Random House in the USA and by Collins in Australia and Great Britain. It was Dahl's first book.

Of all the obstacles which Disney had met, the question of owner-ship was the biggest. One claimant was Charles Graves, author of a history of the RAF, *The Thin Blue Line*, published in 1941. He said that he was the first to have mentioned gremlins in print and that he had subsequently been researching the subject for a book.[30] Disney ought to pay him something, he argued, so that he could in turn pay those he had talked to. He wanted 500 guineas (then $2,100), but was headed off by a tough letter from the Air Ministry pointing out that the film's proceeds were earmarked for the RAF Benevolent Fund.[31]

This was also Disney's reply to another, more credible and angrier-seeming claimant. As early as the autumn of 1942, newspaper stories about the project had reached Dahl's erstwhile travelling companion Douglas Bisgood.[32] As they had crossed the Atlantic together, Bisgood had entertained Dahl with his own version of the gremlin story. The Fifinellas, the Widgets and the rest were, he now claimed in a strong letter to Disney,[33] 'family names which I claim as being my originals' and which he was putting into a book of his own. Bisgood also wrote to Dahl reminding him of all this, and taking the opportunity to joke sourly about the contrast between Dahl's 'pleasant appointment in America' and his own recent return to England 'ferrying a bomber over, which necessitated the risk of running into bands of hostile "Gremlins". He had tired of training new pilots in Canada, he said, and had volunteered to return to his fighter squadron, which was stationed near Aylesbury, close to Dahl's mother's new home. Bisgood didn't mention that while making a meteorological flight in bad weather he had run into and single-handedly attacked three German bombers, sending one burning into the sea, an exploit for which he had been awarded the Distinguished Flying Cross.[34]

Dahl brushed aside Bisgood's letter, telling Disney that while 'Bissie . . . is without doubt an eminent Gremlinologist . . . I am quite sure that he will not cause any trouble.'[35] (He didn't, and was eventually killed, still flying for the RAF, soon after the end of the war.) Dahl had in any case always made it clear that the myth wasn't his own invention. Around the time that his book was published, at least two others like it appeared: *Sh! Gremlins* by 'H.W.' and *Gremlins on the Job* by Judy Varga. But it was Dahl's version that Disney made famous, and it was to Dahl that the popular credit soon went for having dreamed up not only the story but the very word 'gremlins' – a claim he soon became increasingly willing to adopt.[36] Isaiah Berlin remembers: 'He initiated gremlins. That is to say, they were already there, in the Air Force, but he put them on the map. He was extremely conceited, saw himself as a creative artist of a high order, and therefore entitled to respect and very special treatment.'

Certainly, Dahl not only wrote down the gremlins legend but gave it the beginnings of his own style. There is the hint of auto-biography in the pilot Gus, shot down, injured, but determined to get back into action. There is the button-holing, direct manner, with its assumption that the story-teller and his audience are in the same room. And there is the confidence – however glibly rhetorical – of the opening phrases:

> It was some time during the Battle of Britain, when Hurricanes and Spitfires were up from dawn to dark and the noise of battle was heard all day in the sky; when the English countryside from Thanet to Severn was dotted with the wreckage of planes. It was in the early autumn, when the chestnuts were ripening and the apples were beginning to drop off the trees – it was then that the first gremlins were seen by the Royal Air Force.

Although *The Gremlins* never reached the screen, the project was enough to make Dahl 'bankable' as a writer. In 1943 he was taken on by a literary agent, Ann Watkins, and by the autumn of the following year he had published 'Shot Down Over Libya' in the *Saturday Evening Post*, 'The Gremlins' both in *Cosmopolitan* and in book form, 'The Sword' in *Atlantic Monthly*, 'Katina' and 'Only This' in the *Ladies' Home Journal* and 'Beware of the Dog' in *Harper's*. Like any young writer, he was trying out styles. 'The Sword' is in the manner of a florid nineteenth-century orientalist yarn:

> In September the northeast monsoon begins to blow across the Indian Ocean, and the Arabs in the Persian Gulf turn towards Mecca and give thanks to the Prophet for his goodness. Then they load up their dhows and, trusting to the wind and to the

stars, they sail down the Gulf of Oman, around the Cape of Ras el Hadd, and westwards to the coast of Africa.

They come from Muscat and Shinas and Sohar, and they carry in their ships great bundles of carpets from Khuzistan . . .

This appeared in the prestigious *Atlantic Monthly* in August 1943. (Dahl never reprinted the story, but more than forty years later, with his usual frugality, worked much of it almost verbatim into the second of his books of memoirs for children, *Going Solo*.) A few months later the *Ladies' Home Journal* published 'Katina', which was written in his Hemingway mode. It begins:

Peter saw her first.

She was sitting on a stone, quite still, with her hands resting on her lap. She was staring vacantly ahead, seeing nothing, and all around, up and down the little street, people were running backward and forward with buckets of water, emptying them through the windows of the burning houses.

Though the styles are not original, they show Dahl's verve and fluency, and it is easy to see why editors noticed his stories. Wartime conditions had greatly expanded the market for fiction. Magazines were greedy for propaganda. Headline writers such as those at the *Saturday Evening Post* (in which 'Shot Down Over Libya' appeared) were enjoying a particularly easy time: 'Hitler Has You Card-Indexed'; 'Specialists in Sudden Death. The Fighting Marines in Full Color'. Leader-writers followed their leaders ('Nazism isn't an ideology but just a skillfully contrived program for conquest.') And contributors delivered accordingly. In the *Atlantic Monthly*, under the title 'Cracking the German Dam', Guy Gibson first tried out the story which was to become *The Dam Busters*, John Pudney contributed 'Missing' and other poems, and John Buxton his sonnets from the prison camp Oflag VIB. In the *Ladies' Home Journal* Eleanor Roosevelt tackled readers' questions about the war, while romantic fiction supplied answers of its own: 'The Sarge whistled, 12,000 miles away, and a red-haired girl in Georgia heard the music in her heart.'

Each one of Dahl's stories which found a publisher during the years most dangerous for the Allies contained some overt propaganda. In the case of *The Gremlins*, it is true, the objections of Disney's lawyer Gunther Lessing led to the removal of an episode in which Hitler, 'sputtering a flood of unintelligible German', complains to Goebbels and Goering that British newspapers have been crediting the Gremlins with all the good work done by the Luftwaffe. (The scene was to have been interrupted by the entry of Mussolini 'looking pretty battered [and] holding his hands up sort of like an Italian chef describing a dish of spaghetti'.) But the story kept its main theme: that nothing would stop our boys from getting back at Jerry. 'The Sword' delivers the same message. In Dar es Salaam in 1939 the English narrator's servant, a bellicose Mwanumwezi tribesman, hears that his master is at war with the Germans. Taking a prized Arab sword from the wall, he slips out of the house and decapitates a local sisal farmer who has unwisely stayed on in what used to be German East Africa. Again, in 'Katina', set during the British evacuation of Greece in 1941, there are two moments of defiance: one when a fleeing RAF pilot unexpectedly makes telephone contact with a German and tells him he'll be back; the other at the story's climax, when Katina runs across the airstrip shaking her fists at a squadron of Messerschmitts, and is killed.

Like several of the other stories Dahl wrote at this time, 'Katina' has a throb of adolescent mysticism: the Greek mountains silently take part in actions which, to them, are of no more importance than the battle of Thermopylae. There is also a straightforward human warmth in his war fiction which would soon disappear, although not (as the religiosity does) for ever. These semi-autobiographical fictions are full of naïve camaraderie and a protective, if sentimentalized, affection for the people whose countries have been caught up in the fighting.

In part this represents Dahl's response to the last bars of the British imperial symphony: tunes which he had learnt at school and in Shell. But there is also a humanitarian revulsion against war, which comes through most strongly in stories such as 'They Shall

Not Grow Old' and 'Death of an Old Old Man', which he was unable to publish until the war in Europe had ended.[37] But among the earliest pieces put out by the young man what is most noticeable – apart from their energy as narratives – is the fact that one, *The Gremlins*, takes the form of a children's story and another, 'Katina', is centred on a child. The Greek episode in particular has a strong vein of romance in the men's relationship with the little girl – for example, when she enters the mess tent and they all automatically stand up. There was already more than a hint of paternalism in his make-up.

Outside his published fiction, Dahl was becoming in his own person a kind of walking magazine of stories, a conduit of rumours and revelations. Whenever the British intelligence services wanted to weaken somebody's credit in Washington, they had only to dig out a little scandal from the ample supply made available by the mail censors and slip it to the gregarious assistant air attaché. By the next morning it would be in circulation.[38] Dahl in turn secretly relayed back whatever he picked up on his social rounds.

His former diplomatic colleagues tend now to play down this aspect of their work, and the details are inevitably murky. So far as they concern Dahl, the official story is that he was in Washington to represent British air interests and to liaise with representatives of Allied air forces. Dahl's own version was that he was sacked from the official embassy staff and immediately taken under Sir William Stephenson's wing at British Security Co-ordination (BSC).

Stephenson was a figure of legend, to Dahl as to others. A pilot in the First World War, he had travelled widely in the 1920s and 30s on various business projects, particularly involving steel. Among the uses of these journeys was that they enabled him to keep Churchill informed about the rearming of Nazi Germany. Once Britain was at war, Stephenson was sent to collect information about anti-British activities in the USA. After Pearl Harbor, he organized British collaboration with the US secret services and superintended a vast number of independent British activities, ranging from covert propaganda to more dangerous operations.

Stephenson's staff identified and (sometimes fabricating the evidence) discredited German agents and businesses collaborating with Germany. They used a woman agent on a Mata Hari-type mission to infiltrate the Vichy French Embassy in Washington, which was passing military information to the Germans. They manned the colourful, somewhat uncontrollable training and supply centre at Ottawa where Ian Fleming among others learnt the technical tricks of spying. It was Stephenson's 'outfit' which arranged the escape of the Danish nuclear scientist Niels Bohr on a torpedo boat. More fantastically, it came up with the idea of using Hitler's former astrologer to make damaging public predictions about him which, it was hoped, would both alarm the Führer and give comfort to his opponents.[39] Under these excitingly novelistic auspices Roald Dahl, according to his own account, was promoted to Wing Commander, made discoveries which set Downing Street alight and at the end of the war was 'commissioned to write the official history of the Strategic Intelligence Service'.[40]

As for the idea that he was sacked, it may be in the nature of things that we have only Dahl's later word for it. His friends, including some at the heart of the embassy, say that they heard nothing of the sort at the time.[41] Nor can the Ministry of Defence find any indication of his having served in even the acting rank of Wing Commander. This may have been an improvisation of Stephenson's to help Dahl impress the Americans.[42] Friends remember his having been an acting Squadron Leader, which is consistent with the lower, 'substantive' rank of Flight Lieutenant recorded as his final position in both the Air Force List and his RAF personal file.[43] As for his role in writing the official history, this was, like most such projects, a collaborative venture. It was based in Oshinawa, Ontario, and run by Tom Hill, director of Section One of BSC. Three others worked on it with Hill during the summer of 1945: the head of Stephenson's secretariat, Grace Garner; Hill's colleague Helen Lillie; and 'Wing Commander' Dahl.[44]

There is no doubt, though, that Dahl had been recruited as one of Sir William Stephenson's thousand or more regular informants in the proliferating network of British Security Co-ordination.

A familiar problem of intelligence gathering is that in some cases, what is discovered turns out to have been a secret to no one except the discoverer. This seems to have been true of at least one of Dahl's exploits as a spy.

According to his own story,[45] he was at Charles Marsh's house one evening in the summer of 1943 when Marsh gave him a 'sheaf of cabinet papers' to read which had been left behind by the Vice-President, Henry Wallace. Wallace was a radical socialist and there were many who wanted Roosevelt to ditch him – as in fact he soon did, in Truman's favour. Dahl saw that the papers mentioned both the British Empire and US plans, after the war had ended, 'to take over Europe's commercial airlines'. He excitedly summoned a colleague and passed him the material, which was taken away, photographed and speedily returned, Dahl cunningly skulking by the lavatory all the while in case he needed an excuse for his delay. The copy, Dahl later boasted, was given to Bill Stephenson, who sent it to 'C' in London, who passed it straight on to Churchill. The Prime Minister, Dahl claimed, 'could hardly believe what he was reading' and was stirred to 'cataclysms of wrath.'

Wallace's document certainly didn't favour British interests. Among other proposals for the post-war world it urged the decolonization of large parts of the British Empire, including India. But none of this was either secret or a statement of US government policy. It was the draft of a polemical pamphlet written for the Vice-President by two State Department experts and published the following spring by the Institute of Pacific Relations.[46] Although the pamphlet's appearance did elicit an official British protest about Wallace's 'regrettable' comments on the internal affairs of an ally, everything in it had been a matter of public discussion by US politicians and other commentators throughout the war. British rule in India (where Dahl's ambassador, Lord Halifax, had been Viceroy from 1925 to 1931) had been under attack for decades and was a topic of widespread criticism in the USA,[47] not least when Gandhi was locked up in 1942. As for the post-war airlines, even if it might never have independently occurred to the British that Pan American Airways hoped to dominate the world, plenty of warnings were being given. PanAm's own advertisements at the time emphasized the need for US supremacy in civil aviation, and in February 1943 Dahl's friend Clare Boothe Luce had caused a stir by supporting this line in her maiden speech in Congress.[48] Her remarks – which were of course summarized in the British Embassy's weekly report to London – were generally seen as countering criticisms of the industry's expansionism made much earlier by none other than Henry Wallace. In fact, the Foreign Office had not only already identified the problem, but had been urging Churchill to act on it (he finally turned it over to Beaverbrook) since the autumn of 1942[49] – almost a year before Dahl 'discovered' these dangerous notions in the draft of Wallace's pamphlet, so recklessly left in the home of Charles Marsh.

Still, it made for an exciting evening. In Dahl's friendship with Charles Marsh, both during the war and after, work was mixed up with a theatrical kind of pleasure – theatrical in that you had to suspend disbelief in order to enjoy it and that it used up a lot of surplus energy. Sometimes, as in the case of the imaginary correspondence with Halifax, the whole thing was a big practical joke. At others, whatever anyone else thought they were doing, both men took themselves more seriously.

Important matters could be at stake after all, and although neither Dahl nor Marsh was a key player, they were close to people who were very close to people with power. Marsh's newspaper empire in particular gave him a degree of personal influence on public opinion, especially in Texas, as well as first-hand knowledge of the personalities, ambitions and activities of individual politicians. He could be useful to the British, and their approach to him through Dahl was well calculated to flatter his already well-developed sense of his own political value. In March 1943 for example, shortly after a visit to the USA by the British Foreign Secretary, Anthony Eden, Dahl sent Marsh eleven precise questions.[50] Some asked for detailed information concerning the minuter aspects of Roosevelt's chances of re-election in 1944.

Others were more far-reaching. The Allies were beginning their long-term preparations for the Yalta summit, which would decide the shape of post-war Europe. Preliminary meetings were being planned, and the British wanted to know which of the Americans involved had most influence in this area, what their relations with each other were and who was likely to be leading the side at what everyone called 'the semi-final'.

Marsh's twelve-page reply was full of informative side-glances and showed him at his least injudicious.[51] He described the protagonists' exact shades of opinion *vis-à-vis* the Soviet Union, accurately predicted the run-up to the negotiations, gave a good sense of the impression that those concerned had formed of Eden, and warned Dahl that any attempt by Britain to make an independent early deal with the Russians would be brushed aside by Roosevelt. He also summarized some likely key factors in post-war US economic planning. But for all this show of statesmanship, Marsh was generally happier with a mixture of gossip and speculation. He added a note about a past quarrel between two politicians over a private business contract in Ohio, and described other feuds with a keen attention to detail, dialogue and narrative shaping which the writer in Dahl must have enjoyed.

The intelligence-gathering aspect of the friendship never spoiled the fun. In June 1944, for example, Marsh wrote to Dahl from Austin about why the Texas Democratic convention had gone against 'your friend Roosevelt'. 'Had you been here to advise me and report all that Isaiah [Berlin] knew in advance,' Marsh grumbled, 'I would not have been caught short.' But this was little more than a parenthesis in a letter mostly given over to boisterous sexual gossip and innuendo. There was an element of both exhibitionism and voyeurism in the relationship, and not only in the obvious sense of Marsh's boasting to the younger man about his exploits. All his letters were dictated to his secretary, Claudia Haines, whom he would marry after Alice left him. Both Claudia and her teenage daughter were devoted to Dahl and figure in the letters Claudia herself was typing. In the summer of 1945 Charles dictated: 'Claudia is too conceited to call herself your mother. She will settle on the Aunt position, though I strongly suspect that she wants to be more than the big sister. No woman will settle for anything less than being a woman.'

Son, nephew, brother – these were roles which Dahl understood and could manage. Claudia Marsh still describes him as 'part of the family'. Many who knew him at the time thought that his sexual dealings, on the other hand, were not happy. David Ogilvy believes that Dahl was interested in women to the extent that he could boast about them, and 'when they fell in love with him, as a lot did, I don't think he was nice to them'. Helen Lillie, with whom Dahl drove to Canada when they began work together on the history of British Security Co-ordination, says much the same.[52] Martha Gellhorn concluded that he hated women, and that his main interest in her was as a means of access to Hemingway. (When in 1944 she enlisted Dahl's help in getting both her and her husband to Britain to report on the invasion of France, he found an aeroplane seat for Hemingway and left Gellhorn to trail behind by boat.)

But at least one of the women whom Dahl met at this time thinks differently. The French actress Annabella spent most of the war in the USA, starring in morale-boosting plays and films such as *Bomber's Moon* and *Tonight We Raid Calais*. In 1944 her husband, the actor Tyrone Power, was in the Pacific with the US Air Force, and Annabella came to Washington in the pre-Broadway run of Franz Werfel's play *Jacobowsky and the Colonel*.[53] At the first-night dinner she found herself sitting next to Dahl. He had by now perfected his social trick of trying out his stories on people. It was a way of monopolizing attention (and avoiding the necessity of small talk) but also of assessing, and sometimes dominating, his listener. The story he told the petite actress was to be published three years later as 'Man from the South'. It is about a sinister foreigner who bets his Cadillac that a younger man can't make his cigarette lighter work ten times in succession. The stake he wants from his rival is the little finger of his left hand. There is a more than usually grim twist at the end, when the suddenly cowed Cadillac owner is taken away in mid-bet by a minder, a woman, three of whose fingers are missing.

Annabella listened attentively and when Dahl had finished, she asked calmly, 'What happened next?' He was delighted by her sang-froid and asked if he could see her home. At lunchtime the next day he showed up as if by chance in the dining-room of her hotel, at the next table. Soon they were lovers. As Annabella says now with a shrug, 'During the war, it's life against death.'

She went back to New York, where *Jacobowsky and the Colonel* was to run for over four hundred performances (one of which would be interrupted so that Annabella could announce that Paris had been liberated). Dahl visited her there often, sometimes on his way to or from the OSS headquarters in Ottawa. On one occasion he asked if he could leave his uniform with her for a few days while he went somewhere in civilian clothes. He told her never to ask why, because it was not his secret. She enjoyed the conspiracy, and was amused by the impossibility of Roald's disguising himself: 'He was so tall and good-looking – you *had* to look at him!'

After Tyrone Power came home from the war, Annabella says, 'The crazy thing [with Roald] was off. It came back from time to time when we were . . . thrown into each other's arms. But it was like we were twin brothers. Romantic? Not really. Physical, some-times. But most important, we had a complete understanding, and he trusted me.' It was an understanding based in part on her strong practicality and courage. As a girl she had become in effect the only female Boy Scout in France, when her father, Paul Charpentier, introduced the movement to his country from Britain. His daugh-ter wore the uniform, attended rallies and camped rough, insisting that she sleep in straw like the boys rather than on one of the camp beds provided for her and her father. It was good training for the last months of the war, when she joined the Red Cross and went up through Italy with the US Army.

She and Dahl were to remain close for the rest of his life – long after her marriage to Tyrone Power ended, and for longer than any other relationship either of them had had with one of the opposite sex. She speaks of him as a great figure, a hero, and she clearly loved him. Would she then have considered marrying him? 'Certainly not,' she says without hesitation. 'Because – he was kind of impossible.'

Dahl gave his own account of love, some years later, in a piece on the subject which was commissioned by the *Ladies' Home Journal*. With the schematization of a school essay, he divided his topic into two and then subdivided it by percentages. On the one hand there is family love, between parents and children or between siblings. This kind, he said, is always clear and uncomplicated. The other sort, heterosexual romantic love, is very difficult. Here the most common form of relationship is seventy per cent based on sex and only thirty per cent on mutual affection and respect. If only 'our moral and ecclesiastical codes' permitted temporary liaisons for the pleasure and satisfaction of those concerned, without their contracting marriage, 'then this kind of love would form an excellent basis for such activity'.[54]

It can't have helped that in Washington he was professionally encouraged to practise opportunism, duplicity, entrapment. It is not far from these to the cynicism of his post-war short stories. One of them, 'My Lady Love, My Dove', concerns a couple who decide to bug the bedroom of a pair of weekend guests.[55] The idea is the wife's, but her husband's complicity seems to confirm her understanding of their relationship: 'Listen, Arthur. I'm a *nasty* person. And so are you – in a secret sort of way. That's why we get along together.'[56] At any rate he admits to his excitement in fixing up the microphone. What they overhear turns the tables on them. Their young guests have worked out a complicated technique for cheating the older couple at bridge. The spiral of conspiracy and exploitation continues as the hosts decide to learn from their example.

The fiction owes at least one detail to Dahl's connection with the secret services. Bill Stephenson's intelligence operation in the USA often seemed wayward and over-independent to its ostensible masters in Britain, and sometimes came under close scrutiny. On one occasion, it is said, Churchill's trouble-shooter Lord Beaverbrook sent a man to Washington to find out exactly what Stephenson was up to, and Stephenson encouraged Dahl to lay a trap for him.[57] Dahl gave the investigator lunch at his home in Georgetown, where he had set up a concealed microphone. As one drink followed another, Dahl began to ask leading questions about Beaverbrook. The sleuth was satisfactorily disloyal and the recording was sent to his employer, who as a result lost confidence in the eventual report. Some of Dahl's former BSC colleagues are sniffy about the episode ('I thought it was a dirty thing to do against his own country – a terribly dirty thing to do to a man who was your own fellow, er ... '[58]). But it may have helped to maintain their freedom from outside interference.

Dahl's bugging story eventually appeared in *The New Yorker*. In 1953 it was included in the collection *Someone Like You* – the first book of his to be published by Alfred Knopf, and the beginning of an association that would last for almost thirty years. Knopf were not the first publishers of Dahl's adult books, although they might have been. In July 1943 their senior editor Arthur W. Wang read Dahl's story of the outbreak of war in Dar es Salaam, 'The Sword', in *Atlantic Monthly* and wrote congratulating him and asking if he had written anything longer.[59] Dahl, who was staying with Alice Marsh at Falmouth on the Massachusetts coast, sent him 'Katina', which had not yet appeared.[60] They soon met, but Wang said what all publishers used to say – that short stories don't sell except in magazines.[61]

5

In the Valley of the Dahls

Decades later Tessa Dahl was to call the Vale of Aylesbury 'The Valley of the Dahls'. In 1945, long before the joke could have been made, the description was already apt. Sofie Dahl had moved from Kent to Grendon Underwood, a straggling village on a rise of land between Aylesbury and Bicester. Alf, now in her thirties, was in the next village with her Danish husband Leslie Hansen. Else, since 1940 Mrs John Logsdail, lived twenty miles down the road towards London, in Great Missenden. The twenty-five-year-old Asta, who had spent the war in the women's branch of the RAF, was still unmarried.

Sofie would soon move twice, first briefly to Grange Farm, Great Missenden, then to a village house in nearby Amersham. Her children usually called her Mama, but her son often referred to her as 'the mother', as if there could be no other.[1] For the next six years wherever she went, he went. It was from the long, rather bleak scatter of cottages in Grendon Underwood that he wrote to the Marshes saying that he was living contentedly, surrounded by cattle and sheep and rustic characters with straw in their hair,[2] but the way of life continued wherever they were. At Grange Farm, according to Dahl's count, they kept a cow, eight dogs, seven ducks, one pair of ferrets and another of canaries, and eventually a parrot.[3] There was also a goat in which he saw a strong resemblance to the pro-Roosevelt Senator Claude Pepper; this, Dahl said, gave him a thrill of uncertainty every day when he milked her.[4]

He had decided not to go back to Shell but to try to earn his living as an author. It was very hard adjusting to being back in post-war England, away from the excitements and illusions of Washington, but he picked up some of his pre-war hobbies, particularly greyhound racing, and settled into rural existence.

His enthusiasm for gambling brought him into regular contact with working-class people for the first time since he had left active service with the RAF. Among them was a butcher named Claud Taylor, a man of his own age who worked in Old Amersham.[5] Taylor helped Dahl to breed and train his own dogs, and they had a run of luck which made them unpopular among the local gypsy greyhound-owners.[6] Taylor also taught Roald to poach pheasant and tickle trout. Dahl made notes of the things he said in an old cardboard-bound accounts book – jokes, poaching yarns, pieces of rural lore. He especially liked to hear about the ferocity of females of any species. (It was a lifelong preoccupation. In his seventies Dahl joked to a BBC interviewer, 'There's one group of spiders where the female is so fierce that the male has to weave a web around her and wrap her up and as it were handcuff her before he can mate her – which is wonderful, I think. You could apply that to some females of the human species.'[7]) He used what he had learnt from Taylor in a series of country stories which he hoped would make a novel, but which he eventually left as a loosely-linked group called 'Claud's Dog': tales about dog-racing, rat-catching, cow-bulling, maggot-farming, a corpse in a haystack.[8] They are sour pieces: the only people in them who are vividly characterized are the unpleasant ones, and Dahl determinedly crushes any false literary idealism about the countryside. Much later, he sentimentalized those 'sweet days many years ago' in which he lived 'a pleasant leisurely life'. As he came to remember the time, what he wrote then was 'nothing but short stories . . . I worked on nothing else. I was totally preoccupied with the short story.'[9] In reality, he made more than one attempt at a novel and his mood was often one of intense gloom, anxiety about the state of the world, and preoccupation with his own lack of a clear sense of direction.

These difficulties were in part no more (or less) than those experienced by many people in adjusting to peace and to the impoverishment of post-war Britain. But Dahl was also still suffering from the effects of his accident, which in 1946 took him into the Military Hospital for Head Injuries at Wheatley, near Oxford: the latest in what was to be, for one reason and another, a lifetime of hospitalizations, especially because of back problems and his damaged nose.[10] In addition he was facing a psychological struggle: that of being a writer and – for the time being at least – nothing else. Amongst other things, this meant adapting to the fact that peacetime England was a place much more sceptical about literary talent than wartime Washington had been. Sensitive ex-RAF officers were plentiful in the Home Counties, and the fact that Dahl hobnobbed with famous Americans like Hemingway and Lillian Hellman when they were staying in London cut no ice with the Eton-and-Oxford types who held most of the literary power. Dahl was ignored, and often complained about the fact to his American friends, particularly Martha Gellhorn.

Gellhorn saw another source of complication in his return home. He was in his early thirties and on the face of it perfectly marriage-able. But his domestic circumstances could seem a deterrent to women friends. She remembers him taking her home to Wisteria Cottage in Amersham High Street, where she met his mother and what seemed like 'a thousand sisters'. There was 'a suffocating atmosphere of adoration of him . . . and I was treated with hatred by these women, because nobody could be good enough for our boy.' It was all 'very boring and very heavy'. She thought it could not have been a good situation either to have grown up in or to have returned to.

It was in these complicated psychological circumstances that Dahl made his first attempt at a novel: a pacifist fantasy about nuclear war.

In the short stories he had written in Washington the mood was already increasingly grim, closer to Wilfred Owen than to Rupert Brooke. 'Someone Like You', for example, is a conversation between two bomber pilots getting drunk in a bar. One has been through the whole war and has become obsessed with the arbitrar-iness of the fate he has been dealing out:

77

I keep thinking during a raid, when we are running over the target, just as we are going to release our bombs, I keep thinking to myself, shall I just jink a little; shall I swerve a fraction to one side, then my bombs will fall on someone else. I keep thinking, whom shall I make them fall on; whom shall I kill tonight. It is all up to me . . . It would just be a gentle pressure with the ball of my foot upon the rudder-bar; a pressure so slight that I would hardly know that I was doing it, and it would throw the bombs on to a different house and on to other people. It is all up to me.[11]

'Someone Like You' supplied the title for a later book by Dahl, but was itself collected with most of his other war stories in his first book for adults, *Over To You*. Because of Arthur Wang's doubts about short stories, Knopf had passed up the chance of publishing it,[12] so *Over To You* went to the enterprising but short-lived Reynal and Hitchcock, who brought it out in 1946. It was published soon afterwards in England by Hamish Hamilton. Noël Coward noted in his diary that the stories 'pierced the layers of my consciousness and stirred up the very deep feelings I had during the war and have since, almost deliberately, been in danger of losing'.[13]

Few British critics were keen on the mystical elements in the book – the moving mountains and Fin's heavenly landing grounds. The no-nonsense *Times Literary Supplement*, for example, said that Dahl 'is safe with men in the air or on the ground; he is less easy with mysteries'.[14] But the *TLS* liked Dahl's 'combination of ease in the telling and of cumulative suspense'. In the USA the *Saturday Review of Literature*'s reviewer Michael Straight went further, seeing him as 'an author of great promise'.[15] Straight – a novelist and political writer of Dahl's own age, whose *Make This the Last War* had appeared in 1943 – defended the phantasmagoric aspects of some of the stories in *Over To You*, which he found true to the psychology of exhausted pilots. For this reason he saw Dahl as having achieved a more powerful kind of realism than, say, H. E. Bates in his RAF fiction. *Over To You* offered something 'more intense and conceived on a larger scale'.

This was certainly true of one of Dahl's next pieces, which nags away at the problem that agonizes the bomber-pilot in 'Someone Like You': people's interchangeability. The new story, 'The Soldier', involves a situation which was to become common in his writing: an obsessive man dominated by a stronger woman.

In this case the man has returned from the war full of fears of aeroplanes and imaginary gunfire, and suffering from what seems to be a neurological complaint which confuses his senses: he can't always feel pain or tell hot from cold. He longs to return to the stability of childhood, to seaside holidays with his mother. He is treated by a doctor but gets worse. Ultimately he confuses his wife with another woman and is about to attack her with a knife. She disarms him by humouring him and then, choosing her moment, hitting him hard in the face.

Dahl complicates the narrative by letting it take both sides. The dramatic tension – will the man kill his wife? – is counterbalanced by a psychological ambiguity intensified by her behaviour. She has been acting unsympathetically, at least in his eyes. Now she pretends (or admits?) that she is not his wife at all: 'I told you Edna's gone out. I'm a friend of hers. My name is Mary.'

The situation is Pinteresque, but 'The Soldier' was written almost twenty years before Pinter's *The Homecoming*. Dahl began it in 1947 and sold an early version to the BBC's new high-culture radio channel, the Third Programme, in the summer of the following year.[16] This first draft, called 'People Nowadays', contains some extra clues about Dahl's state of mind at the time. Admittedly, the version lacks the inner terrors he later developed from it. It is both more explicit and more sentimental, with an us-against-the-crazy-universe ending denied to 'The Soldier'. The wife murmurs to her husband that the situation they are in cannot be real: what is wrong with everyone today? He can't answer her except by saying that they all seem to have gone crazy. But if in this draft of the story the madness may be the whole world's, rather than just the soldier's, his explanation for it is revealing: 'It was the war talk that did it. He knew it was the war talk, and the talk of new weapons and the talk of another war coming soon for certain.'

Given Stalin's ruthless expansionism since 1944 and the dawning public realization of the implications of Hiroshima, many people had such fears, assuming that the enemy would be a nuclear-armed Soviet Union. One of those with whom Dahl discussed the possibility was his friend Dennis Pearl who, whenever he was on leave, would come to stay at Wisteria Cottage. Pearl had spent most of the war in a Japanese prisoner-of-war camp after being captured at Singapore, but had decided to stay in the army after his release. He was now based in the Middle East with the 3rd Infantry Division, preparing to counter an anticipated Soviet advance into what is now Iran. At the time, Pearl says, 'It didn't seem to many of us that peace had really broken out.' Dahl's frequent letters to Charles Marsh are consumed by such anxieties and by his irritation at what he saw as Marsh's new political complacency. Marsh took Henry Wallace's side, deploring the anti-Communist mood in the USA. Dahl replied that it was not Communism he was frightened of but war. If Marsh went on kissing his beloved Russians, he said, they would sooner or later bite off his tongue.[17] He told Marsh that expert opinion in London predicted a new war by the spring of 1950.[18] It was 'the saddest goddamn thought, the saddest craziest thought that it is possible to think'.[19] Throughout the spring and summer of 1946 – two years before the Soviet Union blockaded Berlin and took over Czechoslovakia, three years before it exploded an atom bomb, four years before the war in Korea – he thought and wrote about little else.

The main fictional product of his anxieties, a novel called *Sometime Never*, was published in the USA in 1948 by Scribner's and in England a year later by Collins (who had also published *The Gremlins*). It flopped, and was scarcely heard of again. Even in Dahl's commercially successful last years, when practically everything he had ever written was reissued, recycled or simply reshuffled into a 'new' collection under a different title, he never tried to revive it. In 1979 *My Uncle Oswald* was promoted as Dahl's first novel – a mistake which Auberon Waugh was among the few critics to notice. (Peace-loving Holland is the only country where *Sometime Never* has been reissued: the 1982 Dutch translation has remained in print ever since.) Yet it was the first novel about nuclear war to appear in the USA after Hiroshima. For that reason alone, it deserves a close look.

There had been several pre-war fantasy fictions on this subject. According to Paul Brians in his expert and readable survey of them,[20] they go back almost as far as the discovery of radiation – Robert Cromie's *The Crack of Doom* appeared in 1895, almost twenty years before H. G. Wells' better-known *The World Set Free*. But during the Second World War the topic had been banned. Some brave editors of science-fiction magazines, particularly John W. Campbell Jr, editor of *Astounding*, ignored the censorship, but it was thorough, and in US-occupied Japan continued until well after the war had ended. There, despite what many people had good reason to know for themselves, fictional references to the effects of radiation were officially deleted, under the pretence that they were untrue.[21]

Such deceptions were harder to practise in the West, particularly once censorship had been lifted. Dahl himself didn't have far to look for reliable information on the subject. In November 1945 *Atlantic Monthly* published a whimsical short story by him called 'Smoked Cheese'. (It seems to have been intended for children. Thirty-five years later in *The Twits* he reused the main element of the plot, in which a man plagued with mice disorientates them by glueing his furniture to the ceiling.) The same issue of the magazine carried stories by Eudora Welty and Frederic Prokosch, and a piece by Raymond Chandler about writers in Hollywood. But even in this company Dahl was unlikely to have missed an article on the atomic bomb by Albert Einstein. 'As long as there are sovereign nations possessing great powers,' Einstein wrote, 'war is inevitable.' The only hope lay in a form of world government.

These ideas found their way into Dahl's novel. It is evident both from his letters at the time and from the book's preliminaries how ambitious and how serious he felt about it. (He even opens with an epigraph from Isocrates: 'The age in which we live should be distinguished by some glorious enterprise, that those who have been so long oppressed may, in some period of their lives, know what it is to be happy ... We stand in need of some more durable plan which will forever put an end to our hostilities and unite us by the lasting ties of mutual affection and fidelity.') In his foreword Dahl writes confessionally, in the spirit of the pilot in 'Someone Like You', about having been a licensed murderer and about the likely destruction of all civilization. So it comes as a shock when he immediately slips back into a newly extended but not much less juvenile version of *The Gremlins*. The book begins where the earlier one did, in the Battle of Britain, but continues to the end of human civilization.

Dahl may, as will become clear, have had Tolkien in mind in writing the story (he liked *The Hobbit*). There are echoes too of Lewis Carroll's mixture of the irrational and the commonsensical. But these elements are combined with the realism of his tougher war stories. The book cannot decide whether it is for adults or for children, and the resulting clashes of tone are bizarre. So, for example, one paragraph about the Blitz begins: 'You can remember how it was, how the scream seemed to come from high up, directly overhead, a female scream, a thin high wailing scream.' The next drops into baby talk: 'And I happen to know that many of the people behaved in the funniest ways when the siren woke them, especially if they were alone.'

This unsureness of style reflects other confusions. Dahl wrote the book at speed during the spring and summer of 1946 – at the height, that is, of the war crimes trials at Nuremberg. Yet plentiful revelations about Nazi anti-Semitism and the Holocaust did not discourage him from satirizing 'a little pawnbroker in Houndsditch called Meatbein who, when the wailing started, would rush downstairs to the large safe in which he kept his money, open it and wriggle inside on to the lowest shelf where he lay like a hibernating hedgehog until the all-clear had gone.'[22] Elsewhere the story delights in its Gremlin dictator, 'The Leader', as if Hitler and Mussolini had never existed.

The Leader of the Gremlins is a prototype of Mr Willy Wonka in *Charlie and the Chocolate Factory*. Between the imagined Third World War and the all-destructive Fourth, he rules whimsically over an underground kingdom, alternately bullying his subjects and appeasing them with sweet fruits called snozzberries. And the book anticipates other aspects of Dahl's later stories – their cheerful misogyny ('the female of any type is always more scheming cunning jealous and relentless than the male'[23]), their cartoon-strip satire – for example, at the expense of the Political Gremlins (who hang upside down and out of whose mouths comes hot air) – and their anal humour (the best way for Gremlins to short-circuit the sparking plugs of Spitfires is to sit on them: 'It is a delightful sensation anyway'[24]). All this sorts oddly with an otherwise grim attempt to imagine both a global nuclear war and a new form of world order.

The book's politics are alarmingly straightforward. Part Two imagines a world dominated by Communism, a system Dahl describes as one in which people 'too brainless even to amass coin-collections for themselves, preach . . . that all coins should be shared by all people.' This free-market theme prompts a lugubrious passage imagining the destruction of London in World War III, where Dahl seizes on the fate of Regent Street: Austin Reed, the Kodak shop, Hamley's, Liberty's, 'everything was gone, all the fine shops . . . They were all gone now.' Then there is talk of an alliance between China and India, the latter a country of 'crafty sunburnt men' who 'are copying and improving upon the weapons of other nations'. While human self-destruction draws near, developments are keenly watched by the Leader, who has devised his own internationalist, libertarian, anti-industrial dictatorship, a kind of proto-Green Fascism whose most appealing regulations (handed down to the men, whose responsibility it is to pass them on to the women and children) are that everyone may eat the fruit of any snozzberry tree and that 'No one shall covet his own wife to the point where he becomes a bore.'[25] But at the book's J. M. Barrie-ish end the Gremlins' dream cannot be realized. They themselves, we are reminded, are purely fictional creatures, dependent for their existence on the imaginations of humans – who have now become extinct. 'We haven't really existed very much, have we? Just a little bit, here and there and then only . . . how shall I put it . . . only in a rather imaginative sort of way.' Only insects are left to begin the process of life over again.

There are some enjoyable moments in all this, and some memorably grim ones, and given much more thought and a skilful editor, a popular allegory might conceivably have been made out of it (especially since this was the period of *Animal Farm* and *Nineteen Eighty-Four*).[26] As it stands, though, apart from its place in the history of war fiction, the book's main interest is in its revelation of Dahl's volatile mood at the time. This is particularly true of the character of Peternip, a former RAF pilot, now a music critic, whose thoughts are fatalistic and despairing and who 'ever since World War II had walked with an irregular, short-long . . . limping gait which reminded one somehow of the swing of a maladjusted pendulum'.[27] Dahl himself was slightly lame since his accident, and his own gloom was lifted by his enthusiasm for classical music and modern painting as well as for writing.

The period immediately after the war was difficult for many authors, Dahl among them. Paper shortages led to long delays in book publication – *Sometime Never* did not appear in England until 1949. Magazine editors seemed less receptive in peacetime than in war. As a result, Dahl sometimes became uncertain not only about the best direction for his writing, but about whether he should be writing at all.

Uncertainty was not the impression he gave to the people with whom he dealt professionally over his stories. In the summer of 1946 he took time off from *Sometime Never* to write about the recent, accidental discovery of a Roman treasure hoard at Mildenhall in Suffolk. The piece was bought by the *Saturday Evening Post*, which had published 'Shot Down Over Libya' and whose editor, Stuart Rose, had recently visited the Dahls at Grange Farm near Great Missenden. Rose's sub-editors wanted to cut the article and Dahl fired off a long letter, enraged that they thought they could write better than he did, insisting that none of his recent work had been shortened, and lamenting the fate of other, tenderer authors if their efforts were so abused.[28] In what was to become the

1 Dahl's mother, Sofie Hesselberg, c. 1910, before her marriage to Harald Dahl.

2 The Norwegian Church in Cardiff, where Dahl and his sisters were baptised.

3 At Elm Tree House School, Llandaff. Dahl's sisters Asta and Else are on the far left, Alfhild in the middle of the same row.

4 Dahl at Repton, aged seventeen, from the Priory House photograph album.

5 The Priory House football team, Repton, winter 1932. Dahl, who played outside left, is in the middle of the back row.

THE SATURDAY EVENING POST 29

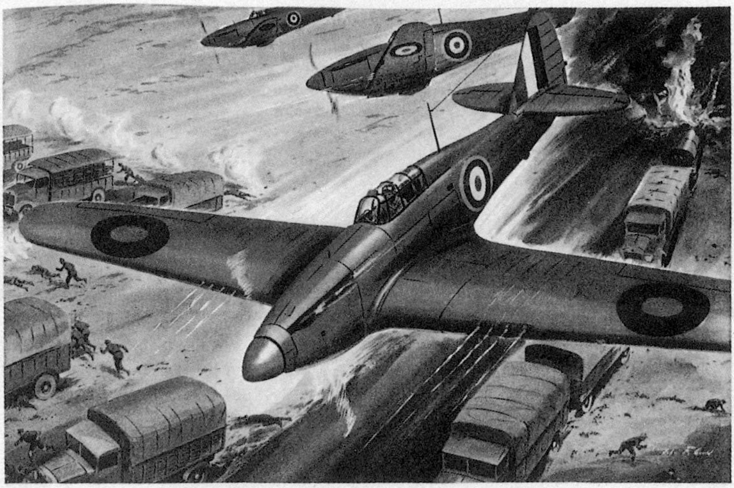

The place was stiff with lorries of all sorts, and as we came down I could see the soldiers running about all over the place. I saw one stumble and pick himself up and go on running.

Shot Down Over Libya

"One of our planes is missing, but the pilot is safe," the communiqué said. Here is that pilot's report.

6 Dahl's first story, as published in the *Saturday Evening Post*, 1 August 1942.

7 One of Matthew Smith's portraits of Dahl, painted in 1941.

8 Matthew Smith in London, early 1940s. (above left)

9 Charles Marsh, shortly before the Second World War. (above)

10 Alfred Knopf. (left)

11 Annabella (Suzanne Charpentier).

12 Patricia Neal.

Annabella

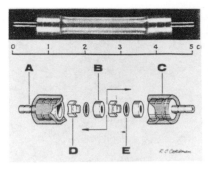

13 The Wade-Dahl-Till Valve, as illustrated in the medical journal *Lancet* in 1963.

14 At Great Missenden in 1964 after the announcement of Patricia Neal's Oscar for *Hud*, with Tessa aged seven and Theo, three.

15 On the way home from Los Angeles in May 1965, three months after Patricia Neal's strokes, with Ophelia, Tessa and Theo.

signature tune of such complaints, Dahl opened with a bribe and closed with a moral outburst. He said that after Rose's visit he had found a set of old wineglasses and bought them for him; they had been waiting for his return. But he ended by warning that a writer at the outset of his career could be crushed by such editorial ruthlessness – particularly if the only way he could feed himself was to submit to what was asked. Dahl added that such behaviour on an editor's part was 'a great crime . . . and I know that you, for one, would not wish to be accused of it'.

With the BBC he was more ingratiating, partly because the relationship was new. He was encouraged to try the medium by a friend of Alfhild's, Archie Gordon, an aristocratic writer and broadcaster who had often stayed at Oakwood before the war. Dahl's first approach, in the summer of 1948, was to send in a letter about a radio talk he had heard on the subject of dog-racing. He was invited to turn the reply into a talk of his own, which he promptly did, modestly pleading that he would be more than grateful for any suggestions about changes and taking the opportunity to offer some of his stories.[29] With the help of a recommendation from Archie Gordon, they were looked at by the South African poet Roy Campbell, who was on the BBC's staff. He immediately accepted 'People Nowadays' (Dahl's first draft of 'The Soldier') and passed two others to H. N. Bentinck, a colleague in the more popular Home Service: 'A Picture for Drioli' (later called 'Skin') and 'The Menace' (later 'Collector's Item' and finally titled 'Man from the South'). Bentinck said that both were too long for his purposes, but he would take the second if it were shortened, which he thought would anyway improve it – a suggestion Dahl meekly accepted.[31]

Things did not carry on so smoothly. Bentinck didn't like Dahl's next submission, 'The Sound Machine', and rejected it.[32] Dahl in his turn complained that the BBC's reader of 'People Nowadays' had talked like an adult addressing a child, which (although this is often Dahl's own tone, both in that story and elsewhere) he didn't think appropriate.[33] He now tried two more stories on Roy Campbell but without success.[34]

85

Dahl's side of the correspondence became increasingly irritable, and he was soon sardonically comparing 'the discriminating literary gentlemen of the Third Programme' with their richer and more full-blooded counterparts on US magazines. In 1951 he visited Germany with Charles Marsh and told Archie Gordon that he had dreamed glorious dreams in Hitler's former retreat at Berchtesgaden: absurd fantasies, such as selling a story to the BBC.[35]

If he was annoyed with the BBC, he was sometimes annoyed with himself too – for example about his article on 'Love' for the *Ladies' Home Journal*, which earned him a more than useful $2,500 (in today's terms about $8,750[36]) but which he now thought was 'bullshit'.[37] Writing well was hard to do and the rejections made it harder.[38] In May 1949 Scribner's, who had published *Sometime Never*, turned down the idea of a new book of his short stories.[39] Still, there were some successes. A compromise had been reached over the piece about the Mildenhall treasure (it appeared under the straight-to-the-nub title 'He Plowed Up $1,000,000'[40]). 'Man from the South', the psychological thriller about a sinister bet for a young man's little finger – with which he had entertained Annabella when they first met – earned him $2,250 from another American magazine, *Collier's*, before he sold it to the BBC. And Dahl was right to think that not all the refusals were deserved. The story which became 'Skin' is an eerie satire on the picture-dealing world where – in a metaphor which the story enacts with chilling literalness – people would take the hide off someone's back to get a painting they valued. Both this and 'Man from the South' owe something to *The Merchant of Venice*. They contrast business contracts with humaner dealings; material possessions (a Cadillac, a picture by Soutine) with flesh and blood. 'Man from the South' ends like Shakespeare's play with a surprise reversal and the humiliation of the Shylock-figure by a woman. 'Skin' is set in war-devastated Paris in 1946. A starving old man is forced to sell a picture of his wife by Soutine to a ruthless dealer. In doing so, he is literally selling his own skin: thirty years earlier the artist had tattooed the portrait on his back. It is left to the reader to guess whether or not he survives.

Post-war Europe, as 'Skin' suggests, was a continent of ruins and in some areas, starvation. Dahl was affected not only by the hard personal adjustment between millionaire society in Washington and the relative privations of post-war Buckinghamshire, but by the larger plight which he saw around him and about which he read in the papers. Britain fared better than some countries, and rural people there less badly than Londoners, but the winter of 1946–47 had been brutally severe, and was followed by an economic crisis worsened by the fact that the first of Britain's repayments on its war debt to the USA was already due. Dahl's apocalyptic mood extended to domestic politics as well as the Cold War, and he blamed much of the dereliction on Attlee's Labour government: 'I wish them dead,' he wrote to Charles Marsh. Although he was 'nearly a Socialist now,' he said he would gladly see the whole cabinet of incapable, greedy, vengeful, joyless, arrogant, physically unattractive and morally minuscule men dead.[41]

Marsh had various reasons for being concerned about the national and international situation which Dahl described to him. He was genuinely philanthropic and cared even more than most Americans that, having helped to win the war in Europe, they shouldn't lose the peace. He wanted to help his young protégé by giving him work to do. And he saw opportunities for himself, both as a businessman and as a collector.

In 1949 he formed a charitable trust, the Public Welfare Foundation. It still exists, spending millions of dollars a year in education, social welfare, medicine and emergency relief for poor countries. The beginnings were more modest. As early as 1945 Marsh arranged with Dahl to set up a project in Limehouse, East London. The parish rector was asked to select two hundred needy families, each of which would be allowed up to $200 per month for a period of six months.[42] The scheme was quickly extended to nearby Rotherhithe, and because what was required couldn't always be bought easily in Britain, the Foundation also arranged to send vitamin pills, as well as apples from Marsh's farm in Rappahannock County, Virginia.

For some time Dahl worked hard on the project, but he was torn between zeal and cynicism. He wrote to Violet Attlee, the Prime Minister's wife, publicizing the Foundation's activities, but made jokes about her when she gratefully replied.[43] Similarly, he congratulated Marsh on his gifts which, he said, both fed people and gave them enjoyment; but he scorned Marsh's offer of vitamins. The poor 'do not give a fuck for vitamins and do not understand them', he told Marsh – they wouldn't eat them even if they were told they were aphrodisiacs.[44]

He may have been right about that, but he may also have been less wholeheartedly sympathetic to the poor of East London than his more impassioned letters made him seem. Much of the population there was Jewish, and in August 1947 Dahl sent Marsh a copy of an answer he pretended he had given to Sydney Rothman, treasurer of the Stepney Jewish Girls' (B'nai B'rith) Club and Settlement, who had asked for help.[45] The letter was a joke, in the style of his correspondence with Marsh about Lord Halifax and 'sex-manhood'. It was almost certainly meant for no one's eyes but Marsh's. But it was typical of Dahl's increasingly contradictory character that his most generous, constructive impulses were accompanied by something with a less pleasant taste. The reply Dahl pretended he had sent to the Settlement said that since he knew that Jews never asked for money, he assumed the Treasurer's request to have been a mistake; but in case it might be repeated, he wanted to warn Rothman that Charles Marsh was a committed pro-Arabist, prone to 'sudden fits of violence during which all the Jews in the neighbourhood tremble and fear for their lives'. Marsh had once bitten off the finger of a Jewish waiter, Dahl said, and when a Jewish woman tried to seduce him, he put itching powder into her face-cream and pulled out her fingernails so that she couldn't scratch. Previously, the 'East Side Club for unmarried Yiddish mothers' in New York had asked Marsh for money, but the philanthropist's response was to buy up their premises, throw out the women and turn the place over to Arab sailors as a hostel. Dahl ended by listing the names of those to whom copies of his letter had supposedly been sent: joke Jewish names such as Miss Alma Finckle, the Rev. Rubin Ruderman and so on.

The letter was a private amusement between friends, and arguably belongs to that realm of friendship which Martin Amis, with
Philip Larkin in mind, has temptingly called 'the willing suspension
of accountability'. But irrespective of whether consenting adults
should be held answerable for their private jokes, they do reveal
certain things, and there is no question that although Dahl had
several Jewish friends, his anti-Semitic jokes were of a piece with
an underlying dislike of Jews in general and Zionists in particular.
Around the time of this letter – 1946–47 – Dahl lamented to Marsh
that the USA should have been giving Britain more support in
Palestine. He approvingly saw the difficult last years of the man-
date, before the founding of the state of Israel, as a war which the
British (among them Dennis Pearl) were fighting on the side of
the Arabs.[46]

His humanitarian concerns were more steadily in evidence closer
to home. Charles and Claudia Marsh paid several visits to
Buckinghamshire, bringing lavish presents for all the family and
involving themselves in various small local agricultural projects of
Dahl's devising. Marsh could never resist a business opportunity.
Even as he crossed the Atlantic, he would be negotiating with the
ship's purser to buy up his surplus supplies – especially of bourbon
– at the end of the voyage. Dahl began trying to interest Marsh in
Norway, where he saw scope for a mutually advantageous timber
project which could supply his patron's businesses with badly-
needed paper, while giving employment to Dahl and Norwegian
members of his family – among them, his enterprising cousin, Finn,
who had spent the war in the Resistance, shipping refugees across
the North Sea to Britain.

There were other schemes. In May 1946 Dahl had written to
Marsh in apocalyptic terms about the starvation in continental
Europe. Separate tours of inspection were arranged over a period
of several years. Piled into a limousine, Dahl, the Marshes and
assorted relations would race through the ravaged countryside,
stopping occasionally so that Charles could send one of his party
to find the local mayor and ask what was needed.[47] It was on one
of these philanthropic holidays, in 1951, that they went to Ger-

many and visited Berchtesgaden where, Dahl wrote, he sat in Hitler's mountain-top redoubt and indulged in fantasies of fame and triumph.[48]

Some years earlier, back in the USA, Marsh had dreamed a more realizable kind of dream. In the summer of 1946 he dictated a letter to Dahl from a car which was travelling, he boasted, at seventy miles per hour on the road from Monterey, California, to Laredo, Texas. He was interested in seeing what kind of trade could be done with Cyprus. He knew that the island was hungry, but also that it had a surplus of ancient vases: 'I believe these folks . . . will take a pick and shovel and dig up a few more . . . So if we can feed the folks over there with what we can sell over here, we might start something, particularly as there are no tariff charges on antiques coming into this country.'[49]

Marsh had already benefited from Dahl's instinct as a collector by commissioning him to find British antiques for him: a chess set used in Victorian times at Simpson's, the old eating-house in the Strand; eighteenth-century tables and chairs bought from a dealer in Thame.[50] Dahl also acted for his patron in purchases of paintings, and within five or six years had built up a promising part-time career as a dealer in the bullish market for European art, acting on behalf of Marsh and other wealthy friends. He had renewed his friendship with Matthew Smith and spent many weekends in Paris with him, cruising the galleries by day and the red-light districts by night. Dahl found it difficult to get Smith to part with any of his own work,[51] but by 1950 had persuaded him to move to a studio in Amersham. While Augustus John's daughter Poppet was decorating the place, Dahl stored fifty-four of Smith's paintings in a spare bedroom at home. Charles Marsh paid a visit that August and sent a note to Claudia, asking her to write a memo about an arrangement through which he planned to buy a large number of the pictures without having to go through Smith's gallery, Tooth's. 'It is all right for Smith to know what has been taken,' Marsh wrote, 'but emphasize no sale until after his death.' Whatever Smith was told, it was a confusing business: he was old and in some ways timid, and although he complained about Tooth (because of the dealer's alleged rapacity, Smith and Dahl called him 'Dog's Tooth') and particularly about his failure to promote him in the USA, he stuck to the letter of their agreements. At one point he became convinced that Dahl had stolen one of his canvases. Dahl said he had simply taken it to have it framed, but the quarrel badly upset them both.[52]

In the autumn of 1950, Dahl, the Marshes and their friends Ivar Bryce and Ralph Ingersoll were together involved in various other transactions, one of them concerning a Rouault which Dahl priced at $6,000.[53] He also negotiated on Marsh's behalf for a Vuillard.[54] The following year Dahl was enlisted to persuade Jacob Epstein (whom he had met through Matthew Smith) to sculpt Marsh. He also at some point made a trip to Switzerland, where he bought another Rouault – a cartoon of President Wilson – and a painting of a nude boy by Redon. These two cost him £190. When he took the Rouault out of its frame to transport it home, he found a self-portrait by the artist on the back.[55]

There was a steady improvement in his fortunes during these years, a reward partly for his sheer hard work and partly just for his friendship with Marsh, kept up in frequent letters but also on their working holidays together. Dahl not only accompanied his patron on his frequent trips to Europe but made several visits to Jamaica, where Marsh owned a resort at Ochos Rios near Kingston and where Ivar Bryce, Ian Fleming, Noël Coward and other friends had houses. Charles and Roald were still like teenagers together, alternating between intense, sometimes maudlin discussions on the state of the world and schoolboy jokes which ran on for years. There was what they called the 'Joy Through Length Project' and its parallel investigation into bow-leggedness in women. There was a plot to seduce a royal lady-in-waiting as a means of persuading the Queen to advertise Pond's face-cream. They fantasized that a famous Russian pianist was a spy passing coded messages through his playing; and that Interpol was conducting an investigation into Marsh's private life. (One piece of evidence was a story published in the *Evening Standard* about a feminist conference where one of the speakers was 'Miss Charlotte

"Charlie" Marsh, of Chelsea, S.W. – known in the pre–1914 campaign as the "beauty" of the suffragette movement'.)[56] On a trip to France with Dahl and Matthew Smith, Marsh handed wine waiters his personal corkscrew, which was shaped like a penis. When the cork was drawn, Marsh would insist that the waiter and everyone else sniffed it. It was in Paris, too, that Dahl and his brother-in-law, Leslie Hansen, put cards in the windows of bistros on the Left Bank, announcing that a wealthy American businessman needed a secretary to go with him to the USA. Applicants were directed to the Hotel Maurice, in the rue de Rivoli, which had to close its doors against the impoverished French girls who formed a queue around the block.[57]

Meanwhile, Marsh was planning more substantial ways of helping his protégé financially. He set up a trust in Dahl's name with investments in the Marsh oil companies worth $25,000.[58] In the summer of 1950 Dahl organized a business trip to Scandinavia, where they visited Oslo, Stockholm and Helsinki. During the trip the deal first mooted by Dahl four years earlier was finally agreed, and Marsh's Public Welfare Foundation put $10,000 into a Dahl family forestry operation in Norway. Marsh made it clear that he didn't want any of the money back.[59] In return Dahl was able to scratch his patron's back, not only as an agent for his art collection but by introducing him as an investor in various business projects, including the purchase of Universal Newsreel by another OSS acquaintance, a lawyer and entrepreneur named Ernest Cuneo.

He was also now beginning to do well on his own account, as a writer. In April 1948 he had written that he was worried that he 'was going through a non-money-making period'.[60] Almost immediately things had begun to look up. There were the deals with *Collier's* and the BBC and his rueful acceptance of the *Ladies' Home Journal* commission. Now, in May 1949, he sold a story to *The New Yorker* for the first time. This was not 'Taste', as Dahl later remembered, but 'The Sound Machine', another fantasy about obsession: a man's belief that he can hear noises made by plants, and his anxiety over their suffering. The story had been rejected by the BBC – more evidence that he was better appreciated in the USA than at home.

Further confirmation of this followed. *Collier's* bought 'Poison', the story about an imaginary snake. In August 1951 it was the turn of 'Taste' to be sold to *The New Yorker*. The next month Dahl had dinner with Lillian Hellman, who was staying at Claridge's. She told him tearfully about the plight of her lover, the detective writer Dashiell Hammett, imprisoned as a result of Senator Joseph McCarthy's notorious purge on 'un-American activities'. Dahl's main concern was that this would turn the socialist Hellman 'more and more against her own country'.[61]

It was a country about which for the moment he didn't want to hear anything bad. He had applied for, and had just been given, a permanent US visa. His work was doing well there, whereas in Britain its only steady-seeming patron, the BBC, had lost interest. In New York he felt that he could move among literary people on equal terms.[62] The muddy charms of Buckinghamshire had temporarily faded. He wanted to get back to sophistication and wealth.

Perhaps, too, even Dahl sensed what Martha Gellhorn had seen, that life with his mother, and so close to his sisters, was not entirely good for a bachelor. But if he was escaping one family, he immediately moved back in with another. The Marshes had room for him in their New York house. They were at present in Europe, and he asked if he might join them on the return voyage. The sooner the better, he said. 'Any boat any date is allright with me.'[63]

6

Yakkity Parties

Dashiell Hammett was in jail from July to December 1951. Among
the women who missed him was Patricia Neal, an ambitious young
actress whose first Broadway role had been in Lillian Hellman's
Another Part of the Forest in 1946. That was how Hammett met
her.[1] He took to turning up daily at the rehearsals, usually drunk.
She was twenty; tall, with unspoilt, country-girl good looks that
would have been bland but for her high, wide cheekbones – so
wide that the *New Yorker* critic Brendan Gill said later, 'the camera
can sort of pan across a face of that kind'.[2] Hammett couldn't
disguise how attractive he found her, but with Lillian Hellman he
did his best to. 'Pat's an awfully pretty girl', he told her, 'if you
don't look at her hands and feet and can ignore that incredible
carriage. She's very much the earnest future star at the moment and
thus not too entirely fascinating if you don't think her career the
most important thing in the world.'[3]

This was written from Hollywood, where Neal had been hired
by Warner Brothers after her Broadway success. Hammett took her
out to dinner a lot there and heard what he didn't already know
about the story of her life. She was much talked about, not least
because she had begun a long affair with Gary Cooper, with whom
she co-starred in King Vidor's film version of Ayn Rand's *The
Fountainhead* (best remembered for a scene in which Neal watches
longingly while Cooper drives a pneumatic drill into a rock-face).
It was the second film she had made. The first was *John Loves
Mary* with Ronald Reagan and Jack Carson.

She worked with Reagan several times, including on *The Hasty*

Heart, which was shot in England. Reagan found post-war conditions there so grim, even at the Savoy, that he had his steaks flown in from New York – a story which encapsulates something not only about Hollywood, but about Anglo–American differences in general. After she had lived in England for the better part of twenty-five years, Patricia Neal still wrote of her days at Elstree in the terms of someone who had spent a period as a voluntary entertainer in a Third World refugee camp.[4] Her Warner Brothers salary was on a scale rising from $1,250 to $3,750 per week: enough to have kept someone adequately for twelve months in England at that time.

Patsy Neal, as she was christened, liked what money could buy. Her autobiography *As I Am* (1988) is among other things a catalogue of fur coats and necklaces, and she talks frankly of how in her earliest days she got around her father for presents. He was a manager for the Southern Coal and Coke Company in Packard, Kentucky, the son of a tobacco plantation owner and a member of the fifth generation of his family to live in the old South. Her mother was the daughter of the town doctor, German by origin. They were unsophisticated people but comfortably off: a telephone, plenty of toys, ready cash from Pappy and holidays on his Virginia farm. In 1929, when Patricia was three, the family moved to a bigger town, Knoxville in Tennessee. It was at school there that her theatrical ambitions were first encouraged. She went on to Northwestern University and was a big success as a student, but after her father's early death left to pursue her ambitions in New York. There she met Eugene O'Neill, the first of several famous men who would fall for her, most of them married and ranging in age from middle-aged to elderly. Before she was twenty-one she had been lunched by Richard Rodgers (of Rodgers and Hammerstein), pursued by David Selznick, had turned down one Broadway role in favour of another, and had made the cover of *Life*.

The affair with Gary Cooper began in 1947. By 1950 his wife Rocky knew and had joined battle. (On one occasion Neal received a telegram: 'I HAVE HAD JUST ABOUT ENOUGH OF YOU. YOU HAD

BETTER STOP NOW OR YOU WILL BE SORRY. MRS GARY COOPER.'5)
Eventually it was Rocky who won, but not before her husband
made Pat pregnant and persuaded her to have an abortion, letting
her know about the arrangements with the memorable words,
'Our appointment is tomorrow afternoon.'6

It was a wretched time. Neal longed for a child. The gossip
columnists called her the woman who was breaking up the Coop-
ers' marriage, which she only wished she could manage to do.
Warner Brothers did not renew her contract, and when she moved
to Fox they lent her out to other film companies. Concentrating
once again on her stage career, she appeared in 1951 in T. S. Eliot's
new play *The Cocktail Party*, which Cooper called 'The Yakkity
Party'. All she remembers about it is that she was the character
(Celia) who has 'long, mystical speeches' and 'ends up crucified on
an anthill in Africa'.7 Then Cooper developed an ulcer. His mother
told Neal that she was to blame. Guilty and scared, Neal called him
to say that it was all over. He didn't ring back.

This was around the time of Dashiell Hammett's imprisonment
and Dahl's dinner in London with Lillian Hellman. Hellman's play
The Children's Hour, about two teachers suspected of being lesbian
lovers, was about to be revived. Neal successfully auditioned.
Shortly before rehearsals began Hellman asked her to a dinner
party. One of the guests was Roald Dahl, who had just moved to
New York.

Dahl was thirty-five, and although most of his friends were rich
and successful, by their standards he himself was neither. In New
York he lived at the Marshes' empty house on East 92nd Street,
which they lent him rent free in exchange for his keeping an eye on
the installation of a new phone system. He wrote all day. Stung by
The New Yorker's initial rejection of the art-dealing story 'Skin', he
dashed off another satire on the cultural market-place, this time
specifically literary: it was about a man who uses an early form of
computer to generate the kind of fiction which would satisfy what
Dahl saw as the formulaic demands of commercial editors. 'The
Automatic Grammatizator', a high-tech version of Edgar Allan

Poe's story 'How to Write a *Blackwood* Article', was rather crudely intended to make fun of *The New Yorker* and when they rejected it too, Dahl thought that it was because they were 'very peeved'.[8] By then he had rewritten 'Skin' and persuaded the magazine to take it, but they didn't like his H. E. Bates-ish stories of Buckinghamshire life, 'The Ratcatcher' and 'Rummins', and sent them and four other pieces back in the course of 1952. Among these was 'Nunc Dimittis', another fiction about painting, and 'Lamb to the Slaughter', a comic crime thriller in miniature which was to become one of his best-known stories, and whose plot must be among the first ever to depend on a domestic freezer. According to Patricia Neal, the idea had been given to Dahl by Ian Fleming one night over dinner. A woman kills her unfaithful husband by hitting him on the head with a frozen leg of lamb, which she then cooks and serves for supper to the police, made hungry by their unsuccessful search for the murder weapon. Dahl had confirmed the practical details with the help of the Marshes' cook, Mary. 'He spent all one morning talking to her about techniques of freezing,' Marsh's daughter recalls. 'Everyone thought he had gone mad.'[9]

These rejections apart, even the success of 'Taste' was diminished in Dahl's eyes by the fact that the story had previously been turned down by the BBC.[10] In it, a wine buff bets his daughter's hand in marriage that a dinner guest can't precisely identify what he is drinking. Dahl had researched the story thoroughly, reading up clarets in André Simon's *A Wine Primer* and calling at the author's home in Carlisle Place to ask him to check the details.[11] Despite all this, one of the BBC's readers, the novelist P. H. Newby, reported that although he found the story 'fun' it was 'completely bogus. The dilemma is unreal.'[12] Not only the dilemma, one may think, but the characters themselves, although the story includes a convincing dissection of the host Mike, an arriviste who:

> knew that he was not really much more than a bookmaker – an unctuous, infinitely respectable, secretly unscrupulous bookmaker – and he knew that his friends knew it, too. So he was seeking now to become a man of culture, to cultivate a literary

and aesthetic taste, to collect paintings, music, books, and all the rest of it. His little sermon about Rhine wine and Moselle was a part of this thing, this culture that he sought.[13]

Whether Dahl was attacking the social world around him in this story, or in some way himself, there is no question about the predominant mood. It is envy. He was too competitive not to want to succeed in New York, but hated many of the people he met there. Not for the first or last time he longed to beat the system, but knew that in order to do so he had to be accepted by it: an acceptance he didn't always easily win, and for which – as in Groucho Marx's joke about club membership – he despised himself when he did.

Nothing he wrote at this time shows any affection for its characters, whom he angrily exploits as agents in plots of trickery and table-turning, competitiveness, greed and revenge. As in a cartoon strip, or a play by Ben Jonson, the mixture of exaggeration and detachment is part of the point. Readers can see their own worst motives being acted out, while being spared the kind of psychological penetration that might otherwise call up conflicting sympathies and difficult judgements. Whatever else they have in common, the adult stories which Dahl wrote during these years are almost all about manipulation: the characters' manipulation of each other, and the author's of his reader. Mike Schofield in 'Taste' sets up a drama and a test – this is his idea of what makes a party go. It sometimes seemed to be Dahl's too, as many of those who have been in the same room as him recall. 'Razzing people up', he called it according to one admirer, who added that Dahl 'had the mind of a slightly naughty eleven-year-old genius'.[14] He was bored by small talk, but had to endure quite a lot of it in the social world to which his behaviour paradoxically guaranteed him an entrée.

This was well before the white-wine-or-Perrier era. Sherry was the weakest drink on offer in New York society, and most people preferred hard liquor, especially Bourbon Old Fashioned: a little sugar, a few drops of grenadine, a lot of bourbon, orange, and a cherry. Everyone, Dahl among them, smoked all the time, including at the dinner table. As in wartime Washington, a rude guest was yet another desirable stimulant. It was a world in which detraction was as much part of the life-blood as admiration, and where people's gossip at its best had a derisive exuberance of which you can still sometimes hear echoes. 'The most conceited man who ever lived in our time in New York City,' Brendan Gill unhesitatingly pronounces of one of Dahl's friends after all these years. 'Vain to the point where it was a kind of natural wonder. You could sit there and listen to him praise himself as you might go to see the Niagara Falls fall. He was full of grace, there was no impediment between him and this narcissism.'

Scorn was an increasingly important part of Dahl's own social armoury. Another weapon was to shock. The habit stuck throughout his life. When he was quite an old man, a woman friend sat him next to her at an official dinner where her husband was the host. Dahl started to talk loudly about circumcision. Enjoying her embarrassment, he explained to a stranger sitting near by, 'Angela was just saying she wonders whether you're circumcised.'[15] A different gambit was simply to ignore people. At her party before rehearsals of *The Children's Hour* began, Lillian Hellman placed Dahl beside Patricia Neal. She was beautiful and famous. She was also young – ten years his junior – and Dahl hadn't previously been attracted to many younger women. Perhaps this is why he said nothing to her and spent the whole evening talking across the table to Leonard Bernstein. But soon afterwards he asked her out to a restaurant where he 'knew the owner, who was John Huston's father-in-law', and where he talked to her impressively about 'paintings and antique furniture and the joys of the English countryside'.[16] He seemed to be interested in everything and acquainted with everyone.

In the famous friends stakes, of course, they were well matched. If Dahl boasted (exaggeratedly, according to Martha Gellhorn) of knowing Hemingway very well, Neal had recently been taken to stay with Hemingway in Cuba by his friend Gary Cooper. Dahl was extremely close to the film star Annabella; Neal was about to co-star with Annabella's ex-husband Tyrone Power in *Diplomatic*

Courier. She had also, for that matter, appeared with Jack Carson and John Wayne. But then Dahl's friend Ivar Bryce had recently married Josephine Hartford, who owned the A&P (Atlantic and Pacific) chain of grocery stores, and his other chums included David Ogilvy, now an advertising mogul, and Bunny and Gena Phillips 'who had connections with the Russian royal family and the queen of England'.[17]

A little later Dahl was to make a new best friend in New York who had no grand connections. An arriviste in the most literal sense, Colin Fox had turned up by accident in the Bahamas on a yacht which he had sailed single-handed from England – a rare feat in those days – having (according to his own account) made and lost a fortune in smuggling at the end of the war.[18] A former merchant seaman, he sometimes claimed to have been brought up in a children's home in Worthing, having been abandoned there by a grand Irish mother.[19] Now a successful model, he repaid the affection of his succession of intimate friends with adulation or disdain, or both. Dahl and he competed in running down their mutual acquaintances: this one was a simpering jerk, that one a show-business Jew, the women all gushing sycophants. Fox still mimics their voices: 'Bobo and Woofy and Valerian, hello!' But he longed, he says, 'to be like the people in books – to know algebra' and he frankly idolized the young Dahl, who in turn was fascinated by Fox's background and personality and saw in him 'tremendous things'. With Fox, Dahl could give full rein to his complex, divided personality. For example, he boasted to him about his work for the Public Welfare Foundation but was derisive of such efforts by others, ridiculing the philanthropic Rhode Island Senator Claiborne Pell – whom Fox had met and liked – as 'a prick who gave out food parcels to the reindeer keepers in Finland'.

Understandably enough, not everyone thought that either Dahl or his address book were an unmixed social asset, and some of Patricia Neal's friends say that after she met him she became less nice to know. In the opinion of one, 'She adopted Roald's values, and one of them was a prodigious amount of name-dropping, and a prodigious amount of gossiping about the people they were name-dropping about. And also, a tremendous attention to money. Who was rich and famous was important.' Others disagree, saying that on the contrary Pat 'treats everyone in the same way'. But it seems possible that she was flattered by the attentions of a man to whom status was so important. Certainly she was touched by his attentiveness. During the run of *The Children's Hour* he began to collect her every night after the performance. And when she first visited his apartment, his photographs, particularly those of Else's three children, showed her an unexpectedly home-loving side of his personality to which, broody since her abortion, she responded. Still, there was something tyrannical in the way Dahl treated her and while it made her grateful for his few words of praise, it continued to bother her friends. When, without quite knowing why, she suddenly began telling people that she was going to marry Roald Dahl, a few tried to warn her off. She says that Leonard Bernstein told her she was making the biggest mistake of her life.[20] Dashiell Hammett wrote a shade more tolerantly to his daughter: 'I think [Dahl]'s a very silly dull fellow but Lillian – through whom Pat met him – and – I guess naturally – Pat both tell me I'm wrong and have only seen him at his worst. The ring isn't bad looking, though, and I told her I was glad she was getting that out of it because she didn't look as if she was getting much else.'[21]

The ring had in fact been lent by the Marshes, who from the start took a keen interest in the affair. On the one hand, they thought it was time Roald settled down, and were encouraged in this by his mother, who was beginning to fear that he would never marry.[22] On the other hand, he couldn't yet support himself, let alone a wife, in the style to which he had become accustomed. According to Patricia Neal, when Dahl took her to meet Charles Marsh, the old man was quick to ask her how much she had in the bank.[23]

Dahl had told her – truthfully, it seems – that he had lost in a stock exchange gamble his share of the money which his father had left to each of his children to buy a house.[24] But he was not penniless. Marsh was continuing to help in various ways and early in 1953 wrote that he was trying to get him on to the payroll of

General Newspapers.[25] Meanwhile, some stories were bought by television, among them 'Taste' and 'Dip in the Pool' (which also appeared in *The New Yorker*). Dahl said he was 'living like a miser, spending nothing and getting a peculiar sensation from watching the bank balance grow'.[26] He now had around five thousand dollars, he said – which was then worth twelve or thirteen times as much as today. Dahl's bank balance was to improve still further as a result of the interest now taken in him by a new father-figure-to-be.

In March 1952 the sixty-year-old publisher Alfred Knopf, who was a wine connoisseur, read 'Taste' in a recent back number of *The New Yorker*. He thought it 'stunning' and dictated a memo to his editor Harold Strauss complaining 'I don't know how we all missed this one.'[27] He told him to look Dahl up and see 'who he is & what he has'. Strauss replied a little stiffly that they hadn't missed Dahl. He filled his employer in on the author's previous stories and reminded him that Dahl had offered them a collection some time back. But he had told them that there was no prospect of a novel 'so we let him go'.[28] Knopf over-rode the objection and by June there was a deal. He told Dahl's agent Ann Watkins that he was 'tickled pink' to have him on the list.[29]

The collection which Dahl delivered to Knopf early in 1953 began, naturally enough, with 'Taste' and included all the other stories which *The New Yorker* had taken. There was the eaves-dropping tale 'My Lady Love, My Dove',[30] 'Skin'[31] and 'Dip in the Pool', a fable in which a compulsive gambler travelling on an ocean liner tries to rig his bet on the distance the boat will travel that day. Having chosen a low number, he throws himself over-board so as to hold up the voyage, trusting a woman whom he has met to raise the alarm. The idea was thought up by Charles Marsh, who had fantasies of scooping the pool on the Cunard liner Albert Ballin. Dahl added his own sour twist. The gambler in the story doesn't realize that the woman whose help he has enlisted is mad. She leaves him to drown.[32]

Then there was a dog-racing story, 'Mr Feasey', which came at the end of the book after the three related country life pieces which *The New Yorker* had rejected.[33] Of these, Harold Strauss would really have preferred 'The Ratcatcher' to be left out, and encouraged Dahl to tone it down. Strauss also disliked, and persuaded Dahl to omit, the anti-German story 'The Sword',[34] which he said he couldn't understand, although there is nothing at all mysterious about it.[35] And he got him to reduce 'The Wish' – about a child's obsessive, imaginary horrors – to a fifth of its original length.

On the strength of Knopf's backing, some other pieces which Dahl had unsuccessfully offered to *The New Yorker* were now accepted by various magazines, to appear just before the book's publication in the autumn of 1953: *Harper's* took 'Lamb to the Slaughter'[36] and *Town and Country* 'Galloping Foxley', the story about a commuter's obsession with schoolboy bullying.[37] *Collier's*, which had already printed two stories intended for the book ('Man from the South' and 'Poison') now published 'Nunc Dimittis'.[38]

'Nunc Dimittis' is about an artist, John Royden, who likes to paint married women in the nude and then, in a kind of slow-motion reverse striptease, adds their clothes, sitting by sitting, until the portrait is suitable to be taken home. The narrator, Lionel, is a middle-aged bachelor who has many women friends but never becomes entangled with them. He is discontented, frustrated, regretful about something, in a way that amounts to eccentricity.[39] He is also a connoisseur. He says that owning a good collection of paintings (in a long list of artists, he mentions Matthew Smith) can create a frightening atmosphere of suspense around a man such as himself – 'frightening to think that he has the power and the right, if he feels inclined, to slash, tear, plunge his fist' through the canvases he possesses.

For some time Lionel has been taking out a young woman called Janet de Pelagia. His friends are beginning to wonder whether he will marry at last. But one of them, an older woman, tells him that Janet has complained that he bores her, endlessly taking her to the same restaurant for dinner and going on about paintings and antique china.[40] Lionel decides to avenge himself. He commissions John Royden to paint Janet's portrait. When he gets it home he patiently takes off the top layer with turpentine. At a large dinner party to which he has invited her, he unveils the picture in front of everyone: 'Janet in her underclothes, the black brassiere, the pink elastic belt, the suspenders, the jockey's legs.'[41]

The story may have been prompted by Goya's famous pair of paintings *The Naked Maja* and *The Clothed Maja*, which were favourites of Matthew Smith's. Dahl was also fascinated by the jealous upheavals in which Smith's own portraits of women sometimes involved him (one husband, a man in public life, angrily made his wife sell the paintings of her by Smith, with whom she had had an affair).[42] The unctuous Royden doesn't resemble Smith, and Lionel is in obvious ways unlike Dahl: he is older, much richer and the story makes great play of his sexual inexperience. Despite all that, it isn't clear how far Dahl stands from Lionel's physical revulsions – at John Royden's bearded mouth, 'wet and naked, a trifle indecent', or at Janet's bandy legs, or at the older woman's 'loose and puckered' face with its folds of fat and its mouth pinched 'like a salmon's'[43] – passages which were left out in the version published by *Collier's* magazine.

Perhaps if Patricia Neal had read 'Nunc Dimittis' she might have given more thought to her friends' warnings, but she was never a great reader. The wedding was held at Trinity Church, New York, on a stifling July day in 1953. Dahl tore out the lining of his suit to make it cooler. Neal wore pink chiffon. Her friend the actress Mildred Dunnock was matron of honour, Charles Marsh best man. Because of temporary British restrictions on the amount of money people were allowed to spend on foreign travel, Dahl's family would have had difficulty in coming, so in fairness to both sides the occasion was kept for friends only. But the Marshes assured Roald's mother that she would like Pat, whom he was planning to take home to England at the end of the honeymoon.

Dahl arranged their trip to Europe with enthusiasm. (Patricia Neal says drily, 'He had an enormous appreciation for anything he generated.'[44]) They drove a Jaguar convertible up through Italy from Naples and on via Switzerland and the French Riviera. Dahl wanted to visit various famous acquaintances, such as Rex Harrison, along the way, and as early as May had suggested to Matthew Smith that he might like to join them.[45] As things turned out, they didn't see him until they reached England in August.

At Great Missenden the couple were to stay with Else and John and their children, whose pictures had made such an impression on Pat. The arthritic Sofie Dahl, walking with the aid of two sticks, came down the drive to meet them and simply said 'Hello'. Straight out of Broadway, Pat was surprised by the fact that 'there was no kiss. No embrace,' either from Sofie or from any of the rest of the family. She soon learned that some northern Europeans of the time had their own forms of welcome. After supper, Alfhild's husband Leslie Hansen entertained everyone with an impromptu display of fart-lighting.

During the following days there was a party where she met other relatives, friends and neighbours: Roald's half-sister Ellen and half-brother Louis; Matthew Smith; the local GP, Dr Brigstock, and his wife; the cookery writer Elizabeth David; and many others. Dahl's youngest sister Asta had just given birth to her third child, Peter; Roald and Pat drove across to their house in High Wycombe to see them. Meanwhile, the two Mrs Dahls began to take one another's measure.

Sofie had been wondering how well Pat would get on with her unusually close-knit family.[46] It was a reasonable anxiety for both of them. Patricia Neal never pretended to be a domestic kind of woman. She was used to getting up late and spending the morning in her dressing gown talking on the phone to friends. The contrast between her Hollywood habits and the sterner regime of a Norwegian housewife in rural Buckinghamshire quickly made for tensions, which Roald felt if anything more keenly than his mother. Sofie said that her concern was more whether her son would make his wife happy than the other way around. She wrote to the Marshes that she hoped Roald would be kind to Pat. 'He is not easy to live with,' she told them. Nor, she recalled, had his father been.[47]

To Pat herself, her mother-in-law came across as critical and forbidding, but one thing they had in common was a liking for babies. Roald was unusually devoted to children and was good with them, Sofie thought.[48] Pat had wanted a child ever since she began her affair with Gary Cooper, and when she told Dashiell Hammett about her forthcoming marriage, her main concern seemed to be not with her prospective husband but with what to call her first child: Neal Dashiell or Dashiell Neal. Hammett wrote to his daughter that the child had better hurry up and be born, 'regardless of which sex it picks out . . . or she'll go out and adopt one because this waiting around nine months might be well enough for some folks but it's a long time if you really want to play at motherhood.'[49]

In the event she had to wait almost two years, and the couple's frustration and anxiety on this score may have contributed to their difficulties in settling down together. There was also the problem of Roald's need to dominate. Friends of Pat's were horrified by how demanding, perfectionist and intolerant he was with her, and how he always seemed to be putting her down.[50] Measured by show-business levels of kissing and embracing, he like the rest of his family could also seem cold. But there was also what seemed to Pat a harsh vein of prudishness, which revealed itself on the honeymoon when Dahl saw her looking at herself naked in the mirror; in a reaction that would have left many a yearning movie-goer aghast if they could have been there, he shouted 'My God, will you stop that! Put some clothes on.'

As soon as they got back to New York they set about moving from their separate apartments into 44 West 77th Street, a fantastical gothic block next to Central Park and overlooking the Natural History Museum. Rents were lower on that side of the city so they could afford a small extra bedroom for Dahl to use as a study. The move was an opportunity for clearing out, and he urged Neal to sell her pictures, which he disliked, as well as the jewels she had been given by Gary Cooper. Her past relationships were more of a trouble to him than his were to her. Pat says that she was still hankering after Cooper and that Dahl was also jealous of, or simply disliked and was bored by, many of her confidants, particularly her loyal future agent Harvey Orkin, a close friend of Cooper's; Dahl complained that Orkin was both loud-mouthed and Jewish.[51]

Nor did he have much time for her family, whom they visited together for the first time that Christmas, almost six months after the wedding. Pat's mother was an unadventurous southerner, limited in her interests and irritated by the social changes around her – particularly black emancipation. Dahl simply couldn't get along with her. A friend who later saw them together excuses him: 'He was no snob. He loved the famous and he loved earls and all that kind of thing, but he was just as fond of village people. What he did mind was if people were intolerant and parochial.' Relations weren't eased on this first meeting when Dahl suggested that his young brother-in-law Pete instead of going to university should leave school and start up a petrol station. No one could have been expected to understand that to Dahl, this represented a romantic ideal.[52] But the Neals may have been right to suspect another motive. Ever since her father died Pat had paid for her brother's education. She continued to do so until he finished university and became a teacher.[53]

Dahl was feeling bloody-minded anyway. Soon after their stay with her family, he suddenly told Pat that he wanted a divorce and wrote a long letter to the Marshes explaining what was wrong.[54] He liked Pat for her courage and frankness, he told them, but they had different friends, no interests in common and little to talk about. Beyond that, of course, there was also 'the question of one's mother'. All his life, Dahl said, he had watched Sofie – like Claudia Marsh or 'any other good wife' – organizing the household, making sure it was kept clean and tidy, and up to a point acting as what he called her husband's servant. However capable and self-reliant the husband was, Dahl said, it was natural to a man to be waited upon. But Pat 'is not able to bring herself to this.'

One difference, of course, was that Neal was the main money-earner. Dahl's mother had never gone out to work and no one would have expected her to. As for Claudia Marsh, Pat saw her as a kind of geisha – which is indeed how Mrs Marsh herself, from the perspective of the 1990s, now amusedly describes her role at that time.[55] But from Dahl's point of view, one of the things which annoyed him was that when he was writing Neal seemed to think he wasn't doing anything. So she stayed in bed talking on the phone while he made the coffee and got his own lunch out of a tin. He accepted, he said, that it was hard to be both a wife and a career woman, but he supposed that those who managed it did so by doubling their efforts.

Some of Pat's friends believe that his expectations were at bottom more complex than this. According to one, Dahl gave out conflicting demands in the unconscious but powerful hope that the person at the other end would fail to meet at least one of them, thereby guaranteeing his own supremacy: 'One message was, you must go out and be an actress and be a success, and the other was, you must stay at home and be a good mother.' And in this there was another double bind. They wanted a child – but was the marriage fit to support one? Dahl said that it wasn't and used the danger of pregnancy as a reason for them to separate.[56]

Naturally enough, when he relented and asked Pat to go on holiday with him, she refused. But she had agreed to join the Marshes in Jamaica, and Dahl asked their advice about whether he should come too. It would, he said, be cruel and stupid to draw out a process which he thought was bound sooner or later to end in failure. Charles told him that both he and Pat were thinking too much about themselves and too little about each other.[57] Yes, Roald should certainly come to Jamaica – but for a vacation, not to 'wash emotional dishes'. Charles himself was not well enough, he hinted, to stand for that. But he told Dahl that 'service' was a mutual matter, and that he was in danger of turning into a martinet.

Patricia Neal didn't know about the exchange of letters, or that Marsh had given Dahl any advice.[58] A shrewd arbitrator, the older man encouraged each side to think that the other was probably right after all. Certainly, his advice to her couldn't have been more favourable to her husband. Dahl should handle all the money, Marsh told her, even if it was she who was earning most of it. And she should do all the cooking and housework. She accepted what he said, and for a while the formula worked, more or less.

Within a year of suggesting it, Marsh contracted cerebral malaria as the result of a mosquito bite in Jamaica.[59] For the remaining nine years of his life he was in effect speechless. His collapse would have been a worse blow to the couple but for the fact that he had helped them to give each other more support. Patricia went back to New York with Roald. He seemed more easygoing; she, more houseproud. A new gynaecologist diagnosed blocked Fallopian tubes and blew them out. By the summer of 1954 Pat was pregnant. Meanwhile, in the Valley of the Dahls Roald's family had been busy on their behalf. A house was found on the edge of Great Missenden, where Roald had suggested that he and Pat might spend their summers. Little Whitefield, as Gipsy House was then called, stands on its own in a country lane, an ancient drove road which runs from a medieval abbey turned country mansion, under the railway bridge and uphill into a beech wood. The house had three bedrooms and five acres of land, full of old fruit trees: apples, pears, cherries, plums. The price was £4,500, of which Sofie Dahl found one half, Pat the other.

7

A Very Maternal Daddy

Someone Like You was published in the USA in the autumn of 1953. (In Britain, Secker and Warburg brought it out the following year.) Dahl's recent marriage added to the plentiful publicity material the Knopf team already had to work on. He asked them to tone down the jacket blurb which they had drafted (he was beginning to be nervous of the phrase 'wounded in action'), but he provided an impressive list of people to whom complimentary copies should be sent. An internal memo observed that he was well connected.

The sales reps liked the book, and so did most of the influential reviewers. The *New York Times*'s critic rhapsodized:

> At disconcertingly long intervals, the *compleat* short-story writer comes along who knows how to blend and season four notable talents: an antic imagination, an eye for the anecdotal predicament with a twist at the end, a savage sense of humor suitable for stabbing or cutting, and an economical, precise writing style. No worshipper of Chekhov, he. You'll find him marching with solid plotters like Saki and O. Henry, Maupassant and Maugham ... The reader looking for sweetness, light, and subtle characterization will have to try another address. Tension is his business; give him a surprise denouement, and he'll give you a story leading up to it. His name in this instance is Roald Dahl.[1]

Other critics compared his black humour with that of the gothic *New Yorker* cartoonist Charles Addams, and his plot situations with those of the now-neglected expatriate English writer John Collier, whose pungent serio-comic tales of bizarre marriages and trick revenges had taken him to Hollywood in the mid-1930s. There was a dissenting voice in the *Buffalo News*, whose reviewer argued that such resemblances were being exaggerated and that 'Dahl's art . . . is not very likely to develop further for the sufficient reason that it is already in full flower.'[2] The tales, he said, 'are sardonic specimens of pure story, devoid of all social significance.' For the most part though, the reviewers, of whom there were a lot, settled for variations on a theme of 'never a dull moment'. They all assumed that readers would know who Dahl was. He was Patricia Neal's husband.

By Christmas, 7,500 copies had been sold, which Alfred Knopf told Dahl he thought was some kind of a record for short stories. The book was in its third printing, and Dahl was still doing promotional appearances and interviews. He was a natural subject for journalists – confident-seeming, opinionated, cantankerous, unpredictable. He lectured them about his ambition to remake the short story as an art form, and compared himself with Picasso breaking away from Corot and Monet.[3] When an interviewer from the *Post* of Houston, Texas, asked if he was writing a novel, he silenced her with a fierce glare: ' "No novels," Mr Dahl looked grim. "It's a mistake to try to do both." '[4] She was either too unnerved or too ill-prepared to remind him of *Sometime Never*, and when he went on to speak enthusiastically about D. H. Lawrence – one of the many authors who have successfully written both short stories and novels (and in his case, poetry too) – she didn't pick him up on the point, but simply asked who was his favourite British author. Loyally, or perhaps just to bamboozle her further, he named a great friend of Matthew Smith's, the avant-garde novelist Henry Green, then having a success in New York. What did she think of him, he demanded?

One-upmanship and turning the tables were favourite techniques. Another was the easy phrase-making that had marked him out even at school. 'A short story has to be two things,' he told the audience at a book-signing session in Dallas. 'It has to be short, and it has to be a story.' Too many fictions in the better magazines were disguised essays or mood pieces. 'I think the short story ought to entertain.'

By February 1954 *Someone Like You* was in its fourth US printing, and was being offered by the Book of the Month Club, which paid a $4,000 advance for it. In April it won a Mystery Writers of America award (an 'Edgar', to chime with Oscar, but also to avoid its being known as a Poe). There were plans for a play to be based on three of the stories. There was even talk of an opera. But Dahl was most pleased by the fact that a Norwegian publisher had expressed interest in the book. Gyldendal, who brought it out in 1955, are still Dahl's publishers in Norway – the longest continuous association of his literary career.

Norway was quickly followed by other Scandinavian countries: Sweden, Denmark, Finland. Meanwhile, Secker and Warburg published the collection in England, although without much success. The *Times Literary Supplement* complained about its 'morbidity and a certain irresponsible cruelty'. Dahl had a gift for suspense, the journal acknowledged, 'but the after-impression is one of heartlessness and distortion'.[5]

Nowhere were these ambiguous qualities put to more effective use by Dahl than in two stories he wrote around the time of his temporary split with Patricia Neal – too late for publication in the book. Like all his best writing for adults, they suggest a bleak, if comical, kind of self-awareness. Both are about tyrannical husbands, and both give memorable victories to the downtrodden wives.

'The Way Up To Heaven', published in *The New Yorker* in January 1954, is about a woman with a pathological fear of lateness. Her husband tortures her by procrastination. At last, she finds proof that his delays are intentional. In the course of one of them, he accidentally gets stuck in a lift – as had recently happened to Charles Marsh, in his house on East 92nd Street. Unlike the tolerant Claudia, Dahl's heroine leaves her husband there to die.

The second story, 'William and Mary', has lasted no less well. It can be seen as a counterblast against political correctness *avant la lettre* – but in its fascination with the minutiae of brain surgery it also turned out to have a grim element of prophecy in relation to Dahl's own family. The tale was, he told the Marshes, 'a stinker' in itself and a stinker to write. As early as October 1953 he was on his third complete draft, working every day until midnight and 'slightly dotty with it all'. He didn't finish it until the following summer.[6]

The plot concerns a philosopher who is encouraged by a neuro-surgeon to let him preserve his brain. (There is an element of sadism in the doctor's description of the process to William, and this echoes William's own cruelty to his wife.) By the time the story opens, the philosopher has died and the experiment has been successfully carried out. All that is left of William is his living brain, floating in a bowl of fluid, still attached to one active eyeball which gazes tetchily at the ceiling. Mary is at home, reading a long letter he has left for her, setting out the situation and telling her how she should comport herself in her widowhood: no drinking cocktails, eating pastries, watching television, using the telephone or, particularly, smoking cigarettes. But Mary has notions of her own. She goes along to the laboratory to visit the ex-William, lights a cigarette and pleasurably blows a thick cloud of smoke into his enraged eye. 'Isn't he sweet?' she says to the surgeon in the story's closing words. 'Isn't he heaven? I just can't wait to get him home.'[7]

'William and Mary' (which Dahl first called 'Abide With Me') was later successfully adapted for television, and is now one of his best-known stories. He had no success with it at the time. *The New Yorker* rejected it in 1954 and again in 1957. It may have been thought too close to Curt Siodmak's novel *Donovan's Brain*, first published in book form by Knopf in 1943, which is about a scientist who successfully keeps a brain alive using methods very like those described in Dahl's story. The resemblance ends there, but *Donovan's Brain* was well known, having been often reprinted (including in Britain), and twice filmed. The second movie version, with Lew Ayres and Nancy (Reagan) Davis, was released shortly before Dahl began writing his story. If he knew Siodmak's book, or the film, he had forgotten that he did. In 1954 Pat Neal wrote to the Marshes, 'Roald finished his difficult story. Then horrors! He discovered that this strange story had already been written. It was done in 1943 & called Donovans Brain.'

Whatever the reason for its rejection, 'William and Mary' was part of a new run of failures with *The New Yorker*, where Dahl's editor Gustave Lobrano had fallen ill and been replaced by the woman who had been his predecessor, the formidable Katharine S. White. Dahl seems not have known about the change-over. He wrote to Alfred Knopf, complaining that he was no longer seeing eye to eye with *The New Yorker*: 'The last polite letter to the chief fiction editor, whom I've known well, didn't even get an answer. So regretfully I'm having to move away and just put the stories in a drawer.'[8]

He had never in fact had as smooth a run with the magazine as he later remembered. And as his complaint to Alfred Knopf implies, he was meeting resistance elsewhere too. New values had been creeping into Anglo-American fiction, as into other aspects of the culture, and Dahl found the kind of stories he was now writing increasingly hard to place, even in the men's magazines – especially *Playboy* – which from now on would be their chief outlets. To earn money, he took on work of a kind which, however estimable by comparison with the average contents of *Playboy*, he like many writers affected to despise: movie-writing – at this time, helping with the preliminary screenplay for the John Huston/Ray Bradbury film of *Moby Dick*. It was the beginning of what would for a time, from the late 1960s, become his major source of income.

It didn't help that a play he had written, *The Honeys*, was a flop. Dahl had tried to combine several of his stories in a plot which involved irascible twin brothers and their long-suffering but eventually murderous wives. Disposing of the men required, as *Time* magazine described, 'a stalled elevator, tainted oyster juice, a skull-bopping with a frozen leg of lamb, and a medicinal drink containing tiger's whiskers'. The play, *Time* said, was 'happier in its details than its fundamental design'. It suffered by comparison with its obvious rival, the venerable *Arsenic and Old Lace*, because its murderers weren't so lovable and its plot complications weren't so insane. In Dahl's play, 'When people aren't actually attempting murder, they are making good, bad and indifferent jokes about it.'

The try-out tour – New Haven, Boston and Philadelphia – was a disaster, with one director being fired and another bringing in new writers to doctor the script. Neal, however, sitting on an unfamiliar side of the footlights, wrote loyally to the Marshes that she would rather be married to a poor but happy short-story writer than to a rich playwright who was in misery.[9] She was heavily pregnant and, after some false alarms, feeling good. The baby, a girl, was born in New York on 20 April 1955. Dahl flew to the hospital from Boston, where *The Honeys* was running. They called the child Olivia after Pat's first stage role at Northwestern. For her second name Roald suggested Twenty, because of the coincidence of the date and the number of dollars per day he was getting in expenses on tour.

From the start, he was a doting father. There had been only his mother to teach him parenthood, and according to Patricia Neal he was 'a very maternal daddy'.[10] Soon he was telling the baby's nannies what to do, when he wasn't giving them the sack.[11] One nurse, whose credentials had impressed him because she had worked for the Churchill family, proved too ugly, and had a persistent cough which irritated him.[12] Another was confused by having to take orders from the baby's father. Pat wrote to Claudia Marsh, 'This is the first American house she has been in where the woman didn't dominate. Next she will have to see yours.'[13] Dahl occasionally escaped the crowded Upper West Side apartment for an outing to the ball game or to play cards, but he took a keen interest in every detail of the household management, particularly when Pat returned to work. He was intensely protective of Olivia, and told friends he wouldn't allow the baby to be left on her own in the apartment with 'some tyrannical nurse'.[14]

There was in fact little danger of that, since his mother-in-law was enthusiastically involved in New York and his sister Else when they were in England. Fortunately so, because whenever Dahl returned to Great Missenden he was reluctant to leave again, and from Olivia's first months a fair amount of her life was spent crossing the Atlantic. Even in Manhattan the family was on the move, between West 77th Street and a more spacious apartment across the Park at East 81st and Madison which had been vacated by Neal's friend Mildred Dunnock. Their life was hectic, especially for Neal, who was both acting and still trying to follow Charles Marsh's advice about wifehood. During the run of Edith Sommers's *A Roomful of Roses*, 'I rose early to bathe and feed my now six-month-old, walked her in the park and did the shopping. I made breakfast and lunch for my husband, conferred with the nurse, cleaned the apartment, prepared supper, did the dishes and made it to the theater for an 8.30 curtain.' Within months she was performing again on Broadway, in *Cat on a Hot Tin Roof* directed by Elia Kazan. At the end of the run Kazan asked her to Florida to discuss her return to Hollywood, as the lead in *A Face in the Crowd*. 'Hollywood' was on this occasion a figure of speech. They rehearsed the film in New York and shot it in Arkansas in the heat of August.

By then Neal was pregnant once more. She left Olivia behind at Little Whitefield, where Dahl had begun to make improvements, building a guest cottage, installing and restoring a gypsy caravan of Alfhild's, and adapting a garden shed as a place in which to write. 'It's marvellous, isolated, quiet,' he wrote to the Marshes. The only occasional disturbance was from some heifers, bought for his butcher friend Claud with a grant from the Public Welfare Foundation, which grazed in the orchard outside. Dahl said he occasionally heard their tongues scraping against the windows. If he left them open, the cows ate the curtains.

His writing hut represented part of an effort not only to recreate his own early childhood, but to improve on it. As a boy in the 1920s, Roald used to hide up a tree in order to write his diary;[15] at Repton there had been the photography dark-room. His garden shed was a more substantial place in which to work, and where he could commemorate, and fantasize around, his past. On a side table he gradually accumulated shards of himself.[16] There was his father's silver and tortoiseshell paper-knife. There was the heavy ball which he had made at Shell out of the wrappings of chocolate bars. There were souvenirs of his time in North Africa – a stone 'star of the desert' picked up in Libya and a tablet fragment with a cuneiform inscription found in Babylon. As he grew old, other relics were added: his own femur, for example, and fragments of his spine, saved from operations. For much of his life he was to spend several hours of every morning and afternoon surrounded by these fetishes, snugly wrapped in a sleeping bag, sitting in an old armchair, his feet on a trunk which was filled with blocks of wood and tied to a leg of the chair to prevent it from slipping. Here he transported himself back to his earliest infancy. Even beyond. 'It's a lovely place to work', he told an interviewer. 'It's small and tight and dark and the curtains are always drawn and it's a kind of womb – you go up here and you disappear and get lost.'[17]

The New Yorker turned down seven stories by him between February 1957 and March 1959.[18] Dahl was being pressed by Alfred Knopf to put together a new collection, but told the publisher that he found ideas harder and harder to come by and was beginning to fear that they would run out altogether. But the real difficulty perhaps wasn't lack of ideas so much as a change of heart, stemming from his new experiences of parenthood. His stories were still 'clever', cynical, vengeful: but these attributes – skilfully deployed in the best of his earlier post-war stories – seem over-contrived in the fiction he was now writing. Perhaps he was beginning to suspect that human dealings required something different of him, both as a man and as a writer, but he wasn't yet sure what it was. The new tales often focused on children, and they carry their burden of malice with a rather artificial air. In one, a delighted couple, Hitler by name, none of whose previous infants have survived, manage to bring up a son called Adolf. In another, a baby is fed on royal jelly and frighteningly turns into a bee. A third piece, 'Pig', is about an orphan brought up as a vegetarian who ends up slaughtered in a butcher's abattoir.

None of these sold. Fortunately, Neal was also busy and earning enough for all the family. Apart from US film and television per-formances, she began to get roles in English productions of US plays. The first was a BBC version of *The Royal Family of Broadway*, about a tribe of actors. Gradually the couple established a busy, unpredictable but well-rooted existence, commuting between the English countryside and Manhattan, and rapidly extending their busy household. On the surface, it looked like an idyll. Dahl toured the countryside buying antique furniture, some of which he restored. He planted about a hundred varieties of rose and began to grow vegetables, especially onions, which were his favourite. He built an aviary and, imitating an idea of Ivar Bryce's at his Eliza-bethan mansion Moyns Park, filled it with brightly-coloured bud-gerigars – white, pink, yellow, green – which flew in clouds around the garden or sat whistling in the trees.

In April 1957 their second daughter was born at Oxford, and named Chantal until her parents noticed the rhyme and called her Tessa instead. Pat's mother paid a visit. As before, she and her son-in-law quarrelled. She criticized his obsession with the rich; he complained about her southern cooking. Peace was resumed when she went home and the Dahls took their annual holiday in Norway, fishing and scuba-diving and visiting his family.

There were frequent summer outings closer to home. Sofie was in her seventies now and crippled with arthritis. She lived with a housekeeper in a wing of Else and John's house, Whitefields, in Great Missenden. Roald visited her often with Pat and the children, and for the rest of the family he would organize picnics on the river Thames or a trip to the Cotswolds. Some evenings he played snooker with men from the village, or drove to the grey-hound stadium at White City, twenty minutes away in west London. Or he and Pat would leave Olivia and Tessa with the nanny and drive down to London for dinner. One memorable night when they were at the fashionable restaurant Prunier's with Matthew Smith, Pat took a liking to a pair of silver sugar tongs and Roald pocketed them for her. As they left, a waiter unsuccessfully accosted the shifty-looking painter, but didn't dare to confront Dahl himself.[19]

They also spent occasional weekends at the Bryces, in company divided equally between the international rich and the decayed European aristocracy. Bryce's heiress wife Josephine Hartford had helped him to buy back the magnificent house and estate where he had spent part of his childhood. He was infatuated with writers, and according to a young woman friend, admired Dahl personally as 'a kind of Viking: strong, manly, adventurous – a throwback.'[20] The two men had much in common: a family fortune made in shipping, and then partly lost;[21] war years spent in the USA; enthusiasms for gambling and for art. (Bryce collected famous fakes, which some think revealing about him.[22]) Both Roald and Pat relished the atmosphere of raffish luxury at Moyns, where they played cards until the small hours and were brought large breakfasts in bed by uniformed servants.

More often, though, they saw local friends, comfortably-off people with children of the same ages as Olivia and Tessa: the Kirwans, for example, a retired brigadier and his wife who farmed on the other side of the hill behind Gipsy House; or the Stewart-Libertys, in front of whose big old farmhouse in The Lee stands a ship's figurehead taken from one of the hulks which were broken up to supply timbers for the family's mock-Tudor department store, Liberty's in Regent Street.

The Stewart-Libertys' place was much less grand than Moyns Park, but none the less had a Hollywood level of opulence which made Pat feel at home. Because of her work, she was still often in southern California, sometimes taking the family with her. Early in 1958 they stayed at Yul Brynner's house in Laguna Beach, where they saw a lot of the painter Alden Brooks, another friend of Matthew Smith's.[23] Back in England that summer, Pat made her West End debut in Tennessee Williams's *Suddenly Last Summer*; Kenneth Tynan said she played her 'dark brown voice' like a cello, and compared the performance to Maria Casares' *Phèdre*.[24] And Dahl at last had a breakthrough with *The New Yorker*, where Katharine White's son and assistant Roger Angell accepted a story about pheasant poaching entitled 'The Champion of the World'.[25]

Dahl rebelled against Pat being so continually busy,[26] but it went on throughout the following year and began to take an emotional toll. Neal made a film at Elstree before returning to New York to rehearse a play about Helen Keller, William Gibson's *The Miracle Worker*. Dahl didn't like the piece and told the author so, at which Pat told him to 'keep your fucking nose out of my business and let me make my own enemies'.[27] Although they often got on well, they were also more and more inclined to quarrel, especially after they had had a few drinks. Roald in particular seemed jealous of Pat's success, and was prone to needling her with jibes against Americans or against theatre people.[28] In such moods, each brought out in the other the characteristics he or she found most irritating: Roald's tetchy, sometimes supercilious presence encouraged Pat to be compensatorily laid back; while her chaotic-seeming ease with the children drove him to pace up and down restlessly until he could stand no more and disappeared to write. But a combination of work and children meant that they were rarely alone together for very long, and their squabbles were countered by the powerful physical attraction between them. Maturity made Pat more beautiful than ever, with her sad dark eyes and her strong-boned face. The allure of the now middle-aged Roald was less easily definable. Untidily dressed, sharp-nosed, with a high forehead, gangly body, very long hands and flat feet, he looked, Pat said, like Virginia Woolf in drag, except that he was going bald. But women were attracted both by this battered appearance and, when he could be bothered, by the attentiveness, energy and humour of his conversation. He gave an impression of being both strong and vulnerable. And because he was hard to please, when he liked you, you could easily find yourself liking him back.

Soon, Pat was pregnant again. In March 1960 Roald, Patricia, Olivia, Tessa and the nanny sailed from New York to England. The new baby, Theo, was born that summer. Ivar Bryce was one of his godfathers, and put him down for Eton.[29]

The crossing had been eventful. Dahl's London agent was with them on the *Queen Elizabeth*. So was his first patron, C. S. Forester. So too was an ambitious British publisher, Charles Pick, recently appointed managing director of Michael Joseph.[30] Dahl's new collection of stories *Kiss Kiss* had just appeared in New York, and Pick bought a copy to read on the voyage back. Although the author had not been writing well recently, the collection contained his two unforgettable stories 'William and Mary' and 'The Way Up To Heaven', as well as another which was to become a popular favourite: 'Parson's Pleasure', about an antique dealer who buys a Chippendale commode from some men whom he thinks of as yokels, pretending that it is worthless to him except for its legs. While he is fetching his car, the men obligingly cut off the legs and smash up the rest for firewood.

Heavily promoted by Knopf, the collection was a success in the USA, and as soon as Pick was introduced to the author he offered him a £350 advance for the British rights, with a royalty starting at 12.5 per cent (the usual figure would have been 10 per cent). Dahl accepted. When they docked at Southampton, Pick telephoned the literary editor of the *Sunday Times* and persuaded him to print 'The Way Up To Heaven' as holiday reading.[31] He reckons that within a couple of years he had sold around 20,000 copies of *Kiss Kiss* in hardback in Britain, about ten times what he would normally have expected for a collection of short stories. Next, seeing an opportunity in the newly expanding paperback trade, Pick bought the rights in the out-of-print *Someone Like You* and invited the editorial director of Penguin to dinner.

In later life, Dahl always claimed to have been ignored by the British literary establishment, but *Kiss Kiss* was respectfully received in Britain. The *Times Literary Supplement* compared the book with the early work of Angus Wilson, and talked of 'the verisimilitude of [Dahl's] caricature of human weakness, showing this to the edge of extravagance, revealing a social satirist and a moralist at work behind the entertaining fantast'.[32] And Malcolm Bradbury, then a young lecturer in the Adult Education Department at Hull University, wrote enthusiastically that Dahl 'gets straight A's in *my* creative writing class'.[33] Bradbury, who had recently made his name with *Eating People Is Wrong*, was writing in the *New York Times Book Review* and commented tellingly on transatlantic differences for writers of short stories: not only the fact that the USA provided the only substantial market, but also the effects of this on Dahl's fiction. Dahl's England was, he rightly said, a curious place, 'rather like the England in British Travel Association ads in *The New Yorker*. Deliberately, he makes it a bit more rural, a bit more quaint, a bit more lively than it really is, a foreigner's England, perhaps.'

It was the US critics who now proved harder to please. Some linked *Kiss Kiss* with the new vogue for sick humour, and Robert Phelps made the point that Dahl's stories are in fact rather like jokes: you can tell them to people.[34] But if they could be retold, not everyone thought they stood up well to being reread, and another reviewer, Paul A. Bittenwieser, said that they were becoming increasingly predictable.[35] Several critics also found something childlike in the book. Phelps was reminded of cartoons: 'there is only the simplest, generic characterization – the Priggish Professor, the Mousy Parson, the Grouchy Millionaire.' Bittenwieser commented on Dahl's fairy-tale use of superlatives: 'an antique is not merely valuable, it is a Venus de Milo of the furniture world; a certain new food is not only delicious, it is worth five hundred an ounce.' Another critic who saw the stories as fairy-tales, with the old-fashioned intention of scaring their readers, was the Canadian novelist and playwright Robertson Davies. But out of the eleven tales in *Kiss Kiss*, Davies was disappointed that 'Mr Dahl only made me shudder with one'.[36]

None of this discouraged book-buyers. In the USA *Kiss Kiss* was published early in February 1960, with massive advertising linking it to St Valentine's Day. Knopf spent in all $8,000 on publicity for the book, and by April the firm had sent out 16,000 of the 24,000 copies printed.[37] Continental European publishers eagerly bought the rights, not only in Scandinavia, but in countries where Dahl's books had not previously been translated: France, Germany, Holland, Italy. In each case, he was taken up by one of the leading literary houses: Gallimard, Rowohlt, Meulenhoff, Feltrinelli. Most of them bought *Someone Like You* too for good measure. And in Germany and Holland, where the collections were quickly successful, translators soon began work on his book of war stories *Over To You*. It would be some time before Dahl saw a big financial return on his writing, but in the German language alone during the next thirty years his books for adults were to sell five million copies.[38]

So when preparations began at Knopf for his next publication, the author was in high spirits. To start with, he had been diffident about it – even slightly ashamed. Alfred Knopf had been pressing for yet more stories, or better still for a novel. Dahl again admitted that he hadn't any ideas, and that the stories in *Kiss Kiss* had come with increasing difficulty.[39] There were only eleven to show for the six years since *Someone Like You* and of those, the best two were in draft even before the earlier collection appeared. However, he had been making up tales for Olivia and Tessa, who were now five and three years old: lively and enthusiastic girls, the younger somewhat fractious, the elder charming and unmistakably intelligent. Their father apologized to Knopf in advance, saying he knew that juvenile fiction was not up his street, but here was a typescript anyway. He later told Knopf that more than once in the course of writing it he wondered, 'What the hell am I writing this nonsense for?', and that when he delivered the draft he had mentally seen Knopf hurling it across the room and asking, 'What the hell am I *reading* this nonsense for?'[40]

The story – even more pronouncedly than his adult fiction, a mixture of folk tale and cartoon strip – was about an orphan who lives with a pair of repulsive and cruel aunts. James meets a man with some magic powder which makes a peach tree in the garden grow like Jack's beanstalk. James climbs into one of its giant fruits, and finds it occupied by a group of large and vociferous insects. The peach rolls away, crushing the aunts and carrying its passengers to various adventures at sea and in the sky, before becoming safely impaled on the top of the Empire State Building. The travellers decide to stay in the USA, where 'Every one of them became rich and successful.'[41]

Alfred Knopf was cautious about *James and the Giant Peach*

123

and said nothing until he had tried it on his children's books editor Virginie Fowler. Her immediate enthusiasm encouraged him, and in July, two months after Dahl sent the typescript, Knopf wrote to him, 'I have just read with absolute delight your juvenile. If this doesn't become a little classic, I can only say that I think you will not have been dealt with justly.'[42]

Knopf's decision came in the course of a leisurely correspondence with his author, much of it about wine. The older man was planning a trip to Burgundy and the Gironde to see the vintage, and he and Dahl traded oenophiliac anecdotes. Dahl had bought an odd lot of claret at a London auction, where it went cheap because the labels had rotted away. As he began to open the bottles, the names on the corks revealed that the wines were first class – Margaux, Lafite – and of vintages dating back to before the First World War. 'Rather fun,' he lordlily boasted.[43]

With Knopf's staff, Dahl's tone was now an even more pronounced mixture of the joky and the grand. He was understandably impatient at their request for yet another potted autobiography, and under 'Brief summary of principal occupations' entered that he had run the harem of an Arab sheikh in the 1930s. But this good humour soon faded, and when he was asked to name authors and critics who might supply a phrase or two to be used in advertising the book, he complained that publishers 'are doing this to me all the time and I hate it. The book they send me usually stinks and I have to tell them so.' The blurb writers also asked for a brief description of *James and the Giant Peach* so that they wouldn't misrepresent it. He answered menacingly, 'You won't.'

There was good reason for his self-confidence. He had already finished the first draft of another story he had been telling to the girls, which he provisionally entitled 'Charlie's Chocolate Boy'. This was at the end of August 1960. Roald and Pat were then at Great Missenden with the girls and the new baby Theo, now a month old. Life was not perfect perhaps, but in the light of the tragedies that were to follow, it would soon seem to have been.

8

Punishment and Pain, Unhappiness and Despair

Roald Dahl longed to be powerful enough to be able to conquer illness and other misfortunes. Whether or not the dream stemmed from the early deaths of his sister and his father, he was fascinated by medicine, and often said he wished he had become a doctor. In Manhattan, through Patricia Neal, he became very friendly with a successful surgeon, Dr Edmund Goodman.[1] Dr Goodman lives with his wife Marian on the north shore of Long Island, on the estate of Averill Harriman, who was one of his first private patients. The Goodmans were friendly with another couple, the Cusicks, and as all three families had children of similar ages, they saw a lot of each other. Mrs Goodman stresses two things about Dahl. He was wonderful with children, to whom (particularly Missy Cusick[2]) 'he would tell marvellous stories . . . and be in total communication with them.' And he would have excelled as a physician.

The story-teller and the healer manqué were one and the same. Dahl's children's books are full of all-solving wizards and magicians – the old man in *James and the Giant Peach*, Mr Willy Wonka and the BFG with his dream potions – and their child-equivalents, such as the girl with the Magic Finger and Matilda. Dahl had no truck with the iconoclastic attitude of writers like L. Frank Baum, whose wizard ruler of Oz is exposed as no more than an anxious little bald old humbug. Dahl's magicians make mistakes, and some of them (particularly Mr Willy Wonka, and

George in *George's Marvellous Medicine*) are cavalier in their dealings with inconvenient people, but they are still heroes and hero-
ines. He himself often said that he dreamed dreams of glory;
literally so, according to Neal. 'When he went to bed, he would
make himself go to sleep by being a hero. Let's say there was a
game which he played beautifully, and they needed someone.
Roald would come forward and say "I will play" – and they would
win.'[3]

For the moment, his triumphs were confined to games (one of
the pursuits he shared with Ed Goodman was golf) and to the
social contests he liked to arrange, whether or not the participants
knew what was going on. One friend of Pat's remembers having
dinner with him some time around 1960 and his delightedly
recounting a trick he had recently played. He had bought some
very good wine, drunk it, kept the bottles, filled them with the
cheapest stuff he could find and served them to his unwitting and
politely admiring guests. She found it 'appalling and indicative of
Roald' that he wanted 'to diminish and demean people, and to
crow about it.' Well, it was only a joke. Other acquaintances saw
something at least as analytical as ill-humoured in Dahl's tricks –
an interest, as one of them put it, in seeing 'what effect they had on
one. He was detached from it. He did things sometimes almost like
a scientist.'[4]

In the light of future events, it would become harder than ever
to separate the detached, para-scientific, sometimes cruel-seeming
Dahl from the kindly magician; the bully from the hero. But his
first big challenge was the accident to four-month-old Theo, to
whom Dahl was unambiguously devoted. Whomever else Dahl
bullied, Theo wasn't among them.

He was Dahl's only son. Put another way, he was the only person
to whom Dahl could be what he himself had lacked for most of his
own childhood: a boy's father. The doctors said Theo was going to
die.[5] His pram had been hit by a cab on the corner of 85th Street
and Madison as the nanny pushed it across the road, bringing
Tessa home from her nursery school for lunch. The taxi threw the

pram into the side of a bus, crushing the child inside. Pat was out shopping near by and heard the sirens.

An ambulance took Theo to Lenox Hill Hospital, where by a miserable coincidence, Pat's old friend Dashiell Hammett was dying of cancer. Ed Goodman, along with the Dahls' paediatrician, saw the baby there. His skull was broken in many places, and there was a 'tremendous neurological deficit.'[6]

Dahl's instinct in this emergency was to become increasingly typical of him: put yourself in charge, and get all the help you can from anyone you know. He didn't trust the treatment Theo was getting – particularly after a nurse mistakenly gave the baby an overdose of anticonvulsant, which the doctors had to pump out. Within three days he and Pat, driven by Harvey Orkin, took the baby away through the snow to Goodman's own hospital, Columbia Presbyterian.

One result of Theo's injuries was that he developed hydrocephalus, a build-up of cerebrospinal fluid which puts pressure on the brain. To drain it, a neurosurgeon used a relatively new technique which involved running a thin tube from his head into a vein, where the fluid would be dispersed into the bloodstream.[7] This was the best available technology at the time, in spite of a problem which no one had been able to overcome. The tube contained a one-way valve which kept clogging. Whenever this happened the baby developed a fever, became temporarily blind, and had to be operated on again so that the tube and valve could be changed. As it became clear that Theo would live, his parents grew increasingly anxious about the dangers of these repeated invasions.

They stayed at the hospital in relays, having left Olivia and Tessa with friends. According to Pat, 'It was, paradoxically, one of the most married times in our life together.'[8] But Roald was sure that there was something more to be done. The affectionate Goodmans remember: 'Any new problem aroused this wonderful curiosity he had, as well as deep feeling . . . He kept things moving. Roald always did that. Nothing was ever stagnant with him. He wanted to find out if there was anything to be done and to do it or to try and get someone to get at it.'

What Dahl wanted to find out in this instance was whether the problem with the valve was unique to Theo, and if not, whether anyone had come up with a better remedy. He made contact with institutions and experts concerned with hydrocephalus, and discovered that thousands of children were in a similar plight. No one knew of a device which worked better.

Theo came home to East 81st Street in January. Today, a big, sensitive, slow-speaking man in his thirties, he lives with his stepmother in the family home at Great Missenden, where he manages a normal existence, working as a supervisor at a nearby supermarket and keeping up the neighbourly snooker game instituted by his father. In the winter of 1960–61 no such happy outcome could have been predicted. Theo needed continual attention and suffered frequent, terrifying relapses. His parents' anxiety was compounded by the fact that Olivia and Tessa were still making the same daily journey to school. And if New York now seemed a dangerous place to live, medical bills of over $12,000 (in today's terms, almost £50,000)[9] showed how expensive it could be also. It was not clear how much would come from insurance.

To raise money, not only Patricia Neal but Dahl himself did TV performances – in his case hosting, Hitchcock-style, a drama series called *Way Out*. Hideously, the long-planned opening episode was based on his story about brain surgery, 'William and Mary'. Dahl didn't object, but although he was a heavy smoker, refused to let his introduction be turned into a commercial in which he lit one of the sponsor's brand of cigarettes.[10] Meanwhile, new stories inevitably proved even less possible to write than before, and he longed to get everyone back to England where medical treatment was free, where they would all be close to his mother and sisters, and where he could escape into the security of his shed. His wife, although she saw the necessity, was less keen. She was now able to find work in England as well as in the USA, but most of her close friends were American, and she needed their emotional support. However, in mid-April Dahl told Alfred Knopf that they were leaving for Buckinghamshire. They would be there, he said, for at least the whole of the summer, and until further notice.[11]

*

Great Missenden felt, as he knew it would, like the safest place in the world. The narrow high street of shops and pubs wound along its shallow valley through the Chiltern Hills, once the main route between Aylesbury and London. Fields and woods sloped up all around. On one hillside, the grey flint-and-stone parish church with its squat, awkwardly-shaped tower rose above the roofs of the abbey mansion. Most of the other village houses were tiny, lined up in terraces of red and ochre brick: a door, a window, two windows above, then the same again, all beneath a continuous uneven roof of tiles or slate. They opened straight onto the narrow pavement, as did the familiar pubs and shops – the butcher's, the baker's, the ironmonger's with its tall old oil pumps narrowing the entrance.

Behind the main street, the buildings were more widely spaced, and the houses had gardens at the front as well as the back. They were still very small, and it was only by comparison with them that Little Whitefield looked more than a cottage. It is white, slated, originally symmetrical, with a garden all around and a brick wall around the garden: a house of the kind a child might draw. At one stage in its history it had been known as Gipsy House – a contradiction which suited the much-travelling yet home-loving Dahls. The name also prevented confusions with Else's place, Whitefields, so they adopted it in 1963.[12]

In the village, it was known that he wrote and she acted, but relatively few people in England had yet heard the name Roald Dahl, and even Patricia Neal wasn't particularly famous there. The couple were well enough liked, not least because in extending the house and garden, they helped to provide employment. A local builder, Wally Saunders, gradually became a full-time member of the household's staff. 'As the family grew', he later recalled on a television programme about Patricia Neal, 'so the house did. And, you know, it was "Pull that wall down and build up that one", and perhaps the next year it would be just the opposite, you know, "Put that wall back and pull that one down, we made a mistake, we took the wrong one down." '[13]

When, later, Dahl bought a billiard table and had a regular game at Gipsy House, Wally was usually one of the players. Some visitors were unimpressed by what they saw as Dahl's attempt at 'the Hemingway buddy thing', but he really liked to spend time with working men, going to the dog races or playing darts. And where, as with Claud's cattle, he saw a chance to help, he was sometimes able, through the Marshes' Public Welfare Foundation, to provide it. Gratitude then, as well as sympathy, surrounded the couple when they brought Theo home, and they quickly settled into a protective local routine. Tessa was enrolled for the following term at Gateway School, a private nursery in the village; Olivia at Godstowe, a traditional preparatory school for girls, a short drive away in High Wycombe. Their father's share as a chauffeur in one of the Godstowe school runs was duly organized. Meanwhile, summer was coming. To cheer up Olivia and Tessa, who – particularly the latter – showed signs of having been traumatized by their brother's accident, the ever-energetic Dahl took them and other members of the family on various expeditions. A favourite was flying model gliders on a hillside near Amersham. He met another enthusiast there, a hydraulic engineer named Stanley Wade, whose hobby was to make miniature engines for toy aeroplanes.

Practical people like Wade were among those with whom Dahl always got on best locally. He hated the English obsession with class (although with his usual contradictoriness, he also partly shared it: he was infatuated with titles, and complained to friends that Asta's husband Alex Anderson, with whom he didn't get on, was a mere vet[14]). Among the financially better-off of his neighbours, he preferred sophisticated business people like the Stewart-Libertys to the gentry who shot and hunted. Some of the latter reciprocated his distrust. In 'up-county' Buckinghamshire circles, according to one former neighbour, there were people who wouldn't have him in the house – perhaps because the more hidebound they were, the more he went out of his way to offend them. In the early 1960s it would have been hard to find a society less adventurous within similar reach of London. As the neighbour says, 'Roald used to like to shock, and go to a smart dinner party and say something simply frightful.'

That spring and summer, making himself agreeable stood lower than usual on Dahl's list of priorities. His main concern was still with the valve in Theo's head. Dahl now knew that three main problems were involved.[15] Two were related to the surgical operation itself. As the tube containing the valve was inserted into the cerebral ventricle, small particles of organic matter were liable to get into it. Even if it remained clear, there was a danger that the end of the tube would rest too close to the choroid plexus, the structure of blood vessels which generates the cerebrospinal fluid. When this happened, pieces of the choroid plexus might, over time, break off into the tube. Either way, when solid matter entered the valve it became blocked, and infection developed.

The existing valve was a simple affair, a short length of silicone rubber tubing with a tiny rubber dome at each end, slit to let out the fluid. Solid matter couldn't easily escape through the opening, and if it did, another problem was exacerbated. This was that the dome was unreliable in its main job, of preventing blood from returning into the valve, where it coagulated.

The Dahls had been referred by Theo's surgeon in New York to a specialist at the Hospital for Sick Children in Great Ormond Street. He was a senior man, unacquainted with new treatment for hydrocephalus and unimpressed by its success rate. He passed Theo on to a junior colleague, a neurosurgical consultant then in his early forties called Kenneth Till.

All of Till's patients were children, most of them suffering from potentially fatal conditions. He was professionally accustomed to meeting distraught parents. He would explain to them what he proposed. Here was the problem, this was what he would like to do about it, these were the possible outcomes. Did he have their permission? Often, the answer would be no more than a desperate shrug.

Dahl was different – to Till, refreshingly, fascinatingly and helpfully different. He had had plenty of first-hand experience of hospitals. He read everything up for himself and was, in Till's estimation, 'very knowledgeable'. There was also a psychological detachment: 'He had the coolness – I think this perhaps is the word

– the coolness to want to know the pros and cons, the whys and wherefores. He didn't have to hold himself in.'

Whenever Dahl didn't understand what Till proposed, he would make him draw it for him. He studied the problem incessantly, and came up with two ideas. One was simple but frightening: that since the draining system seemed to be harmful to Theo, perhaps they should try just taking it out to see what happened. The other was to devise a better valve. Then he remembered his aircraft-modelling acquaintance Stanley Wade, and put the problem to him.

Within a month, Wade had designed a prototype. In appearance something between the fuse in a household electric plug and the valve of a bicycle tyre, it consisted of a cylinder about seven millimetres in diameter and four centimetres long. Inside were two stainless-steel shutters, each consisting of a disc held within a cage, which allowed both fluid and small solid particles to pass around it in one direction, but which closed tight if any pressure were exerted in the other. Wade also offered a solution to the problem of inserting the tube itself into the brain. He constructed a thin implement of hollow steel, with a flexible extractor to remove any plug of organic material before the permanent tube was introduced through it.

Dahl, Wade and Kenneth Till met regularly at Little Whitefield to discuss progress – and also to fly Wade's aeroplanes. Till remembers an occasion when one disappeared into a nearby field and Olivia brightly parroted her father: 'It's in the bloody cabbages.'

Most medical breakthroughs are expensive: there are development costs, inventors hope to make their fortunes, everyone involved has to be paid. In this case, the men agreed that if the valve were successful, it should be priced at no more than would cover the manufacturing and administrative outlay. Experiments were carried out free by engineering firms with which Wade had connections. The fact that no serious money was involved also saved time. Little more than a year after the family's return to England, a patent application had been lodged for the Wade-Dahl-Till Valve. In June 1962 Dahl wrote to Alfred Knopf, telling him that the first valve had been inserted into a child's head at the

Hospital for Sick Children in Great Ormond Street. So far, there had been no setbacks. He added buoyantly, 'You should *see* the apple blossom in our orchard this morning.'[16]

Within eighteen months, the valve was on the market at less than a third of the price of its earlier rival. It came to be exported all over the world, and Kenneth Till reckons that before it was superseded, it was used to treat two to three thousand children. Some people still have it in their heads today.

As it happened, there was no need to use it on Theo, who unexpectedly but steadily began now to get better. His recovery seemed to bless the whole family's life. At their new schools, the girls quickly made friends who were delighted to be asked home by them. The house with the gypsy caravan in the garden and the coloured birds flying all around had fast earned a reputation as a children's paradise. Olivia's and Tessa's tall, restless father was a little intimidating, but was redeemed by the fact that he kept the glove compartment of his old Humber stuffed with packets of sweets, which he sometimes dished out as rewards for the best story anyone told on a journey. And Pat was beautiful and tolerant. Women who are now mothers themselves, friends at that time of Olivia and Tessa, describe sticking their crayon drawings over the not-yet-famous paintings on the walls, and around Christmas helping themselves to slices off the big caramel-coloured Norwegian cheese which stood in the kitchen all day.[17] Pat's best-remembered phrase, in her husky southern voice, was 'Whatever you want, darling.'

By the autumn of 1962 Olivia was seven and a half, an imaginative, slightly fey girl who made up rhyming poems in the car and charmed visitors by telling them that she had an invisible imp on each shoulder, one good, one bad.[18] Tessa was an imperious, articulate five and a half – plump-faced, and already with something of the look of her mother. Theo was just over two. Early in October their parents went to a dinner party given in London by Alfred Knopf, who was *en route* for the annual Frankfurt Book Fair. The other guests were the popular novelist Storm Jameson and her husband, and the publisher Frederick Warburg. Dahl had just delivered a revised draft of *Charlie and the Chocolate Factory*. He had submitted the first version not long before Theo's accident, almost two years previously, but had inevitably been slow in revising it. Now he was in boisterous spirits, and told Knopf that the family were all well.[19]

A few days afterwards, the parents of children at Godstowe School received a note warning them of an outbreak of measles. In those days, few children in Britain were inoculated against the disease: catching it was regarded as a normal rite of passage, like losing your first teeth. Gamma globulin was hard to obtain, except for pregnant women. Pat tried the husband of Roald's elder half-sister Ellen, Sir Ashley Miles, who was a celebrated physician, the author of a standard textbook on immunology. For once, string-pulling failed. Indeed, Miles's eminence was itself a barrier to any help he might otherwise have given. He had been Director of the Department of Biological Standards, and was well on his way to a senior position in the Royal Society. It wouldn't have been right for him to bend the rules – and besides, he said, it would be good for the girls to get their measles over with.[20] The vulnerable Theo was another matter, and for him the serum was made available.

Soon, Olivia became ill. She had always succumbed heavily to minor ailments, but when she slept for twenty-four hours at a stretch, Pat called the doctor. Roald tried to amuse the child by making little animals with coloured pipe-cleaners, but she 'couldn't do them at all'.[21] That evening, drowsiness became coma. The doctor returned, went white, and called an ambulance. Olivia died in hospital the same night.

As Dahl's early story 'Katina' shows, he had felt a protective tenderness for little girls long before he was a father, let alone a bereaved one. The tragedy would have been shattering to anyone, but in his case it followed two years of intense anxiety and effort over Theo. It also echoed his sister Astri's death, at exactly the same age. He felt like Ben Jonson in similar circumstances: 'O, could I lose all father now!' Two months later, on one of the few occasions when he was ever guilty of understatement, he told

Alfred Knopf, 'Pat and I are finding it rather hard going still.'[22] Neal herself puts it more strongly. She says that her husband all but went out of his mind.[23]

For a writer, one option not readily available at such a time is to take refuge in work. Sitting on his own in the shed, with a blank pad of lined yellow paper in front of him and a pile of neatly-sharpened pencils, there was no escape from whatever pushed itself into Dahl's mind. He gave himself over to private mourning on a Victorian scale. Olivia was buried in the nearby hamlet of Little Missenden, in a large plot – the idea was that it would eventually accommodate her parents too. Dahl went again and again to the grave, and with the help of a horticulturist friend, Valerie Finnis, built an Alpine garden on it, taking an obsessive pride in the number of different species it contained – about 120, he said, including some found for him by a collector in Munich which were exceptionally scarce and had never been grown before in England. He had also imported a tiny cineraria from Afghanistan.[24] He thought about the after-life, and because he believed in always going to the top man for advice, made an appointment for himself and Pat to discuss the matter with his old headmaster Geoffrey Fisher, the retired Archbishop of Canterbury. Dahl didn't think that Olivia could be happy where there were no dogs, and Fisher angered him by saying that the Christian heaven was confined to humans. Whether or not this doctrinal severity stirred Dahl's later, mistaken attack on Fisher in *Boy*, Pat thought that their daughter's death was the end, for Roald, of any residual possibility of Christian belief.[25]

He had always found it almost impossible to talk to anyone about his feelings, and seemed now to cut himself off from friends, relatives, even from his children, in a way which made Tessa at least feel that she could never mean as much to him as Olivia had meant. To a theatre-director friend, Gerald Savory, who spent a lot of time with the couple immediately after Olivia's death, it was as if a shutter had come down.[26] Some months later, Dahl asked Annabella to come and stay, and took her to the grave. But he didn't weep, and said nothing of what he was going through.[27] He was drinking more than usual, and increased his dose of the barbiturates which, whether for back pain or just to calm himself, he regularly took.

When Tessa was fractious, so she says, her father sometimes handed out pills to her too. Because of her later drug addiction, it is a serious claim. Her mother denies it, saying that she and Roald would never have given the children 'grown-up pills', but her youngest daughter Lucy confirms Tessa's story, while pointing out that there was and is nothing unusual about it. Lucy adds that her parents would also quite often give the children wine or whisky if they were feeling unwell, 'and it did make you feel better'.[28] If this is right, some of Tessa's and Lucy's later difficulties may have had part of their origins in the tragedies which hit the family at this time (in Lucy's case, before she was even born) and in their father's escape-routes from them.

Dahl's efforts to write were still unsuccessful. Six months after Olivia's death, he told his publishers, 'I feel right now as though I'll never in my life do any more! I simply cannot seem to get started again.'[29] But for Neal, work was both a ready form of escape and a necessary source of income. Acting brought new surroundings, new friends, and a mind other than her own to occupy. For a time, she accepted almost anything that was offered: a part in a single episode of a TV series, and then an unimportant-seeming role in a film with the provisional title of 'Hud Bannon'. The TV contract enabled her to take the whole family to Beverly Hills for a few weeks. Then the film unexpectedly turned out to be a hit. *Hud*, with Paul Newman, was eventually to win Patricia Neal an Oscar. Meanwhile, other movies followed: Alexander Singer's *Psyche 59*, with Curt Jurgens and Samantha Eggar; Otto Preminger's *In Harm's Way*, with John Wayne. She also quickly got pregnant. In May 1964, aged thirty-eight, she gave birth to another daughter, Ophelia. Theo, who had his own versions of names, called her 'Don-Mini', which – shortened to 'Min' – was adopted by everyone because it avoided painful slips with 'Olivia'. Within six months, Neal was expecting yet another baby, although she and Roald told no one for a time. A new film turned up, and the whole family went on location in Honolulu: Roald, Tessa, Theo, the baby Ophelia and two nanny-housekeepers.

At the suggestion of Pat and Roald, Kenneth Till had agreed to remove Theo's old valve altogether. After a period of nervous experimentation, he was managing well without it and – although permanently impaired by his injuries – was beginning to enjoy the stories his father told to him and his older sister Tessa. Slowly, Dahl struggled back to taking an interest in his work, and in how his published books were doing.

James and the Giant Peach, which he had completed shortly before Theo was born and had dedicated to Olivia and Tessa, had not yet found a British publisher. In the USA it had been widely reviewed and was a steady, if modest, success. The critics – who tended to assume that their adult readers would be familiar with Dahl's short stories – were particularly enthusiastic about the jaunty poems, part Edward Lear, part Hilaire Belloc, which intersperse the narrative. Some made the point that what adults find repulsive, children may enjoy – the description of the hideous aunts, for example. This wasn't what the more specialist reviewers in librarians' journals and educational papers liked to think. 'The violent exaggeration of language and almost grotesque characterizations impair the storytelling and destroy the illusion of reality and plausibility which any good fantasy must achieve,' wrote Ethel L. Heins, a children's librarian from Boston, in the *Library Journal*. 'Not recommended.'[30] For Dahl, it was an early taste of what was to become an increasingly common type of reaction to his work. But another Bostonian, the reviewer in the *Herald*, compared the book with *Alice in Wonderland* and said it 'should become a classic'.[31]

By October 1962, a year after it first appeared and a month before Olivia's death, *James* had sold 6,500 copies in hardback and earned its author $2,000 in royalties. Meanwhile, an offer came from another publisher, inviting Dahl to take part in a project so enterprising that it was denounced by everyone who wasn't involved. Macmillan New York had begun to approach well-known adult authors of the calibre of Arthur Miller, Sylvia Plath and John Updike, inviting them to write an extremely short book for young children. They would be supplied with a vocabulary list thought suitable for the age range, and would be paid $2,000[32]: not a fortune (today it would be worth about £7,000), but the work didn't look arduous, and Dahl was keen both to get back to writing and to make some money of his own. Many authors had already signed up, and he was sent one of the best of the results, Robert Graves' *The Big Green Book*, for which the productive but as yet relatively little-known Maurice Sendak had done the illustrations.

Graves' story could not have failed to appeal to Dahl. It is about a lonely boy who learns how to be a magician. Turning himself into an old man, he persuades his unpleasant uncle and aunt to gamble all they have against him at cards. When they lose, he makes them his slaves. Dahl had already thought up a new tale of his own, and had been telling it to Tessa and Theo. It was an attack on people who shoot birds for sport. (Dahl had some of his Buckinghamshire neighbours in mind.) A girl with a magic finger decides to thwart a trigger-happy family called the Greggs. First she spoils their aim, then she turns them into birds and has them held up at gunpoint by vengeful ducks.

Alfred Knopf was jealous of Dahl's involvement in the rival publisher's scheme, and did all he could to warn his author off. He said that Macmillan was about to go bankrupt, and sent him an article from the *Horn Book* (a journal for specialists in children's literature), sternly critical of the series' word-lists.[33] Dahl conceded that, taken to its limit, the approach would result in a populace whose vocabulary consisted of less than a thousand words, none of them longer than two syllables.[34] Perhaps to appease Knopf, he said that with the exception of Graves' *Big Green Book*, most of the titles so far published were 'tripe' and that the essential idea for the series was grotesque. But he had to consider his family, and from that perspective, 'I was not entitled to turn it down.' Later, having delivered the book and received his cheque, he dismissed the project as unimportant. He would much prefer to be writing for adults, he told Knopf: 'I am trying, but no luck so far.' In any case, he rightly anticipated that an attack on the gun lobby was not what Macmillan's had had in mind. They paid Dahl his fee, but the typescript of *The Magic Finger* sat in limbo. His willingness to deal with a new publisher, however, had sent a warning to Knopf, and Dahl's editors there were quick to take the hint when he began to ask what was happening about his new draft of *Charlie and the Chocolate Factory*, which it was now six months since he had delivered.

Dedicated to Theo, *Charlie and the Chocolate Factory* concerns a poor family – Charlie Bucket, his parents and all his grandparents – who live in a small wooden shack, eating little except cabbage and potatoes. Near by stands a mysterious chocolate factory owned by Mr Willy Wonka. Mr Wonka is enormously rich, and something of a magician. According to Charlie's grandparents, his myriad inventions include a way of making both chewing gum which never loses its taste and chocolate ice-cream which stays cold without being refrigerated. One day, they tell Charlie, Mr Wonka found that some of his workers had been selling trade secrets to his rivals. So he sacked everyone, and for months the factory was silent. When the story begins, it is back in production. Yet the gates remain locked, and no one is ever seen to enter or leave.

So curiosity, as well as greed, is aroused when Mr Wonka announces a children's lottery, in which the five winners will not only be given a lifetime's supply of sweets, but will be taken on a personally-conducted tour of the factory. After several raisings and dashings of his hopes, the starving Charlie finds one of the winning tickets.

The other successful children are the greedy Augustus Gloop, the spoilt Veruca Salt, the gum-chewing Violet Beauregarde, and Mike Teavee, 'A boy who does nothing but watch television.' In the course of their visit Mr Wonka takes against each of them, and disposes of them ruthlessly before the eyes of their doting parents. Charlie Bucket, on the other hand, who is simply described as 'The hero', wins favour, if more through inoffensiveness than for any positive merit. It transpires that Willy Wonka's real purpose was to

find an heir. He appoints Charlie, and whisks off his family –
several of whom are unenthusiastic about the idea – to join him for
ever in his candied underworld.

Knopf's editor for children's books, Virginie Fowler, had written
enthusiastically to Dahl as soon as she received his revised manuscript. But she had run into difficulties with potential illustrators.
The first one she approached, whom she prefers not to name, was
unhappy with the Oompa-Loompas: in the version first published,
a tribe of 3,000 amiable black pygmies who have been imported by
Mr Willy Wonka from 'the very deepest and darkest part of the
African jungle where no white man had been before'. Mr Wonka
keeps them in the factory, where they have replaced the sacked
white workers. Wonka's little slaves are delighted with their new
circumstances, and particularly with their diet of chocolate. Before,
they lived on green caterpillars, beetles, eucalyptus leaves 'and the
bark of the bong-bong tree'.

Virginie Fowler saw the story as essentially Victorian in character – a 'very English' fantasy – so didn't find these passages objectionable, although she had other reservations.[35] But this was 1962,
and there were what she describes as 'civil rights problems' in the
USA which she thinks may have deterred her potential illustrator.
So she thought she would try someone who had approached her,
who was well established in advertising and keen to move into
book illustration: Joseph Schindelman.

By the time Fowler sent Schindelman's preliminary sketches to
Dahl, he was devastated by Olivia's death and did not reply. Some
months later, having forced himself back to work, and also having
read *The Big Green Book*, he suggested they try Maurice Sendak
instead. Fowler investigated, but found that Sendak would not be
free to take on the job until the autumn of 1964, eighteen months
away, and that he would want a share of royalties rather than a
straight fee. Dahl was prepared to wait, but not to lose part of his
income. The following year, 1963, Sendak's *Where the Wild
Things Are* first appeared, and made his name. His work has much
in common with Dahl's – particularly its roots in northern European tradition and its keen sympathy with the crueller sides of a

child's imagination. Their never-realized partnership is one of the more tantalizing might-have-beens of children's literature.

It would be more than fifteen years before Dahl found, in Quentin Blake, an illustrator who, although very different from Sendak, truly complemented his writing. Always inclined to impatience, he was made even more so by his grief, and complained to Alfred Knopf both about the financial demands of illustrators and about what he described as Fowler's unconscionable delays. Among the firm's nervously prompt and soothing responses was one from Robert Bernstein, then in charge of all juvenile publication for the new Random House-Knopf-Pantheon group. Bernstein said he had just read *Charlie*, 'and so have my sons, who are 6, 10 and 11, and it is a wonderful, wonderful children's book'.[36] This was in the superlative vein which Dahl himself used as a writer, and to which he had been growing accustomed from his US publishers. By profession and instinct, the less expansive Virginie Fowler belonged among the specialists in children's literature: teachers and librarians whose responsible but sometimes over-cautious judgements Dahl came over the years increasingly to despise. She was in her fifties, long-established in juvenile publishing, and believed that good books for children followed certain conventions. For example, they shouldn't be in bad taste, and they shouldn't have half an eye on adults. Although Fowler liked *Charlie*, the book seemed to her to break both rules, and she now tried to explain why.

Dahl had tried the stories on his own children. He both understood and shared their taste for bad taste, and couldn't have cared less about the consequences. He also knew that reading aloud is more fun for adults if the story includes something for them too. In the case of *Charlie and the Chocolate Factory*, part of what they are offered is the ruthless, if temporary, elimination of children themselves. Dahl, like Hilaire Belloc in the *Cautionary Tales*, was frank about the fact that most children are obnoxious, both to adults and to each other, some of the time. He entertains by comically allowing the worst to happen to representatives of the very people for whom he is supposed to be writing.

This built-in double standard is one enjoyable joke. Another, again aimed at the adult reader (and the sophisticated child), is Dahl's pantomime trick of making puns that the young won't necessarily get: the buttergin, for example, which Mr Willy Wonka manufactures alongside butterscotch. And then there is the story's direct way of commenting on how children should and should not be brought up, in its ridicule of spoilt children and their parents and its attacks on television.

Virginie Fowler didn't like this. In May 1963 she sent Dahl a list of editorial comments, in which one of her main criticisms was that the story kept commenting 'on an adult level' rather than staying 'on the child's side where the book should be'. But if it should be on the child's side, Fowler quailed at its raucous humour: for example, the disposal of Veruca Salt down the factory's rubbish chute.[37] 'This whole image of smelling stinking garbage makes for a crude image', she sniffed, 'which can be done perhaps in an adult commentary on the current world and written in another form. But, in a fairy tale based on the eating of sweets, one is a bit revolted and unnecessarily too! . . . fish heads and cabbage and stuff have no place in a chocolate factory.' African pygmies, on the other hand ('Are they really made of chocolate, Mr Wonka?'), didn't strike her as out of place there. She says today that she persuaded Dahl to make some changes in his treatment of the Oompa-Loompas, and that the songs he wrote for them, turning them into a kind of comic Greek chorus, were among the results. But there isn't anything about the Oompa-Loompas in her letter and eventually, as we shall see, they were to cause so much trouble that for later editions, these episodes were rewritten and redrawn.[38]

If some of Fowler's objections now seem both finicky and misdirected, no one at Knopf seems to have noticed how the story could be interpreted as a warning about the firm's future dealings with the author. It would be naïve to say that Mr Willy Wonka 'is' Roald Dahl, but they have a lot in common – for example, in the similarity between Dahl's third-person narrative voice and Mr Wonka's own hectic, exaggerated way of talking:

'There!' cried Mr Wonka, dancing up and down and pointing his gold-topped cane at the great brown river. 'It's all chocolate! Every drop of that river is hot melted chocolate of the finest quality. The very finest quality. There's enough chocolate in there to fill every bathtub in the entire country! And all the swimming pools as well! Isn't it terrific? . . .'

The children and their parents were too flabbergasted to speak. They were staggered. They were dumbfounded. They were bewildered and dazzled. They were completely bowled over by the hugeness of the whole thing. They simply stood and stared.[39]

More revealing, as things were to turn out, was Mr Wonka's way with criticism ('No arguments, *please*'), and his jettisoning of those he takes against. But that is to jump many years ahead.

Mr Willy Wonka knows what is good for people, and forces it on them whether they want it or not. At the end of the story, he takes over Charlie's whole family with the same cheerful, dictatorial confidence as he must have used when enslaving the Oompa-Loompas:

'I'd rather die in my bed!' shouted Grandma Josephine.
    'So would I!' cried Grandma Georgina.
    'I refuse to go!' announced Grandpa George.
    So Mr Wonka and Grandpa Joe and Charlie, taking no notice of their screams, simply pushed the bed into the lift.[40]

This was very like Dahl's own approach to family disagreements – for example, the way he moved his family back to England after Theo's accident. By now, though, Pat was again so busy that they were never long in one place. Dahl himself, as the months accumulated after Olivia's death, found more to occupy him wherever Pat happened to be working. In Honolulu in the summer of 1964, he was approached by the then little-known director Robert Altman, and began work with him on an original screenplay *Oh Death, Where Is Thy Sting-a-ling-a-ling*.[41]

The film was never made, partly because Dahl and his Hollywood agent Irving Lazar quarrelled with Altman over money and the ownership of the story-line.[42] There was the excuse of his family's needs once more, and by the time of the dispute, he had to find cash to care for Pat herself. Yet already he was seeing the first glimpses of his later colossal earnings. Olivia's trust fund, when she died, was sufficient to endow a small charity.[43] The children's trusts benefited again in the summer of 1964, when Dahl was paid $30,000 – in today's terms, about £100,000 – by MGM for the film rights in one of his war stories, 'Beware of the Dog'.[44] 'The Visitor' – the Uncle Oswald story he had related so graphically to David Ogilvy[45] – had sold well, earlier in the year, to *Playboy*, after being rejected by *The New Yorker*. In July, his paperback publisher Dell purchased an extension in the rights to *Someone Like You* and *Kiss Kiss*, which were due to expire. In an unguarded moment, Dahl boasted about some of these successes to Harding Lemay at Knopf. He wrote that he was continually amazed by the way his small store of fiction continued, week by week, to earn money, 'and quite big money, too', especially from continental Europe. There was also a steady market in television adaptations, and his work was always in demand for what he called 'the anthology racket'.

In September 1964 *Charlie and the Chocolate Factory* appeared in the USA, to general acclaim. The allegations of racism did not come until later. Even the sober *Library Journal*, which had dismissed *James and the Giant Peach* as crude and exaggerated, was enthusiastic.[46] Within a month, the first printing of 10,000 copies had sold out. The *New York Times* was sufficiently impressed to ask Dahl for an article on writing for children, and he dashed off a diatribe claiming that 'Five out of seven children's books published today are a cheat' and condemning the indolence of all contemporary publishers with the exception of Alfred Knopf, and all contemporary authors with the exception of himself. His own children's books, he boasted, took 'somewhere between eight and nine months to complete, with no time off for other work . . . a big slice out of the life of any writer, and a big drain on his batteries.' It was a drain too, or so he prematurely lamented, on his bank balance: 'For one who is used to writing for adults only, it is . . . an uneconomic diversion.'

9

Centre Stage

Writers are more prone than most people to worrying about money – especially when they are doing well. Like other artists, many of them are continually afraid that their talent, and with it their earning power, may vanish as inexplicably as it appeared. The tastes of publishers and audiences can seem arbitrary: as much so when they are enthusiastic as when they aren't. Few artists, however successful and confident-seeming, do not harbour a doubt that perhaps a mistake has been made, and that sooner or later they will be rumbled.

Roald Dahl was no stranger to these anxieties, especially given the way his adult stories seemed to have both lost favour and dried up at around the same time. His insecurity was increased by the needs of his young children, especially Theo, and at a deeper level by the facts of Theo's accident and Olivia's death. These were events without meaning, yet crying out for explanation. On the surface, both Roald and Pat responded to them with determined rationalism and practicality. They continued to employ the nanny who was pushing Theo's pram on that terrible day. But both of them also felt obscure, potent forms of guilt. Patricia wondered whether Olivia's death might not have been a punishment for her abortion when she was carrying Gary Cooper's child.[1] She also bitterly remembered times when she or Roald had smacked Olivia for naughtiness. Could these tragedies – Theo's at least – somehow have been averted if their way of life had been different, less ambitious and hectic?

Yet Pat found herself working harder and harder. She tried to ration herself to one film a year, and had a clause written into her *Hud* contract guaranteeing her a month free with her children at Great Missenden in the middle of the shooting schedule.[2] In April 1964, heavily pregnant, she decided not to go to Los Angeles to collect her Oscar for *Hud*, and agreed to Roald's suggestion that Annabella should attend the ceremony on her behalf. But she was poor company when she wasn't in the limelight: desultory, lethargic, bored by the household chores, and inclined, like her husband, to drink too much.

The more work she turned down, the more she was asked to do: which in turn brought yet other pressures into the couple's life, in the form of jealousy on the part of the ever-competitive Roald. Some people who knew them thought that they were showing the strain of a deeper incompatibility.[3] Whatever the truth of that, Olivia's death had brought a new degree of grimness to Roald's already often cynical emotional life. The mood was exacerbated by his poor health: in April 1964 he was diagnosed as suffering from a kidney stone.[4] All in all, it was understandable that there was a haphazard-seeming ferocity in his *New York Times* article – in the claim, for example, that most modern juvenile fiction was so bad that after reading it to a child, all you could do was 'apologize . . . and turn out the light and slink downstairs to wash away the memory with a glass of whisky and water'. An editor asked him to tighten up the argument and to cut some of his more punitive criticisms. He refused, so the piece was moved from the front of the Sunday books section, for which it had been commissioned, to an inside page. Dahl grumbled to Alfred Knopf, who bluntly consoled him that 'In your case the point isn't that they should welch at putting you on the front page but rather that they were stupid enough to expect a piece from you that they could print there.'[5]

Knopf knew that Dahl had a specific reason for his bile against the children's literature establishment. He couldn't find a British publisher either for *James and the Giant Peach* or now for *Charlie and the Chocolate Factory*. The most enthusiastic of Dahl's British editors, Charles Pick, had left Michael Joseph in 1962, and it was then that the firm decided, after a year of hesitation, not to take *James*.⁶ Dahl's British agent Laurence Pollinger offered the book to George Weidenfeld, again unsuccessfully. Since plans were under way for the US publication of *Charlie and the Chocolate Factory*, Dahl and Pollinger now decided to wait until they could offer both books together in Britain. The first new attempt, in the autumn of 1964, was with Hamish Hamilton, but Hamilton told Pollinger that the books seemed to be adult stories in disguise – a repetition of Virginie Fowler's earlier criticism.⁷

This was a blow to the author's morale, and of course also to his finances – one made worse by the fact that children's publishers in continental Europe still looked more to Britain for new books than to the USA. *James* was translated into Dutch in 1963, but so far that was all. Dahl complained bitterly to Alfred Knopf's wife Blanche: 'I refuse to peddle these two books around all the publishers of London.' He had told his agent to give up until he learnt what she and Alfred recommended. English publishers were prim, stupid and snobbish, he added. 'I refuse to go cap in hand, and I refuse to be rejected right and left.'

There was nothing much the Knopfs could do, but from Pollinger's list of the remaining interested British publishers, they suggested Dahl start with Chatto and Windus, and then Cassell, Cape, and Collins, in that order – although, Knopf warned, 'I would not trust one of them to risk a shilling on our unsupported enthusiasm for your work or the work of anyone else.'⁸ Dahl went the rounds again, and was yet again rejected. Among those who turned him down this time was Judy Taylor, children's books editor at The Bodley Head, and a future biographer of Beatrix Potter. She remembers having been put off by the tone of Dahl's agent's letter, which – unusually for a writer still little known in Britain – laid down various conditions, including a retail price per copy so low that she thought it would have been 'totally impractical'.⁹ But Taylor has no regrets about the decision. 'As an editor, one has to like a book oneself,' she says. 'I could see that Dahl would be popular with children, but publishing for them has to involve more than that, somehow.'

If these rebuffs were painful in themselves, they further complicated Dahl's envy of his wife's successes. The more famous she
became, the more he seemed an appendage to her career. In the
summer of 1964 they were in Honolulu, where he passed his time
looking for orchids while Pat shot *In Harm's Way* with John
Wayne. She had recently passed up a possible top role in *The
Pumpkin Eater*, directed by Jack Clayton, with a screenplay by
Harold Pinter based on Penelope Mortimer's novel. This was
reported in the *Daily News*'s 'Hollywood' column while the Dahls
were staying at the Beverly Hills Hotel on their way home to
England: 'Pat's getting choosy about scripts since she won the
Oscar. She turned down one that would have given her more
money than she's ever been offered.'[10] The Oscar trophy for *Hud*,
the *News* told its readers, was sitting on her living-room mantel-
piece in Great Missenden. The piece ended by mentioning paren-
thetically that her husband's latest children's book was out that
month.

Film and theatre offers continued to come in while Neal spent
the rest of the summer at Gipsy House with Tessa, now seven, the
four-year-old Theo and the new baby, Ophelia. Dahl was fractious
about his desire to be writing for adults, but managed to turn out
some semi-pornographic, distinctly misogynistic tales, among them
'The Last Act', which he hoped would prove commercial. In his
leisure time, he pottered about in his musty new orchid house,
which stood on its own a little way from the writing hut. He
admired the flawless elegance of the flowers and the intricacies of
their taxonomy, which gave him another area in which to display
expertise. He only grew phalaenopsids, he would say airily.[11]

He and Pat also caught up with their local friends, particularly
Brigadier Kirwan and his wife Patricia, who farmed near by and
whose son James was the same age as Tessa. The Kirwans had a
tennis court, and Dahl often played singles with James's older sister
Angela, a slightly built, conventionally pretty secretary in her early
twenties.[12] Angela was bored with her job and with life in Great
Missenden. She found Gipsy House a 'lovely, unpompous' place,
and often went round there. She admired the glamorous Pat, but

had the impression that Roald didn't much like women, so was taken aback when Pat teased her that perhaps she was a little in love with him. The Dahls were in need of extra domestic help and offered to take Angela to Los Angeles, where the whole family was soon to move for six weeks for the shooting of John Ford's *Seven Women*.

They went in February 1965, just after Chatto and Windus declined *Charlie*. Ophelia was nine months old, and although she told no one other than Roald, Patricia was once again pregnant.

The flight out was unusually tiring – a storm forced them to land in Labrador, where they waited, dressed for southern California, in a temperature that felt like fifty below. From the moment of their late arrival, Neal was occupied with costume fittings, rehearsals, and the visits of countless old Hollywood friends. Kirwan, doubling as cook, secretary and deputy nanny, was flabbergasted by her employer's reception in Hollywood: how busy and popular she was, and how fascinated everyone seemed by every detail of her life.

For the children too, it was a starry existence: one which, to Tessa, helped to compensate for her feeling that she was always being compared unfavourably with her dead sister. Their Brentwood house, rented from Martin Ritt, director of *Hud* and, most recently, of *The Spy Who Came in from the Cold*, had a kidney-shaped pool. Theo had learned to swim while they were in Honolulu, but he was still prone to falls, and it was necessary to take special care of his head. Dahl busied himself with making the place safe for him, padding a stone pillar and other sharp surfaces.[13]

He also finished a piece of fiction which he asked Angela Kirwan to type. She still remembers it vividly. It was 'a particularly horrid story about a gynaecologist who had been in love with some woman who had gone off and married somebody else. She'd then come back to him, I can't remember why, twenty or thirty years later, widowed, and she was obviously menopausal, and he was absolutely beastly to her and just getting his own back on her, and she was having problems with lovemaking, and it had a horrid –

like all of Roald's stories – but a horrid, twist to it. I remember, as a very innocent 22-year-old, being absolutely shattered.'

Dahl hadn't given her any warning about the contents of 'The Last Act'. 'He liked to shock,' Angela Kirwan says, 'so he probably would have been very happy shocking me.' But almost anyone would have been troubled by the way Anna's 'problems with love-making' are anatomized by the gynaecologist, Conrad, as he reaches the climax of his 'bit of unfinished business' with her.[14] The menopausal Anna, whose husband has recently been killed in an accident, is in the middle of a prolonged breakdown when Conrad part-seduces and then rapes her:

> 'No!' She was struggling desperately to free herself, but he still had her pinned.
>
> 'The reason it hurts,' he went on, 'is that you are not manufacturing any fluid. The mucosa is virtually dry . . . .'
>
> 'Stop!'
>
> 'The actual name is senile atrophic vaginitis. It comes with age, Anna. That's why it's called senile vaginitis. There's not much one can do . . . '

When Anna starts to scream, Conrad pushes her away and walks coolly from her hotel room. The End.

The story was bought by *Playboy*, where over the years Dahl was to publish almost as much as he ever had in *The New Yorker* (which turned it down[15]) and more than in any other magazine. It's hard to catch the tone of the *Playboy* pieces. They have a gothic archness which makes it seem off the point to ask for more convincing dialogue and characterization, or a deeper moral sense. Part of the joke is to write about self-consciously 'adult' matters in the voice of a schoolboy – but, of course, that was often Dahl's own voice too:

> Then all of a sudden, Conrad put his tongue into one of her ears. The effect of this upon her was electric. It was as though a live two-hundred-volt plug had been pushed into an empty socket, and all the lights came on and the bones began to melt and

the hot molten sap went running down into her limbs and she exploded into a frenzy.[16]

Is this high camp? Or is it just well aimed at male readers of limited subtlety? Whatever the tone, Dahl's book-loving friend Dennis Pearl didn't like it, and had an argument with him about what he saw as the waste of his talent.[17] Pearl much preferred the sensitive, imaginatively warmer stories in his friend's first collection *Over To You*, and thought that this was the kind of thing he should have been building on. Dahl told him that what mattered was to give readers what they wanted. Pearl – who was beginning to read Saul Bellow and John Updike – said, 'Being a chap who only connects with literature through reading, I think that's wrong. You should write what you want to write. They'll read it if it's good.' But Dahl made it clear that he had to earn a living, and that the *Playboy* type of story was what sold. Besides, he found it amusing to write that way.

However humorous the intention, these stories – especially those collected as *Switch Bitch* (1974) – depend unmistakably on a repelled, vengeful, invasive attitude to sex. In 'The Visitor', Uncle Oswald finds he may have had it with a leper. In 'Bitch', he is assaulted by a hideous woman to whom he himself has administered a powerful aphrodisiac. In 'The Great Switcheroo', two men engineer a means of going to bed with each other's wives without the women realizing. It took Dahl longer to run out of plots like these than out of the situations of his earlier fiction, but eventually they too dried up. More than twenty years later *Playboy* published under his name a tale about a bookseller who blackmails the families of men whose deaths have recently been announced, by sending them a bill for what he pretends were their recent purchases of pornographic books.[18] He is caught when he chooses a blind man as his victim. The plot is filled out with long passages dwelling on the physical repulsiveness of the blackmailer and his woman accomplice, and jokes at the expense of the English establishment types they prey on. All this is in the manner Dahl often slid into when he wasn't particularly trying – an infantile mix of exaggeration, greed and adjectival vagueness ('a dozen Moroccan servants were laying out a splendid buffet lunch for the guests. There were enormous cold lobsters and large pink hams and very small roast chickens and several kinds of rice and about ten different salads.') But if the style is his own, the plot wasn't.[19] It belonged to a story by James Gould Cozzens, which first appeared under the title 'Foot in It' in 1935, and later as 'Clerical Error', under which title it was included in a popular anthology in the early 1950s. Some readers wrote to *Playboy* drawing attention to the plagiarism, but their letters weren't published.

While the forty-eight-year-old Dahl, wretched over his daughter's death, anxious about his maimed son, envious of his wife's fame, desperate to get back into *The New Yorker*, was busy imagining a middle-aged gynaecologist's revenge-rape of the love of his youth, Patricia Neal went each day to the studio, put on a pair of trousers and pretended to be a medical missionary in China 'who scandalizes her Christian sisters with her worldliness – a morality that later allows her to save them by sacrificing herself to the ravages of a Mongol barbarian'.[21] *Seven Women* had begun filming. No one knew that Neal was pregnant – a worry when she found that her part required her to ride a donkey. But perhaps there was no connection between that and what happened at the end of the fourth day of shooting. She was helping the nanny with the children's baths when she felt a violent pain in her head. As she told Dahl about it, her eyes began to lose focus. Recent tragedies made him act with a decisiveness that was urgent even by his own imperious standards. He instantly telephoned a top Los Angeles neurosurgeon, Charles Carton, whom they had met socially and had informally consulted about Theo.

The call saved Neal's life. By the time her husband put the phone down, she was unconscious and vomiting, but an ambulance was racing to collect her and Carton was on his way to meet them at the hospital. She regained enough consciousness to ask, 'Who is in this house? What are the names of the people in this house, please?'[22] They were the last words she was to say for many weeks.

Neal had suffered two successive aneurysms – a form of stroke in which a congenitally weak place in the wall of an artery in the head is ruptured, allowing blood to jet into the soft brain tissue.[23] A third stroke, the worst, happened while she was being X-rayed. Carton spent the whole night operating, using a saw to make a trap-door into her left temple, removing a clot of haemorrhaged blood from between the brain and its coat, cutting into the left temporal lobe (which controls movement and speech) in order to remove another clot, clipping the aneurysm and spraying on plastic to reinforce the artery wall. Before he began, he didn't know whether his patient would survive. When she did, he wasn't at first sure he had done her a favour.

Tessa, who had seen her brother's accident and had been at home when Olivia was taken to hospital to die, also saw her mother being carried away, and was intensely involved in everything which followed. It was an appalling experience for the volatile child. Her father was continually at the hospital, and according to her own memories, she didn't see him for the next three or four days, or her mother for as many weeks. The gates were crowded with reporters and photographers. Eventually, when she was taken to see Pat, she was quite unprepared to find that her famous, beautiful, husky-voiced mother 'could not talk, could not move her right side, had no hair, had a crooked mouth . . . wore an eye-patch and didn't even know how to say my name.'[24] To Theo, by contrast, these horrors seemed familiar; perhaps even reassuring.

Patricia Neal's friend, the actress Betsy Drake, visited her on the night of the operation and saw her immediately after it. Drake says that Neal 'looked as though she was in a storm at sea'. Dahl quickly assumed the role of ship's captain, jettisoned needless cargo in the form of superfluous flowers and messages sent by well-wishers, and repelled visitors whom he didn't like – including some of his in-laws. Those whom he let in were horrified by what they found. But slowly, Neal came back to consciousness. Through some strange quirk of the brain's organization, the words of poetry and songs are stored separately from other forms of communication, so she could sing. And gestures enabled her to indicate when she felt the most important of her needs: to smoke. But her head was shaved, her face screwed up, her paralysed leg had to be supported by a calliper, and when words began to come back to her, they were usually gibberish. She called a cigarette an 'oblogon'; a martini a 'red hair dryer' or a 'sooty swatch'.[25] She was still pregnant.

In March 1965, a month after she had gone into hospital, Neal was taken home to the Ritts' house. Large numbers of friends managed to get through the vetting process, among them Lillian Hellman, Cary Grant, Margaret Leighton, Donald Pleasence, Hope Preminger and John Ford. Another visitor was Anne Bancroft, who had won a British Film Academy award for the part Neal had turned down in *The Pumpkin Eater*, and now stepped into her role in *Seven Women*.

A star was ill, and Angela Kirwan thought that some of the visitors came just to say they had been there. But others – particularly Betsy Drake, Mildred Dunnock and Marian and Ed Goodman – were persistent and helpful. As the weeks went by, Dahl began to see that such goodwill might be translated into something of lasting practical value. With physiotherapy, Neal was beginning to walk, but as far as her powers of communication were concerned, she needed to retrace much of her development since childhood. Although some simple grammatical structures were returning to her, her vocabulary was cruelly limited and still often jumbled. According to the doctors, the early months would be all-important. Dahl's approach was first to announce that his wife would make a one hundred per cent recovery, and then to set about goading her into it. Those who already disliked him saw his behaviour as of a piece with his usual domineering. One describes it as somewhere between that of a dog trainer and a traffic cop.[26] It was his custom, another says, to humiliate people in front of others: that is how he treated Pat.[27] But some, closer to him, were more sympathetic about the strain he was under, and remember how his mood could swing from rigid control to open vulnerability.[28] This was southern California in the mid-1960s. If authoritarianism had not disappeared, it was certainly out of style. When, within two months of her stroke, Neal was pushed by Dahl to go out to dinner and to struggle with the same food as everyone else, many of her friends were scandalized. Undeterred, he began to make plans for a press conference before their return to England in May. He coached his wife in her lines: 'I feel fine. The baby will be fine. I'll be back to work in one year.' But for all her public optimism, Pat mostly felt exhausted, frustrated and miserable.

There were two new members of the returning household. Dahl had persuaded a nurse from the UCLA Medical Center to come back to England with them, bringing a friend to help her. The Marshes' foundation paid everyone's fares. At Heathrow, all the Dahl sisters were there to meet them, and Roald promptly resumed charge of the tribe. 'I called in no doctors', he later wrote; it was a matter that had to be sorted out by the family alone.[29] Pat's speech was not all that was affected. She could not read or write, or do even the simplest sums. She was listless, and prone to bouts of deep depression. 'Unless I was prepared to have a bad-tempered, desperately unhappy nitwit in the house,' her husband recalled, 'some very drastic action would have to be taken at once.' The National Health Service speech therapist could offer no more than two half-hour sessions per week. Dahl persuaded his sisters and various local friends – the Kirwans and a dozen others – to take part in a roster. Pat was to have six hour-long lessons a day, each with a different volunteer. Members of the team also took turns with the children, the cooking and the housework.

When some of the helpers saw Neal for the first time after her return, they went home and cried. Later, working with her regularly, they soon realized that she was not only crippled but in mourning. She was an actress who had lost her speech and her memory: whatever her husband said, she knew that her career could never fully recover. Lame, her face fallen and either inexpressive or wildly melodramatic, she had also lost the best of her looks. This was dejecting for the wife in her, as well as the actress. As for the mother, in a sense she had lost her children too. There were two usurpers. Tessa, if only in her eight-year-old's imagination, took on the roles of hostess and of conversational companion to her father. More obvious to Pat herself was the fact that while the man she called 'Papa' (after Hemingway) did not himself take part in her lessons, he was both their co-ordinator and, even more fully than before, the organizer of the entire ménage. He gave up the New York flat which they had been keeping on, and had an extension built on to Gipsy House for their new staff. He discussed meals with the cook, vaccinations with the nurse, drove the children to school, and arranged for them to see their friends, cousins and aunts. 'Everything was changed,' Pat says now. 'It was sad because our marriage, it had been good, it really was good. I did the cooking, I did the children, keeping the house, the garden, the weeds – and then when I got ill, everything changed in the end. He was the only person who really could control the children, and it was "Daddy! Daddy!". You know, they looked up at him and it was just so irritating to me. Everything was turned upside down. We'd been through so much, and [before,] we did it equally, really.'

Not everyone remembers the pre-stroke Neal as having been quite that much of a housewife, or the marriage as having been such an ideal of mutuality, but it was easy to see why she was irritated and depressed by Dahl's absolute dominance, both over the family – including, it often seemed, the families of his sisters – and over the volunteers, whom some visitors called 'the handmaidens'. For that reason, but also because her well-advanced pregnancy left her even more lethargic, she looked for subterfuges so as to avoid the tougher parts of the new régime, deflecting her teachers into games of dominoes or into making cups of coffee. The weather was damp and cold. She would sit indoors for hours, smoking or eating sweets, bored, isolated and in despair. Quite often, she would tell people that she had lost her mind. She couldn't even make sense of *Pigling Bland* when she tried to read it to Theo. It seemed that her new baby would never be born. And when it was, what kind of a state might it be in?

Dahl, meanwhile, continued to insist that she was on her way to a full recovery. The doctors were sceptical, but less so than they had been, and it was clear to them that his methods, along with

Neal's own strength, were responsible for much of the improvement she had already made. One of those methods was publicity.

That summer, he agreed to a proposal from *Life* magazine that a journalist should come to Great Missenden and follow the last stages of Neal's pregnancy. Barry Farrell was a sensitive writer whose own marriage had been destroyed when his child died.[30] He sympathized intensely with Dahl, and often sat up with him late into the night, drinking his good wine and 'enjoying his large small talk'.[31] Dahl, he wrote, 'is the best storyteller I know, and listening to him often worked a kind of spell on me.' Under this spell, he seems to have written down whatever Dahl told him and put it into his *Life* article and later into a book, the financial proceeds of which were shared between them.[32] The book was titled *Pat and Roald*, but Roald, or his version of himself, was so much at the centre that Pat complained that she scarcely seemed to be in it. Certainly, *Pat and Roald* – both in itself and because it became a main source for other journalists – helped to fix the myth of Roald Dahl in the public mind. Here, readers could learn again how his Gladiator had been brought down in flames by 'a burst of machine-gun fire ... while strafing a convoy of trucks south of Fuka, a village not far from Alexandria'.[33] Farrell also reported Dahl's 'invention' of the gremlins: the very word gremlin, he gasped, 'was Roald's contribution to the dictionary, a word he had coined to name a race of aerial saboteurs during the war'. Every one of his short stories 'appeared in *The New Yorker* as soon as they were submitted'.

This last idea must have been a particularly consoling fantasy to Dahl. His most recent rejection letter from *The New Yorker* (about 'The Last Act') had arrived only three months before Farrell. And at around the same time, his latest book for children – the ill-fated anti-shooting story *The Magic Finger*, which Macmillan had commissioned and then refused – had been turned down by his own editor at Knopf, Virginie Fowler.[34] Fowler preferred Dahl, she says, as a writer of 'wonderful fantasies': the new book was satirical or, as she puts it, 'rather sticky, and much more adult in feeling.'[35] Dahl himself, who had other things on his mind, had been untypically self-deprecating about it, so she let it go without further consultation. Harper and Row then gratefully stepped in and bought the rights for $5,000.

Alfred Knopf didn't seem troubled when he first heard what was going on, but Dahl soon changed that. Abject letters were rushed off to the incensed author, and icy memos to the unfortunate editor. 'While I respect greatly the high editorial standards you maintain,' Knopf told Fowler, 'I think there are cases where the basic interests of the house override, and must override, your opinion of a given manuscript, and that sometimes if an author wants to publish a given story sound policy requires that we publish it regardless of our opinion of it . . . Am I not correct in saying that your decision in this case was never discussed with me, Mr Cerf, Mr Klopfer, or Mr Bernstein?'[36]

Meanwhile, Robert Bernstein quickly set about repairing the damage. He sent Dahl word that the Book-of-the-Month Club had bought *Charlie and the Chocolate Factory* for its Christmas 1965 mailing, and that he anticipated over 5,000 sales. He knew that although Dahl was very busy with his family, he felt he was in need of money. Would he like to edit a book of 'Knock, Knock' jokes? 'I should tell you', Bernstein added, 'that I have still not recovered from the shock of hearing that Harper's was going to publish one of your books. My feeling about you is that you are a wonderful writer and anything that you wish to put your name on we should publish.'[37]

It would be five years and several more quarrels before Dahl had anything to offer them. For the moment, he was preoccupied with three overriding aims. He wanted the new baby to be safely born. He wanted to get his wife not only better, but back at work. And he wanted to become so rich that they would never have to think about money again.

The first proved no problem. With Barry Farrell and his notebook in the back of the car, the couple drove regularly to Oxford to see

Neal's obstetrician. On one of these journeys Pat asked, 'What are you going to name the baby, Papa?' 'Dwight', Dahl answered, confident of a laugh from the back seat.[38] In fact the child, born in perfect health on 4 August, was a girl, and they called her Lucy Neal. The press agencies had the news before Lucy's grandparents. *Life* magazine's photographers were in the delivery room within minutes of her arrival. The pictures show Neal battered but triumphant, her hair still not fully grown back from her operation. Dahl, looking vaguely North African in his surgical gown and hat, gazes enquiringly into the crib.[39]

The birth gave Neal a brief surge of confidence, but she soon relapsed into an ever-deeper depression. Dahl pressed on towards his second objective. In place of the roster of handmaidens, he persuaded someone new to work with her single-handedly in her own home. Valerie Eaton Griffith had herself recently been ill with a thyroid complaint. A spinster friend of Angela Kirwan's parents, she had given up her job with Elizabeth Arden and was living with her father, a mile from Gipsy House. Roald drove Pat over every morning, after he had seen the children off to school, and left her there for most of the day. The two women got on well, and Valerie grew both very fond of Pat and increasingly absorbed in her difficulties and the best approach to their cure.

Dahl, in the meantime, went back to his shed in the garden and set about getting rich.

10

Credits

It was from what had until then been Patricia Neal's world that Dahl was to earn most of the family income in the late 1960s and early 1970s.

There was a lot of sympathy for Neal in Hollywood, and within months of her strokes her husband was offered a chance to write his first big screenplay: *You Only Live Twice*. According to Neal, the James Bond movie paid him more than she had ever earned.[1] But it was with a great show of reluctance that he agreed to do it, telling his publisher that he found the idea 'exceptionally distasteful'.[2] The harder he found it to write prose fiction, the more protective he was of his literary self-image. He told Barry Farrell what he also kept promising Alfred Knopf, that his 'only real ambition' was to turn out a new, 'really solid' collection of short stories.[3]

Of course, he had stooped to films before. His work with Walt Disney on *The Gremlins* had helped to launch his career and, since then, he had contributed to the film of *Moby Dick*, had sold his story 'Beware of the Dog' to MGM for its successful war-thriller *Thirty-Six Hours*, and had written the script for the abortive Robert Altman project *Oh Death, Where Is Thy Sting-a-ling-a-ling*. There were also plans for a film of *Charlie and the Chocolate Factory*, and despite the book's attacks on watching television, a television series based on it was mooted too.[4] Several of Dahl's adult stories had already been successfully adapted for the medium.

For all his grouses, Dahl showed every sign of enjoying the Bond project. Ian Fleming had died two years earlier. Dahl had met him often in Jamaica and in New York, through their mutual friend Ivar Bryce,[5] and had hero-worshipped him. They had much in common: sporting prowess, not having been to university, the secret service, attractiveness to women, interests in gambling and collecting, and a robust, if juvenile, fantasy life. Fleming was the more cosmopolitan, a top-drawer version of many of the younger man's qualities and enthusiasms – so much so that Dahl told Fleming's biographer John Pearson that for him, 'There was a great red glow when Ian came into the room.'

Glow or not, and despite Dahl's much-bruited contempt for Hollywood's cavalier treatment of writers, he made no objection when United Artists abandoned any pretence of following Fleming's original novel. *You Only Live Twice*, published in the year the author died, is far from being his strongest book. Essentially, it is a long sequence of touristic episodes set in Japan, with asides on oriental customs, international politics and (in the encyclopaedia-entry manner which Dahl's own stories often imitated) poisonous plants. The horticultural strand forms part of a more than usually far-fetched intrigue by Fleming's power-maniac, Ernest Stavro, to wipe out the Japanese warrior class.

The film rights belonged, like those in most of the Bond books, to a Canadian–US partnership, Eon, based in London and owned by Harry Saltzman and Albert ('Cubby') Broccoli. Eon had already made four hugely successful James Bond films for United Artists, starting with *Dr No*. So far, each of them had been dramatized by Richard Maibaum. It was Maibaum who established the formula of toning down the novels' sex and violence and playing up their humour and fantasticality,[6] but the screen-writing process had always been complicated. The first script of *Dr No*, for example, was written jointly by Maibaum and Wolf Mankowitz, but subsequently reworked by two others. On the following three Bond films, three writers other than Maibaum earned credits, not to speak of those who were paid for their work but not finally named on screen. Partly to satisfy union rules, the writers chosen for these British-based projects had been, like Wolf Mankowitz, British: Johanna Harwood, Paul Dehn and John Hopkins.

You Only Live Twice involved new problems, both because of the weaknesses of the original book, and because the project faced intense competition from other Bond-type comedy thrillers, several of which had appeared in 1965 and 1966 – among them *Our Man Flint*, starring James Coburn as the agent-stud, and Columbia's *The Silencers* with Dean Martin. Meanwhile, Columbia also hired Wolf Mankowitz to write the screenplay for an Ian Fleming novel which Saltzman and Broccoli did not own: *Casino Royale*. This film had already gone into production, with John Huston as director and a starry cast including David Niven, Ursula Andress, Orson Welles, Peter O'Toole, and Woody Allen as a walking atom bomb.

Broccoli responded by pouring money into the new Eon project (a million dollars were budgeted for the set alone) and hiring a team made up equally of the most dependable of the previous Bond specialists and of some famous new blood. John Stears, who had won an Oscar for the special effects on Eon's previous Bond production *Thunderball*, came into the first category, as did the designer, Ken Adam, and the composer, John Barry. Lewis Gilbert was persuaded, at first reluctantly, to direct. He had had a big success recently with *Alfie*, the film version of Bill Naughton's play about a cockney Don Juan, played by Michael Caine. Gilbert's box-office successes also included *Reach for the Sky* (about Dahl's old Shell colleague, the war hero Douglas Bader). For *You Only Live Twice* he brought in Freddie Young as cameraman; Young had just won an Academy Award for *Dr Zhivago*.

In the spring of 1966 some of the team, including Broccoli, Gilbert, Adam and Young, made a preliminary reconnaissance trip to Japan. They took along a well-established Hollywood scriptwriter called Harold Jack Bloom.

They were looking for ideas, and among other things they hoped to find a coastal fortress like Blofeld's headquarters in Fleming's novel. There wasn't one, but they were intrigued to see a large number of volcanic craters in a national park on the island of Kyushu, and decided to use one of these instead as the film's main setting. It gave them a basis for a new narrative – Blofeld's plot to start a war between the USA and Russia, each side assuming that the other was responsible when their rockets were hijacked in space. The story used current developments in the space race, including the first operations by astronauts walking outside their craft. And it would also eventually feature both a car chase in which the pursuing automobile is picked up by a huge magnet and dropped into the sea, and a helicopter battle, in the shooting of which one of the cameramen lost his leg.

Dahl later claimed credit for every detail of the new plot, and described the film – much of it shot at the Pinewood Studios, near his home – as his one experience of real harmony between producer, director and scriptwriter.[7] This is also roughly the version given by Steven Jay Rubin in his history of the Bond films,[8] although he says that the main new idea – the fortress within a volcano – was Broccoli's, and that the helicopter chase was suggested by the invention of a miniature autogiro by another member of the film's multitudinous crew, Ken Wallis. The director, Lewis Gilbert, is uncertain at what stage in the project he started working with Dahl rather than Harold Jack Bloom, although he knows that it was Bloom, and not Dahl, who went with them on the first trip to Japan. But soon Gilbert and Dahl were meeting almost every day, either at Broccoli's Mayfair office or at his home near by, deciding on the details of each scene.[9] They got on well together. Gilbert thought Dahl 'a brilliant guy', and was surprised that he wasn't hired for any of the later Bond films. He can't remember what it was that Bloom contributed to earn him his eventual credit for 'additional story material'. The official Bond histories don't mention Bloom at all.

It is a reticence Bloom does not himself share. According to him, he 'made up everything you saw on the screen'.[10] The credit was originally to have read 'Screen story by Harold Jack Bloom', but he was later told that if this form of words were used, Ian Fleming's name would suffer unduly – even though, until Bloom started work, 'There was no story at all. The Fleming book was discarded completely.' Bloom says that Dahl changed none of the action in the screenplay. 'We should have been given joint credit at the very least. Had the picture been done here [in Hollywood], I would have been properly credited, but [the British] weren't crazy about using American writers. I was very disappointed.'

When *You Only Live Twice* appeared in June 1967, most reviewers accepted the simple version of events, that the script was exclusively Dahl's. Only the studio-wise *Variety Weekly* mentioned Bloom's name.[11] Most of the more favourable attention, in any case, was concentrated on Ken Adam's set and the special effects. As far as Dahl's dialogue was concerned, the trade papers were polite, but sharper critics such as those in *Newsweek* and *The New Yorker* found the sexual *double entendres* ('It will be a pleasure serving under you') unusually laboured – a cruder version of the comic style of the earlier Bond scripts. As Pauline Kael wrote, 'The gaggy screenplay for this installment coarsens the style. The earlier films had something genuinely blithe about them . . . but in "You Only Live Twice" the sense of play keeps getting lost.'[12]

Whatever the critics thought, the film was an enormous popular success. Dahl always claimed that this was all that mattered, and that his contribution had been crucial. In a film, after all, the guy who gets the credit is the guy who gets the credit, and in his own mind Dahl's importance had been confirmed, while he was at work on the script, by the regular arrival of a chauffeur-driven Rolls-Royce at Gipsy House to pick him up – or sometimes just to pick up the latest pages of dialogue.[13] It was the kind of attention he always craved, and it took his mind off recent events. Collecting Tessa, Theo and their friends Amanda Conquy and Camilla Unwin from school, he would regale them with the adventures James Bond had had that day.

In the autumn of 1967 Dahl sent the ten-year-old Tessa away to her aunts' old boarding school, the grand, expensive and conservative Roedean. He thought that Theo too would soon be self-reliant enough to go as a weekly boarder to a nearby prep school, Caldecote, although Pat wasn't so sure. In the end, neither of these attempts was a success. Tessa was moved after a couple of years to the more liberal Downe House. Theo had a private tutor for a time, before being sent with a local friend to a school in Switzerland for children with special educational needs. Ophelia and the baby Lucy, meanwhile, were still at home with their nanny.

Pat's powers of communication were improving steadily, but she was still lame and bitterly depressed, and Roald was sure that the only remedy was to get her back to acting. As early as January 1966 he had put out another press release saying, once again, that she would be at work within twelve months. That April they appeared on a US television programme, the *Merv Griffin Show*. In the first half of the twelve-minute interview, shot at Great Missenden, Griffin interviewed Neal alone about her illness. He asked whether her doctors thought she would be able to return to acting. Her voice drawling but clear, she said frankly that she hadn't discussed the idea with them. Griffin then turned to Dahl's children's books, and the author came in on cue. He said that although no one in his wife's situation had ever recovered more than she already had, he was confident that she would achieve complete normality. According to one viewer at the time, he seemed 'determined that she will get well, and she is determined that if he feels that way, she will.'[14]

How far Dahl believed his own myth is hard to know. He had given much thought to the best psychological approach to take with Pat, and knew that she would find it all too easy to give up. Sheer determination was involved, on his part as well as hers. When friends tried to help her out of cars or up flights of steps, Roald told them that she must do it for herself. At such moments, even he sometimes wavered, according to Dennis Pearl. Yet domineering came more easily to him than it might have to someone else. In the same way, his optimism was both deliberate and an unavoidable part of his larger-than-life, fantasizing mentality. There was a similar ambiguity, as the months and years passed, in the way he encouraged her to act independently of him; or, as some saw it, got her out of the way. In March 1967 he arranged for her and Valerie Eaton Griffith to go to the USA without him, to speak at a dinner in aid of the New York Association for Brain-Injured Children – a frightening challenge, and one which both women tried to resist. Soon afterwards, he accepted a sizeable role for Pat in the film of Frank D. Gilroy's play *The Subject Was Roses*, about the difficulties of communication between a returned war veteran and his parents. It was shot in New York at the beginning of 1968, less than three years after her stroke.

When Neal asked him if he would accompany her on the first US trip, he refused, saying 'You're on your own now.'[15] It was a larger-scale version of his agreeing to Valerie Eaton Griffith's suggestion that they move Pat's lessons out of Gipsy House into Griffith's place in Grimms Hill. As he said at the time, now he would be able to listen to some Beethoven, before going off to his hut to write.[16] But perhaps he already sensed that as time went by, he would need to put still more distance between himself and his wife. He was determined to do his best by her, but could not disguise from himself how frustrating he found her lethargy, her moodiness, her lack of interest in the things he cared about. It was not until many years later that he could bring himself to talk about these feelings to others, and even then, he wouldn't admit that he might have made some mistakes. He told Valerie Eaton Griffith, 'I'm frightfully good at blocking off one side . . . I get efficient and busy and am more interested in the work side of things. It's very important to keep busy.' Griffith bravely suggested that it was also important not to be *too* busy, but he brushed the implied criticism aside.

In Griffith's subsequent experience with her now nation-wide Volunteer Stroke Scheme, few marriages survive a stroke where the ill partner's communication is seriously affected, unless the couple are well into middle age or older. 'Stroke kills marriages', she says bluntly – among other reasons because, in a literal-seeming sense, the affected partner may no longer be the same person as before. Sexually, despite some early difficulties, Roald and Pat were gradually able to resume relations, but he still often boasted about his attractiveness to women, not least in front of his wife.[17] The attraction went along with, seemed partly to derive from, his arrogance: the easy assertiveness with which he would commandeer girls to go with him as tasters and bag-carriers on expeditions to shop for food or to pick mushrooms. It may only be the subsequent change in manners that makes some remember this approach not only as

seductive, but as strangely humiliating.[18] But among those humili-
ated was, of course, Neal herself. When, while she was pregnant
with Lucy, he had joked with her that he might 'nip into London
and find myself a girl', she gamely answered that he should beware
of a heart attack. But she didn't forget what he said.[19] Her anxieties
on this score made her both give and demand shows of affection, in
a way which irritated, and began to repel, her less demonstrative
husband. 'I love her,' he wrote to a close friend, 'I'll never leave her.
But I have to live with her all the time, and you would go round the
bend within a couple of hours.'

In Dahl's case, going round the bend took the form of a slipped
disc. Ever since his plane crash he had been prone to back troubles
of one kind or another, but in the summer and autumn of 1967
they became acute, and in November he underwent a spinal operation which was a failure and had to be repeated.[20] While he was in
hospital in Oxford – excruciating pains in his neck and lower back
compounded by infected surgical staples and a fissure in his colon –
his eighty-two-year-old mother telephoned him to ask how he was,
and to send her love. She didn't mention that she herself was very
ill. Before he came home, she died. The date was 17 November: the
fifth anniversary of Olivia's death.

With all that had happened since Theo's accident seven years
previously, it was hard for the sick Dahl to feel this new loss. But he
needed the company of strong women. Sofie had long been crippled and housebound, and her son had automatically taken her
place at the head of the family.

There was rarely a day when Else didn't drop in at Gipsy House
for a few drinks, with or without her twin daughters and their
elder brother Nicholas. (Roald introduced Nicholas to an enthusiasm for contemporary art which was to become his career.[21]) Asta
appeared less frequently. She and her strong-willed Scottish husband Alex still lived near by with their three children, but Roald
had never quite forgiven Alex for being a vet, or perhaps just for
not admiring him enough. Alfhild, on the other hand, was a very
frequent visitor, partly to escape from her eccentric husband. One

day she reported that she and their daughter had returned home from a shopping trip to find a gun on the table, with a message from him saying, 'When you get in, please shoot yourselves.'

Roald and Alf always telephoned each other when there was gossip to relate. Tessa remembers that, while all of the family 'loved to discuss drama, they didn't like to discuss the effect on people's emotions.' Still, Roald absorbed himself in all domestic issues, whether they concerned his sisters or the running of Gipsy House. Friends noticed that while he had been away in hospital, Pat had seemed not only more active around the house, but much more cheerful.[22]

School fees and domestic wages remained dominant concerns. After *You Only Live Twice*, Dahl spent some time on a screenplay for Aldous Huxley's *Brave New World*, but couldn't find a way into the story.[23] Cubby Broccoli came to the rescue by signing him up to adapt a children's story, again by Ian Fleming: *Chitty Chitty Bang Bang*. The film's director was to be Ken Hughes.

This time, the original book provided much of the first part of the eventual film. In Fleming's story, on the face of it well suited to Dahl, an eccentric inventor makes some money with a new kind of confectionery, buys and restores a vintage car which turns out to have magical powers, and takes his mother and children in it to France, where they are involved in various adventures. This wasn't enough for Broccoli, who had been enviously eyeing Walt Disney's recent success with the extravaganza *Mary Poppins*. He talked over other possibilities with his director. Ken Hughes was accustomed to writing his own films, which had ranged from an updated, gangster version of *Macbeth* to *The Trials of Oscar Wilde* (known in the USA as *The Man with the Green Carnation*) starring Peter Finch. According to Hughes's own account, he went away and worked out what was to be the eventual story-line of *Chitty Chitty Bang Bang*, which he then passed to Dahl.[24]

Dahl was suffering the first stages of his new back problems. He may also have taken umbrage at seeing the plot of *Chitty Chitty Bang Bang* rewritten before he had even begun work on it. For whatever reason, he didn't communicate with Hughes. After about four weeks, according to the voluble cockney director:

> Broccoli starts to say 'What's going on?'. I said, 'He's the writer, leave him alone', but Cubby got increasingly nervous.
>
> Roald is in his country cottage. Five weeks to the start of shooting, the producer says 'I've got to have some pages' – terrible thing to say to a writer. So finally Roald sent some pages around. He'd hardly got through a third of the script. Cubby read it and went white. I said, 'What do you think?' He said, 'I think it's a piece of shit.' 'Ken,' he says, 'write the fucking script.' So I hit the typewriter and I was still writing the day before we went on the floor. Every fucking word in that bloody script I wrote on my portable typewriter I bought in Maida Vale.

When a *New York Times* reporter visited the Pinewood Studios set in October 1967, the stricken Dahl was nowhere in evidence. Hughes made sure that his absence was noticed. 'You 'aven't seen him around 'ere, 'ave you?', the paper quoted him as asking rhetorically. 'No. I had to rewrite the whole bleedin' scenario.'[25]

In a memorable and just review, Pauline Kael was to describe *Chitty Chitty Bang Bang* as 'almost sadistically ill-planned'.[26] It is hard to see why anyone should want to take credit for it, and Dahl himself was relieved to dissociate himself from the whole unhappy episode.[27] (He never spoke to Ken Hughes again.) Almost all the reviews were bad, and several mentioned the fact that the film had been, as the *Hollywood Reporter* put it, 'patched and retreaded throughout a long shooting schedule'.[28] There was no secret about the troubles with the script, of which a final final rewrite had been undertaken by the James Bond veteran Richard Maibaum.[29] But once again, while the result didn't please the critics, it was a box-office hit, and this time Dahl was on a percentage – or a percentage of a percentage.

He built a swimming pool at Gipsy House and inundated the children with presents. In other ways, too, he spoilt them as much as the absent-minded genius Potts in the movie – who, when his children don't want to go to school, tells them, 'Oh well, it'll give the others a chance to catch up, won't it?' Valerie Eaton Griffith says, 'If they were not happy at school, or if they did not want to do their homework, Roald would always say "Don't bother." ' But as usual he was divided in his behaviour, and in a way which, whether or not they were aware of it at the time, left them permanently confused. When they wanted pocket-money, he would often hand over twice as much as had been asked for, but only after a homily about the importance of thrift.

Such indulgences must have been partly intended to make up to the children for the losses and disasters they had been through – and perhaps also for their father's own occasional moments of harshness. There was a similarly all-too-comprehensible duality in his behaviour towards Patricia Neal. For example, there were the bridge games in which he would encourage her to take part. With a certain amount of tolerance on the part of the other players, and with someone to look over her shoulder, she enjoyed playing cards. But sometimes her husband would humiliate her. Barry Farrell remembered his telling her sharply, one Easter at the Bryces at Moyns Park: 'You must answer your partner with a bid if you've got some points in your hand. You do know how to count points, do you not?'[30] However hard Dahl tried, he was too competitive to lower his game for her. 'He always wanted a slam', Valerie Eaton Griffith says. 'Roald liked the top contract.'

The contracts he procured for Pat in the film business were even harder challenges, and more public ones. Again, they certainly helped her towards a fuller recovery, but Dahl never doubted that the only definition of that process was for her to return to exactly what she had been doing before. Yet, however successfully she could be coached into impersonating the old Patricia Neal, it was obvious that there were some things she would never be able to do again. She was still slightly lame, but more problematically, she found it very hard to remember lines, and sometimes just to utter them. During the three months' shooting of *The Subject Was Roses* in New York, Valerie Eaton Griffith worked as a prompter by day and a governess by night. At the hotel, she discouraged Neal from going out to parties, and took her through her words over and over, night and morning. On the set, she held up 'idiot boards' with Neal's lines written on them for her, or crouched behind sofas and whispered them to her.

A process which might have seemed humiliating to an onlooker turned out to be a triumph. The performances of Neal and her co-star Jack Albertson were generally acclaimed, and each was nominated for (and he won) an Academy Award. (Albertson subsequently played Grandpa Joe in the film version of *Charlie and the Chocolate Factory*.) Yet it wasn't long ago that she had been unable either to walk or to talk. During the shooting, she loved being back in Manhattan among her old friends, who made a big fuss of her. And she told everyone how grateful she was to her husband for forcing her back to work.[31] One weekend, he came over to see her, and she was so keyed up that she couldn't concentrate on filming.[32]

Still, his regime continued to make outsiders uneasy. It was partly a matter of the publicity he, as well as she, was extracting from it all: magazine interviews, profiles on television and radio, each one naturally mentioning his work as well as hers. And now he was turning the situation into one of his stories. Literally so. He had bought the film rights in a new novel, *Nest in a Falling Tree*, a romantic melodrama by Joy Cowley which he planned to adapt as a vehicle for Neal to star in. If MGM agreed to put up the money, the Dahls would work on a deferred-payment basis, only taking their fees when and if the movie went into profit.[33]

In various ways, Dahl based the screenplay on Neal's actual predicament. She plays Maura, a middle-aged woman recovering from a cerebral aneurysm, who works part-time in a Buckinghamshire hospital helping children with impaired speech. (In one sequence, she is shown reading *Charlie and the Chocolate Factory*.) The doctors would like Maura to do more of this work, but – here the film roughly follows the book – she is tied to a crippled mother, a blind old harridan with whom she lives in a run-down gothic mansion. Their existence revolves around the village and the church, a world of gossipy women and, in Dahl's grotesquely off-key version, salacious old men in mackintoshes. Dahl has the villagers obsessed with the vicar's impending operation, maliciously rumoured to be a sex change. The trouble with hospitals, says one leering character, is that 'One invariably comes away with something or other missing.' 'They're just going to snip it off,' the vicar's wife innocently replies. 'It's got a lot bigger lately, and that scares me.'

With an abrupt but temporary shift back to Joy Cowley's novel, a brutishly handsome boy called Billy arrives on a motorbike, having heard that the two women need an odd-job man. Although his story about himself is unconvincing, Maura's mother hires him, and makes Maura give him her own bedroom. Maura inevitably falls in love with him, but the development of the relationship is undermined by the film's slow revealing, and her eventual discovery, of another of Dahl's additions to the plot: that Billy is a serial sex killer. From here on, the film leaves behind both the book and the *Carry On* antics that have been superimposed on it, turning into a thriller-cum-sentimental-melodrama. We see Billy rape and kill both a local schoolteacher and Maura's mother's nurse. Will Maura herself be next? Unexpectedly, her kindness moves him to remorse, and he tells her his secret. They run away together, abandoning Maura's screaming mother in a hospital ward. The couple are seen walking on beaches at sunset and admiring young lambs, Neal in a variety of optimistic shetland jerseys and tam o'shanters. But temptation returns to Billy, and in order to escape it, he throws himself off a cliff.

Films equally bad have been commercially successful, but this one flopped. The *Hollywood Reporter* called it 'a lethargic although artfully photographed mess'.[34] *Variety* criticized its clichés and inconsistencies of motivation.[35] Everyone made unfavourable comparisons with the recently revamped *Night Must Fall*. MGM let the film run for a while in New York, but it was never released in Britain, and neither Dahl, Neal nor the director, Alastair Reid, ever saw any money from it. Even as an exercise for Patricia Neal, it couldn't have been called a success. In the film's all-English context, her accent isn't convincing, and there were embarrassing rows over passages in Dahl's script which Reid and his editor cut on the grounds that she was having difficulty speaking them. Dahl used his power with MGM to force Reid to reinstate a few lines, but when *The Night Digger* was released, he once again publicly dissociated himself from it.

With hindsight, the film's failure was predictable, and arguably resulted from nothing worse than misjudgement of various kinds on Dahl's part. His experience of screenplays was more limited than might at first have appeared to his partners, because much of the previous work of this sort attributed to him had either been started or rescued by more seasoned scriptwriters. He had meant well, but had taken on more than he proved able to manage.

Perhaps this is all that lies behind the slight edginess that comes into the manner of some of the people involved when you mention *The Night Digger*. Yet there is something more than uncomfortable about the ways in which Dahl had altered the story for his wife. However well she had recovered, what did he suppose she would feel about the new scene in which the crippled mother is casually abandoned? Or about the fact that such tension as the plot possesses comes from the possibility that the character she plays will be both raped and murdered by her lover? Reid found Dahl's behaviour exceedingly distasteful. 'He was a bully, a big, overpoweringly enormous guy. He would make [Pat] repeat things in front of people, and treat her like a child. It must have been completely humiliating for her. And he used to talk about her, not exactly behind her back, but as if she wasn't there.' Reid concedes what those closer to Dahl emphasize more strongly, that he may have acted like this in order to 'provoke a spark', but says it seemed as though he liked doing it.[36]

Dahl's work on *The Night Digger* more or less coincided with a bust-up between him and another film director, Mel Stuart, who was making the film version of *Charlie and the Chocolate Factory*. Dahl had contracted to write his own adaptation, and for a time the two projects overlapped. He was in Hollywood without Pat, finishing his screenplay for the children's movie and raising money for *The Night Digger*. Alastair Reid was there too, busy with a different film, and they shared a bungalow at the Beverly Hills

Hotel. Although Dahl was always rude about Hollywood people, Reid noticed that he seemed to enjoy their company well enough. He knew everybody and everybody knew him – less as a scriptwriter perhaps than as Patricia Neal's husband, but now also as a famous children's author. Reid says that kids followed Dahl around in the street like the Pied Piper. He also had in tow a glamorous girl-friend who was staying at the same hotel – the daughter, it was said, of a Chicago gangster.

Dahl and Reid drank and gossiped together, and Reid, then in his early thirties, still remembers the older man's wartime anecdotes: how he had been shot in the back by bullets from his own crashed aeroplane; how Winston Churchill had asked him personally to spy on Roosevelt, who was a deep admirer of his writing; and how MI6 had instructed him to eliminate a double agent, which he did by pushing him off a ship in mid-Atlantic. Meanwhile, Mel Stuart was unhappy with the progress of Dahl's script for *Charlie* and, without telling the author, brought in a young unknown named David Seltzer to rewrite it.[37] Stuart says he wanted the story to be treated more 'realistically', although it is hard to see what this means in relation to the final product, which is unabashedly and enjoyably fantastic. Some of the changes reflected a concern for the sensitivities of a more racially mixed audience than Dahl had had in mind – the film's Oompa-Loompas, for example, are no longer black, but orange with green hair. (It was for similar reasons that the title was altered to *Willy Wonka and the Chocolate Factory* – 'Charlie' being Afro-American slang for a white man. The change was explained in publicity handouts as reflecting an in fact non-existent expansion of Wonka's role.) But other alterations were made simply to add to the fun.

Dahl had returned to Great Missenden by the time he learnt that David Seltzer was – in Hollywood parlance – 'writing behind' him. He was so incensed that in order to appease him, Stuart had to fly to England from Germany, where *Willy Wonka and the Chocolate Factory* was being shot. But the new script stayed. Apart from the additional episodes, Seltzer had redrafted much of the existing dialogue, had given Willy Wonka a taste for literary quotation ('all

I ask is a tall ship and a star to steer her by'), and provided a new ending. Mr Wonka tells Charlie not to forget what happened to the man who suddenly got everything he had ever wanted. When Charlie asks, 'What happened?', he tells him, 'He lived happily ever after.' Dahl hated this, although it seems to fit the story well enough.

Seltzer was not given an on-screen credit for his work (the screenplay is simply attributed to Roald Dahl), but the film helped to launch him on a highly commercial Hollywood career, one of whose successes would be the award-winning *The Omen*, with Gregory Peck and Lee Remick. As Mel Stuart proudly says now, 'he turned out to be as talented as he really was'.[38] The implication seems to be that in Hollywood's terms, Roald Dahl was less talented than he was turning out. The combination of *The Night Digger* and his attempt to adapt *Charlie* in effect brought an end to his career as a scriptwriter. By the time other such offers began to come his way, even he felt rich enough to refuse them.

11

Businessman of Letters

Dahl was glad to give up film work, or to be given up by it. He was bad at collaborative enterprises, and in any case he was beginning to see the commercial potential of concentrating on books for children.

Although he disliked the movie version of *Charlie and the Chocolate Factory*, its release in 1971 increased his fame. But his children's books were already doing extremely well. By March 1968 *Charlie* had sold 607,240 copies in the USA. The figure for *James and the Giant Peach* was 266,435.[1] Knopf's royalty statement showed the author as being owed almost a million dollars. Before the end of that year, all these figures had doubled.[2] And both books had at last broken through in Britain, as well as in France (where *James* was published by Gallimard in 1966, a year earlier than in England). In the course of the following decade they were to appear in Denmark, Finland, Norway, Sweden, Germany, Italy, Portugal, Japan and Israel. But it was success in Britain that mattered most to Dahl. He achieved it in a way that both pleased him very much and allowed him to use his commercial cunning.

Tessa had a school friend, Camilla Unwin, who lived in the next village, Little Missenden. Her father, Rayner Unwin, was a publisher: J. R. R. Tolkien's publisher, in fact, although he didn't specialize in children's books. One day, Camilla brought home copies of the US editions of *James* and *Charlie*, given her by Tessa. A letter from Allen & Unwin was soon on its way to the author.[3]

Unwin didn't know that the books had been turned down by practically every other established publisher in Britain, and Dahl sent him a poker-player's reply. Allen & Unwin, he said, was one of the few British houses which hadn't already approached him. However, the many offers he had received were too hedged about with conditions. His books were unusually successful in the USA and he was ambitious for them in Britain. How could Unwin improve on his rivals' terms?

The usual publishing arrangement in Britain and the USA is one in which the publisher capitalizes the author by advancing him a sum of money before his book appears, and in many cases before it has been written. The author keeps this money whether or not the book turns out to be profitable, but takes a relatively small share of the total proceeds: usually between 10 and 12.5 per cent of the book's purchase price, which must first of all repay the advance. Rayner Unwin is by his own account an old-fashioned publisher, and he suggested to Dahl an old-fashioned publishing arrangement: a partnership of the kind which his father, Sir Stanley Unwin, had very successfully formed with Tolkien, and earlier with Bertrand Russell. Allen & Unwin would print and market the books in full liaison with the author, but without advancing him any money. If sales didn't cover the costs of production and administration, Dahl would make nothing. But any profit would be divided equally between them, and if the books were a success, his share would be bigger than under his other publishing contracts.

Because of his recent earnings, Dahl for the first time didn't feel in need of an advance. He was also impressed by the best-selling names on Unwin's back list. So he accepted, and was soon taking a keen interest in every aspect of the deal. New illustrations were commissioned, from Faith Jaques, for *Charlie and the Chocolate Factory*. In the case of *James and the Giant Peach*, at Dahl's suggestion Allen & Unwin used the pictures drawn for the French edition by Michel Simeon. The books were printed economically in East Germany and bound in hardback but without a separate jacket. As a result, they could be sold at twelve shillings and sixpence (62.5 pence; in today's terms, about £4) – considerably cheaper than most British hard-cover illustrated children's books at the time.

The shy-seeming, gentlemanly Unwin found Dahl extremely

tough to deal with over business matters, and learned to keep his distance from him at home. 'He was a very heavy persuader, and a gambler,' Unwin says now. 'He sort of radiated power. I'm glad he didn't go into politics.' But of course, the gamble paid off. And while Unwin felt similarly squeamish about the extent to which Dahl used his family's personal tragedies as a way of getting publicity, the interviews with him which appeared everywhere increased sales. Talking to journalists, Dahl emphasized both the low price of the books and the shocking effect they had had on humourless American 'female librarians'.[4] Female British reviewers did not fall into the same trap. In *The Times*, Elaine Moss called Charlie 'the funniest book I have read in years' and predicted that it would become a classic. 'Dahl's dialogue in these two books smacks of Carroll,' she wrote, 'his verses of Belloc. But he is a great original.' The review was helpfully quoted in the influential trade journal *The Bookseller* just before Christmas 1967.[5]

In New York, meanwhile, the staff of Knopf were still in a spin about Virginie Fowler's rejection of *The Magic Finger*, which Harper & Row published in 1966. Dahl increased their nervousness by complaining about distribution arrangements at Random House (the group of which Knopf was now part).[6] He passed on a report that a wholesaler in Los Angeles had been kept waiting two months for five hundred copies of *Charlie* which had been ordered for Christmas, but did not arrive until January. Alfred Knopf replied in person, laying the blame on new technology.

A flurry of in-house discussions ensued about what Dahl might be persuaded to write next, and how he could be kept from the clutches of Harper & Row. Random House had responded to the expanding market among educationally anxious parents by launching a series called Beginner Books. In the spring of 1968, when Dahl visited Patricia Neal in New York during the shooting of *The Subject Was Roses*, he met Robert Gottlieb, the new head of Knopf. Gottlieb reported to Robert Bernstein, President of Random House, that they had discussed various possibilities, including a contribution to the new project.[7] They also talked about a sequel to *Charlie and the Chocolate Factory* and about a new collection of stories for adults.

Dahl was hesitant about taking on anything substantial at this stage, but the idea of another short picture-book appealed to him. He started work at once and, early in June, sent in a hastily-written little story – in prose, but with sketches of his own – about ruthless farmers and an embattled family of foxes.

'The Fox', as the story was titled, caused pandemonium at Knopf. The author was earning them millions of dollars, was notoriously touchy and had shown that he could easily be lured away by another publisher. He had in effect been commissioned to write the new book. The problem wasn't only that, as one internal memo put it, 'The writing is poor, the fantasy is unbelievable, the plot is badly worked out and . . . contains a long middle section in which there isn't really much to illustrate'. [8] 'The Fox' also flagrantly incited its readers to become shoplifters. From the point of view of the moral education of children, and therefore of the book's likely sales in a market still believed to be dominated by teachers and librarians, it was, everyone agreed, unpublishable.

Dahl's draft typescript begins roughly like the now well-known book, and is an allegory of how he tended to see his domestic situation at the time. A family of foxes are trapped in their den by men with shotguns, who are waiting for starvation to drive the animals out. Mr Fox has an idea, which is where, in his publisher's view, Dahl's original went most seriously wrong. With his children, Mr Fox simply tunnels from the wood to the nearby town, under the main street and into a supermarket. The young foxes yelp with pleasure at the sight of shelves and shelves of groceries, sweets and toys. 'Fantastic,' cries Mr Fox. 'Grab a trolley!' He warns them not to take too much, so that the losses won't be noticed and they will be able to come back again. The family returns home to a feast, which Mr Fox assures his wife can be repeated every night. 'Mrs Fox smiled at her husband. "My darling," she said, "you are a fantastic fox." '

In New York, hectic discussions ensued about how to salvage the situation, while telegrams began to arrive from Great Missenden asking what was going on. Pat Neal had been away for several months making *The Subject Was Roses*. Dahl told Bob Bernstein that he was feeling the strain of running the house and dealing with his children's, as well as his own, spring viruses and other problems.[9] Tessa, in particular, was miserable at Roedean, where she was being bullied. Dahl himself underwent an operation on his nose that summer. A week later, he took Pat, Tessa, Theo, Ophelia and the three-year-old Lucy to Norway for their annual family holiday, but suddenly began a torrential nose-bleed and had to go into hospital.[10] For a week, his nostrils were plugged with wads which he grumbled were the size of frankfurters.

Bernstein wrote sympathetically, temporizing about the book and pleading staff holidays as an excuse for the delays.[11] Four months and half-a-dozen readers' reports later, the brief typescript landed on the desk of Fabio Coen, an executive editor of children's books in an elevated corner of the newly-expanded Random House empire, Pantheon Books. Coen's objections were no different from anyone else's, but he had a solution, which he summarized in 350 words. The main change is that the foxes steal from their persecutors, the farmers:[12]

> Mr Fox digs out to get his bearings. Finds he has dug right where he wanted to be – in the chicken-coop of farmer No. 1. Mr Fox and little foxes steal eggs and chicken. Meanwhile the three farmers still waiting where we left them. Mr Fox and children carry eggs and chicken back to Mrs Fox, then start digging tunnel in a new direction. They dig and dig right into smoke-house of farmer No. 2. Steal hams and other goodies. Carry back to Mama fox who stores things away and begins to prepare a large meal. Mr Fox and little foxes dig third tunnel in yet another direction. Dig and dig right out to farmer No. 3's cider cellar. Littlest fox particularly delighted, likes cider. Each one steals big bottle of cider, and return to mother fox who by this time has everything ready for a feast. All sit down to huge banquet. Switch back to three angry farmers still waiting with guns for foxes to appear.

Coen was deputed to put his idea to Dahl himself,[13] but Robert Bernstein first prepared the ground with more than one long, circumspect letter, making clear that they wanted to publish everything Dahl wrote, and that if he was not convinced by the proposal, 'in the end we will do it your way'. Dahl had earlier defended his version energetically. He said that he had considered the moral problem raised by the foxes' shoplifting, but decided it was of no importance. In the first place, that is how foxes survive, and he thought children should be aware of the fact. Second, neither Beatrix Potter nor Tolkien had been concerned about such matters, so why should he be?[14] Bernstein could have answered that neither of these arguments might seem as conclusive to a parent or teacher in downtown Los Angeles as in rural Buckinghamshire, but Dahl was in fact sufficiently mollified to agree to considering Coen's suggestions. In the event, he was delighted by them. They were, he joked, 'so good that I feel almost as though I am committing plagiarism in accepting them.' None the less, like the foxes, he would 'grab them with both hands', and start immediately on a completely new draft of the book. It was the first time, he gratefully if untruthfully added, that any of his publishers had ever come up with a 'constructive and acceptable idea' for his writing.[15]

Coen's was the version of the book which finally appeared, and which, decades later, is still a bestseller. *Fantastic Mr Fox* was published by both Knopf and Allen & Unwin in 1970, and soon throughout the rest of the world. Dahl dedicated it to the memory of Olivia.

Dahl was now fifty-four: hard-working and prosperous, but in poor health, balding, and distinctly lame – when he and Neal walked side by side, they lurched into each other like a pair of penguins. The children would hear him in the morning groaning as he reached for his pill-bottle, before he came down in his dressing-gown to breakfast, a pile of letters, and the organization of the household.[16] His wife and his son were both disabled. His eldest surviving daughter was clever and articulate, but, like her brother, unhappy at school: he moved her from Roedean to Downe House, but she didn't like it much better. The fees were enormous, and there were all the others to educate. The youngest, Lucy, was still only five.

If Tessa hated school, she seemed no more contented at Gipsy House. When she came home for the holidays, Lucy remembers, 'all hell would break loose' – particularly if their mother was there too.[17] Both independently and together, they were tempestuous women. Quite often, though, Patricia Neal was away. She appeared in a television drama called *The Homecoming*, made in Hollywood and Wyoming, and as a speech therapist in the film *Baxter*. She was increasingly in demand for US projects concerning illness and disability: lectures about stroke rehabilitation, the voice-over for a documentary on cancer. And through Dahl's advertising friend David Ogilvy, she was soon offered a lucrative contract making a series of television commercials in New York for Maxim Coffee.

When Tessa had been small, the whole family travelled around with Pat. Now Pat either went alone or with Valerie Eaton Griffith. So she was less of a presence in the lives of her younger daughters. Dahl believed that Tessa's problems were largely a result of the instability of her early upbringing, and was determined to provide something different for her sisters. He couldn't depend much on Pat. And having, for most of his own childhood, been without a father of his own, he had to make things up as he went along. In his younger children's eyes, he succeeded wonderfully. Lucy says that to her and Ophelia, with no memories to contend with of Theo's accident, Olivia's death or their mother's strokes, 'It's like there were two portions. There was the Tessa era, with all the tragedies, and then there was my era, which was calm and lovely.'

Her favourite memories are of the many times when she and Ophelia were alone with their father and, in the background, their Filipino cook and nanny-housekeeper. Lucy was a self-contained child, happy playing alone. Ophelia, when she was home from school, followed her father around as he pottered in the orchid house or the aviary. Sometimes, he would take them and the dogs

183

for a walk up the hill behind Gipsy House into the woods, where they looked for rabbits. He made games for them, such as a weighted metal spiral attached to a pencil, which drew patterns on a sheet of paper. At bedtime, he mixed up sweet drinks which he called 'witches' potions' – tinned peaches or pears blended with milk and food colouring. (His own potion would be a large scotch.) Then he told them stories about a friendly giant who concocted dreams in a jar and blew them into children's bedrooms. More than once, after he had left the girls to sleep, he put a ladder up to their window and stirred the curtains as if he were the giant himself. In the way of paternal jokes, it became something of a routine as the years went by – one which Ophelia and Lucy dutifully humoured.

From the younger girls' point of view, Tessa and their mother spoiled such idylls, partly just by being there, and partly because of the pressures they brought to bear on Roald. 'If there's one thing my father hated,' Lucy says, 'it was to be demanded of. He liked to give, but he didn't like to be demanded of.' But of course the others see things in their own ways. To each of the children, Dahl was 'my' father, and Tessa's own relationship with him was if anything more intimate and more jealous than anyone else's. He wrote to her 'almost every day' when she was at school, and she remembers her mixture of pride and agonizing embarrassment when he came to collect her for exeats and holidays, shambling around in his old clothes, tieless, with a flask of coffee or whisky, among the other children's tidier and more circumspect parents.

Pat too has her own happy domestic memories: games of Scrabble with Roald's sisters, outings to the village pub with Roald, dinner parties with friends. And there were their holidays: in the Basque country near Annabella's farm at Saint Jean-de-Luz, or in the Caribbean with the Bryces or with Claudia Marsh (Charles had died in 1964 after his ten-year, silent paralysis). Almost every year, too, they went to the west coast of Norway, where they stayed at the same hotel, the Strand at Fevik, near Kristiansund. Each day, their routine there would be the same: a hired boat, a little voyage to an island, fishing along the way, cooking the catch for lunch.

*

There was a cost to such idylls, and not only in the financial terms which so preoccupied Dahl. The new head of Knopf, Robert Gottlieb (later to succeed William Shawn as editor of *The New Yorker*), visited Gipsy House several times with his wife, the actress Maria Tucci. They describe an atmosphere which was lively, jolly, full of excitement, but not at all relaxed. Dahl was charming, Tucci says, 'completely in charge – a puppeteer, making everything work.' He took her around the garden and showed her his orchids: it was the flowers' perfection that he liked, he told her. Dinner began with jellied consommé, and he proudly drew attention to the fact that it had been made by Pat. But even the food was for the most part his responsibility. He had grown all the vegetables, and when his guests praised the main dish, smokies cooked with cream, it was he who later sent them the recipe.

Maria Tucci was intrigued and moved by Dahl. She had expected something different. Pat's friend Mildred Dunnock, with whom Maria had worked, had warned her that he was snobbish and cruel. She saw nothing of that, but what she did see, she thought was a gruelling performance. Before dinner, on their first visit, Roald had gone to tell stories to the younger children. Passing their open bedroom doorway, Maria saw him off his guard, his face utterly exhausted. She later came to think of him as 'a man whose need for perfection was so extreme that I was very glad I was not his child or anyone close to him.'

If the perfectionism was exhausting, so was the conflict from which it arose. Dahl wanted not only others to be better than they were, but himself too. He complained about how Pat's stroke had intensified what he saw as some of her worst characteristics – her lack of intellectual curiosity, her selfishness, her quick temper. But he knew that he had faults too, such as the restlessness which made him pace up and down in the house which he believed he was making into a haven of calm. He still insisted that anything wrong could be put right. 'Daddy got so caught up in *making things better*', Tessa says. 'He used to say, "You've got to get on with it." ... He used to shout, "I want my children to be brave." ' Dahl's moral universe was one in which there could be no question without an answer, no battle without victory, no irresolvable complexity. This was true of his writing also.

Although he wrote little in the late 1960s and early 1970s, he still hoped to return to adult fiction, and his earlier books for adults now reached an increasingly far-flung readership. As part of a demonstration of enthusiasm after it lost *The Magic Finger*, Random House brought out a selection of his stories in the prestigious classics series, the Modern Library. Other compilations soon appeared and, through Rayner Unwin, Dahl negotiated a deal with Penguin for paperback editions of *Someone Like You* and *Over To You*, as well as of *Charlie, James, The Magic Finger* and *Fantastic Mr Fox*. All of these appeared between 1970 and 1974. Penguin officially claimed at the time that they paid no author a royalty higher than 12.5 per cent, but Dahl got 15 per cent.[18] By 1975, his books were becoming bestsellers in Britain as well as the USA. *Charlie* had sold 225,000 copies here in paperback, 60,000 in hardback; *James* 115,000 and 45,000; *Fantastic Mr Fox* 74,000 and 15,000. Meanwhile, *Kiss Kiss* had been translated into Russian and Japanese and *The Magic Finger* into Indonesian. From now on, as soon as the English-language rights in his books were sold, foreign publishers would be negotiating to translate them.

While he waited for new ideas to come, he occupied himself with various recyclings of earlier work: the sequel to *Charlie and the Chocolate Factory*, entitled *Charlie and the Great Glass Elevator*; a collection of some of his *Playboy* stories, entitled *Switch Bitch*; a children's book based on one of his *New Yorker* stories, 'The Champion of the World'.[19] He was also planning a miscellaneous collection called *The Wonderful Story of Henry Sugar* and a novel developing the character of the salacious Uncle Oswald, first introduced in 'The Visitor'.[20]

Meanwhile, he had made some revisions to *Charlie and the Chocolate Factory*. Although the early critical response to the book had been favourable, some readers had come to object to the book on a variety of grounds. The most glaring was the characterization of the Oompa-Loompas. But this was of a piece with the story's outlook on other human relationships: in particular, Mr Wonka's ready disposal of people he dislikes and his high-handed way with objectors. In 1972 a wide-ranging attack on the book was published by Eleanor Cameron, a leading American writer of children's fiction.[21]

Her article, in the respected journal for children's literature specialists *The Horn Book*, was damaging because of its intellectual weight, and also because it started from ground Dahl had claimed as his own: hostility to the corrupting power of television. This was a theme whose public impact had been increased, since *Charlie* first appeared, by Marshall McLuhan's bestselling books *Understanding Media* (1964) and *The Medium is the Message* (1967), which assumed that television had already taken over from printed books as irreversibly as they had taken over from illuminated manuscripts – and with no less revolutionary effect. Like Dahl, Eleanor Cameron drew a contrast between the values of television and those of literature. But she said that those who want to defend literature must remember that it isn't valuable of itself, irrespective of its quality. Very few books last, or deserve to. You have to sort out the good from the bad. Furthermore (and here she decisively parted company with Dahl), goodness in fiction is partly a moral matter, bound up with 'the goodness of the writer himself, his worth as a human being'.

Cameron claimed that, for all its satire at the expense of the television-addicted character Mike Teavee, *Charlie and the Chocolate Factory* is only speciously opposed to what she saw as the medium's shallow gratifications. The pleasures the book offers, she said, are like those of a game show or of chocolate itself: instantly enjoyable, but temporary. Everything depends on the plot. The human situation, especially Charlie's poverty, is 'phony'. And 'As for Willy Wonka himself, he is the perfect type of TV showman with his gags and screechings. The exclamation mark is the extent of his individuality.' However amusing the book may be for adults to read, and however greedily children consume it, it is underlyingly cheap, tasteless, ugly, sadistic and, for all these reasons, harmful.

Dahl had often complained that critics didn't take him seriously. Now that one had, he dashed off an angry, superficial reply which avoided the main arguments and concentrated on personalities.[22] He 'had not heard of [Mrs Cameron] until now', he said. She, on the other hand, ought to have found out more about him before writing her 'extraordinarily vicious comments'. Her observations about the moral connection between a book and its author showed, he said, that she could not have read either Barry Farrell's *Pat and Roald* or any of the numerous articles on Dahl and his family, which would have told her that they had suffered tragedies from which they had emerged 'quite creditably'. One of these misfortunes had befallen his son Theo, to whom *Charlie and the Chocolate Factory* is dedicated. With more feeling than logic, Dahl said that it must be clear that he would not have written a book which would hurt Theo, or any other of his children, who 'are marvelous and gay and happy', and whose happiness he believed that the book had increased.

Cameron had no difficulty in answering these points, and there the argument stopped.[23] But Dahl's publishers got at least part of the message: that to those concerned with bringing up children in a racially-mixed society, the Oompa-Loompas were no longer acceptable as originally written. The following year, to accompany its new sequel *Charlie and the Great Glass Elevator*, a revised edition of *Charlie and the Chocolate Factory* appeared in which the Oompa-Loompas had become dwarfish hippies with long 'golden-brown' hair and 'rosy-white' skin. From now on, Dahl was often to find his books read – not least by his publishers – with a critical thoroughness he wasn't used to, and didn't always care for.

12

Wham!

Dahl used to boast in those days that he paid the housekeeping bills out of his winnings at blackjack.[1] It was an exaggeration, but Ian Rankin, a friend whom he took gambling at the Curzon House Club half a dozen times, says that he never saw Dahl come away the loser.[2]

He kept his gambling money separate, in a bedroom drawer (which, according to Tessa, some of his children were later to find a useful source of supply). When he went to the Mayfair casino, he would take £200 or so from the drawer. He never spent more than he had either brought with him or won on the night.

Dahl offered to teach Rankin his blackjack method. The minutest calculations were involved, about when precisely to double, when to split, how much to alter your bets in relation to the previous ones you had been putting up. Rankin – an old-fashioned, laid-back Old Etonian with sandy hair and a broken nose – couldn't be bothered to memorize the technique sufficiently well to make it work, and says that even if he had, by the time the table had given him a large whisky he would have forgotten. But Dahl drank little while he was playing, and gave the game his intensest concentration. He was always looking for the moment when he could add his own twist to the method: one which, he liked to claim, changed the odds a little more so that they were fractionally in his own favour. The approach was psychological as well as technical. While playing, he watched for a hint that the banker was nervous, perhaps because there had been a run of play against him, or because, in a changeover, he had newly joined the game. Then Dahl would pile in and win.

His public persona was not, of course, that of a gambling man. And he hadn't yet acquired his later fame as an irritable, ornery sounder-off on political issues. The world knew him as a genial, rather scruffy children's author – a tall scarecrow whose face, under the increasingly bald, high dome, looked both distinguished and in need of repair.

This appearance fitted another role, as one of the people behind what had become the Volunteer Stroke Scheme. The methods which Valerie Eaton Griffith developed by trial and error with Patricia Neal ('she teaching me', Griffith insists) had been taken up next with the writer Alan Moorehead who, after suffering a stroke, rented a house in Great Missenden so as to benefit from the same techniques.[3] In his case there was much less improvement, but the potential of the approach was clear, and Griffith won the support of a scientist in Great Missenden, the Nobel prize-winning chemist Sir Robert Robinson, in planning a national scheme, which eventually found sponsorship from the Chest, Heart and Stroke Association. Moorehead and Dahl encouraged Valerie Eaton Griffith to write a book about her efforts, *A Stroke in the Family*, and helped her to get it published by Penguin in 1970. Gradually the volunteer organization spread, and today it co-ordinates 120 local schemes through ten regional managers and publishes its own books, pamphlets and a quarterly magazine.[4]

Another view of Dahl which he encouraged was as the libertarian father idealized in *Danny The Champion of the World*. The book, first published in 1975, mythologizes a father-son relationship of the kind which, in both roles, Dahl had seen shattered. It is also an ode to a newly-prevalent condition, that of the single parent, as well as to an old one: the rural outlaw. When Danny – the book's narrator – was a baby, his father 'washed me and fed me and changed my nappies and did all the millions of other things a mother normally does for her child'.[5] Yet this male mother is a traditionally macho, omniscient patriarch, a skilled car mechanic and maker of kites, wildlife expert, story-teller and defender, who takes Danny's side against a bullying teacher. He also has a secret. At night, he creeps out of their gypsy caravan and goes poaching in the nearby woods.

In essence, it is an expanded version of the ideal of devoted, piratical fatherhood in *Fantastic Mr Fox*, and we are clearly meant to read the book as another allegory of Dahl's own ménage. It is dedicated to 'the whole family: Pat, Tessa, Theo, Ophelia, Lucy'. The gypsy caravan (on whose roof apples thud with an everyday evocativeness reminiscent of Dahl's earliest stories) is based on the one still parked in the garden of Gipsy House. The petrol station comes from Dahl's first job; Danny's teachers are versions of those at St Peter's, Weston-super-Mare.

Even the nocturnal poaching had been one of his real hobbies. But when the book was written, in the early 1970s, the sport had developed an additional symbolic meaning for him, signalled by a warning which Danny gives to his readers: 'You will learn as you get older, just as I learned that autumn, that no father is perfect. Grown-ups are complicated creatures, full of quirks and secrets . . . that would probably make you gasp if you knew about them.'[6] Such quirks, we are to understand, must be forgiven in both parents and children. They are part of not being 'stodgy'. For as the book's last page insists, 'What a child wants and deserves is a parent who is SPARKY.'

There was no shortage of sparkiness at Gipsy House, although it now often took the form of rows between Roald and Pat, or Roald and anyone else, after he had had a few drinks in the evening. There were also signs that as a recipe for bringing up children, even the most vivid incandescence had its limitations.

After Theo's accident and Olivia's death, Tessa had been upset to a degree which led Pat to suggest they find her some counselling. Anna Freud's name was suggested, but Dahl furiously vetoed the idea.[7] By 1972 a turbulent, slim, six-foot-tall fifteen-year-old with her mother's long legs and wide cheekbones, Tessa was offered a role with Pat in a Hollywood film, *Happy Mother's Day – Love George*.[8] The idea came from Pat, who now thinks it was a bad mistake. Roald was furious, but didn't see how he could stop her. Tessa feels that he didn't try all that hard. Certainly, when she afterwards walked out of boarding school and returned home the worse for a few Bloody Marys on the train, he gave her the impression that he found it all amusing and that in a way, he was proud of her for it.

It was the strongest indication yet that some of his children would be as independent-minded and as troublesome as Dahl himself. But the lives of his daughters, particularly Tessa and Lucy, were to be characterized by an emotional storminess for which he felt partly responsible, which he couldn't calm, and which still continues after his death. As usual, he came up with what he hoped would prove a practical solution: opening an antiques shop called The Witchball in Great Missenden for Tessa to run. If it seems like an idea more in tune with his own interests than Tessa's, that was partly because he was otherwise preoccupied.

According to Annabella, Dahl had had various flirtations since his marriage to Pat and – although there is a discreet haze over the details – these had included at least one long affair, with a million-airess in New York.[9] (She had a famous collection of pictures, and once, when she was away, Dahl took Annabella to the house to see them. 'We were like two naughty schoolboys sometimes,' the actress says.) Pat herself says that since her stroke, there had been the gangster's daughter, an Irish novelist and a woman in Switzer-land – all part of what Tessa describes as 'an endless slew of rich old bags who suddenly wanted to do nice things for me'. Accord-ing to Annabella, 'Roald didn't make passes at women. The women ran to him.' To illustrate his response, she makes a gesture like someone pushing crumbs off a table.

By the early 1970s, someone altogether new overwhelmed Dahl's thoughts. The key to Danny's words about parental secrets and nocturnal disappearances was Felicity Crosland: in her mid-thirties, strong, elegant, Gallic-featured – in some ways a younger version of Annabella herself. She was recently divorced from her husband Charles, a quiet gentleman farmer with whom she had had three daughters, who now mainly lived with their father.

When she first met Dahl, she was employed by David Ogilvy's advertising agency, for which Patricia Neal was making the Maxim Coffee commercials. According to Pat's account in *As I Am*, Mrs Crosland was given the job of helping Mrs Dahl choose the dresses she would wear in commercials in which she poured Mr Dahl his coffee. ('My husband is a writer,' Pat had to say. 'He's terribly fussy when it comes to the coffee he drinks.'[10]) Pat was in need of friends, not least because Valerie Eaton Griffith, who was now busy with the ever-expanding Volunteer Stroke Scheme, had begun weaning her off their daily lessons. Griffith now blames herself for this, thinking she may have over-estimated how independent Neal really was, and how well she would withstand having nothing to do at home. Certainly it seemed to her that under the near-intolerable pressures on Pat, she 'began to behave badly. She was intolerant, she would yell at people, she would crave attention so that she'd overdo almost everything in an actressy way, and make it very difficult for people to live and be peaceful in that house. It was extremely hard for all of them, and very hard on Roald, who had stood square behind her, and possibly that was the germ . . . '

Pat liked the attentive Felicity, and asked her to Gipsy House. A journalist who later interviewed the younger woman described Pat's predicament: 'Imagine the scene. You meet someone at work, get on with her rather well and invite her home to meet your husband. She and he take one look at each other and wham! – you're out of the picture.'[11]

Already smitten, 'Liccy' (pronounced Lissy) returned the invitation. Over dinner with the couple at her Battersea flat, she mentioned that she was going to Paris the next day. With his trick of always giving a woman an errand to run, Roald asked her if she could pick up an umbrella he had left with a friend there. The friend greeted her with the words, 'I hear you are the most marvellous woman in the world.' Soon afterwards, Felicity and Roald met *à deux*. Dahl, then in his late fifties, seemed to her 'a shy Norwegian giant with all the Nordic hangups,' but 'very romantic'. He discovered that Felicity had been born in Palace Road, Llandaff, very near his own birthplace. Her father was a Portuguese surgeon named Alfonso d'Abreu who, Dahl liked to boast, took part in the development of the heart pacemaker.[12] Her mother was born Throckmorton, from a Catholic family which can trace its lineage back to the Middle Ages. One of her ancestresses was a maid-of-honour to Queen Elizabeth I, married Sir Walter Ralegh and when he fell into disfavour under James I, spent a dozen years imprisoned in the Tower of London with him and their children.[13] Llandaff, medicine, royalty, adventure, literature: it was a multiple *coup de foudre*.

They met frequently, both in London and at Gipsy House. Liccy sometimes brought along a man to Great Missenden for cover. Dahl's gambling companion Ian Rankin was one of them (it was through her that he and Dahl met). These arrangements produced their own complications, some of them farcical. One night, taking a walk in the garden after everyone had gone to bed, Rankin set off the burglar alarm by mistake and was arrested by two local policemen. The whole household was woken up, but Dahl's anger seemed out of all proportion, and Rankin wasn't invited again.[14]

Inevitably, people began to find out: among them Tessa. She was now in her mid-to-late teens, often anorexic, heavily involved in drugs and embarking on her own succession of affairs, in which some of her partners can be seen as surrogates of her father: the fifty-year-old Peter Sellers among them. By the time she was nineteen, she would be pregnant. All this may have coloured the account she now gives of those days.

One night at Gipsy House, Tessa says, her father offered her a new kind of sleeping pill to try. It didn't work, and as she lay awake, she heard him talking to Felicity on the telephone in a way that made it clear that they were lovers. Tessa had already suspected this from something her aunt Else had said, but when she challenged Felicity, she had denied it. Now, Tessa told Else what she had heard. Else said that it was best if everyone turned a blind eye. This wasn't Tessa's style, and she confronted her father. He at first denied everything, then rounded on her: 'You've always been trouble, you've always been a nosy little bitch. I want you to get out of this fucking house now.' Whether or not these were his actual words, they are what Tessa remembers hearing. Later, he apologized, and the next day came around to The Witchball and said that Liccy wanted to talk to her.

According to Tessa's understandably emotional account, it was an odd meeting. She was wretchedly confused, not least because Felicity was always very kind to her in her troubles – if anything, more helpful than her own mother. She also saw Else's point, that the energetic but ailing Roald needed emotional support of a kind which Pat did not provide. Above all, Tessa was fascinated by her dawning sense of the power which her knowledge gave her. As she remembers it, Felicity offered to give Roald up if his daughter asked her to. But, again according to Tessa's account, Felicity warned the girl that this would devastate him – and that the marriage would be finished if Pat were told. So Tessa kept the secret.

In doing so, she unavoidably became an accomplice. As she remembers things, the pair gradually came to use her as a go-between and a confidante. Roald in particular, in an attempt at self-exoneration, told her intimate details of his foundering relationship with her mother, and then bribed her – with money, and after her baby Sophie was born, with a house in Wandsworth – to keep quiet. Tessa had always longed to be closer to her father. This wasn't how she had imagined it, but it was something.

The other children knew nothing of the affair, and lived relatively unperturbed in their own worlds of school, friends and horses. Pat herself was often away, and so far suspected little of what was going on. To casual visitors, Gipsy House still seemed a noisy, affectionate, untidy domestic paradise. Everyone describes what successive magazine photographers and film cameramen also recorded: the Constructivist paintings and Picasso lithographs; the log-piles of bottles in the wine cellar; the garden with its gypsy caravan and the unswept writing hut. One newcomer after another learnt what kind of pencil Dahl wrote with (a yellow Dixon

Ticonderoga with an eraser at one end), inspected his armchair
with its writing board covered in billiard-velvet, was offered a
chocolate bar from a well-worn tin box, and heard his disquisition
on the history of the Malteser.

So long as Dahl didn't take a dislike to them, almost anyone felt
welcome. He had built an indoor pool for Pat, but its main users
were children from the village. Friends would turn up at Gipsy
House to play snooker on the recently-acquired three-quarter-sized
table, or just to have a few drinks. Dahl was a man's man, say the
men who liked him, and Gipsy House was a place where you didn't
feel you shouldn't swear.[15] Not all women were made to feel so
comfortable, particularly if they were friends of Pat's. The journalist Gitta Sereny, for example, found Dahl 'very cold, very absent' at
this time.[16]

His publishers were among the most frequent visitors. Robert
and Helen Bernstein and their family came on several occasions,
admired a Henry Moore print, were given it, and were taken to the
Curzon House Club.[17] And there were the many friends who lived
near by: a scientist, doctors, businessmen, but few writers
(Elizabeth David was a special case) and certainly no literary critics.[18] If he liked people, Dahl's charm was such that even to those
who had only met him a few times, he could seem uniquely close.
While few claim that they understood him, many of his friends and
acquaintances thought they were the only ones who knew him at
all. So when, as inevitably happened in a life which was both very
busy and in fact not at all short of lasting relationships, some
of these people found themselves shut out, they could be hurt.
Creekmore Fath was not particularly surprised at the fact that
although he often visited England after the end of the war, his
attempts to make contact with his old Washington buddy always
failed. But David Ogilvy, like Ian Rankin, was surprised to find
himself suddenly dropped. Ogilvy had sometimes been critical of
Dahl's treatment of Pat, and believes too that Dahl may have been
envious of his prominence in H. Montgomery Hyde's book about
wartime British intelligence in the USA[19] – a book in which Dahl
himself does not figure. But when, around this time, he invited the

Dahls to stay at his French château, he was astonished to receive a letter from Roald announcing that they were no longer friends. The rupture, he says, was both 'total and inexplicable.'

A similar but even more hurtful rift occurred with Colin Fox.[20] Fox was one of those who thought themselves special to Dahl. He particularly remembers a day when they were putting up fencing posts together at Gipsy House. As they worked, Dahl told him he mustn't think he could survive for ever as a model and player of bit parts. 'You'll have to do something concrete, or your friends will have to look after you.' Fox heard the second part of the sentence more clearly than the first. A vulnerable man, he was overwhelmed that Dahl should think of looking after him. From that moment, 'always he was in the back of my mind, that here was this great pillar – Gentleman's Agreement.' Years afterwards, near-derelict and in despair, he came to England from New York in the hope of drawing on what he saw as this promise. With pitiful symbolism, Fox says he wanted Dahl to write some words for him, for a play in which he had been given a non-speaking role. He telephoned from a call-box in the Vauxhall Bridge Road, but Dahl said it wasn't convenient, and would not see him.

It is easy to see how Dahl could have been misinterpreted in such a situation. And a lot was going on, not least within the family. Although Pat and Roald fought a good deal, they also had some deceptively happy times together. In January 1974 they went to the Virgin Islands, where Roald played in a golf tournament. Pat now remembers the holiday with irony: 'He was in fine form. Outrageously witty, too. He charmed everyone at the event. Including me. We got along so well that I started to think of Tobago as our second honeymoon.'[21] That spring, she successfully underwent cosmetic surgery on her stroke-slackened face, and Felicity brought 'an armload of presents' to the hospital. In the summer, instead of going to Norway, Roald, Pat and the children joined Liccy and her daughters on holiday in Minorca, together with another friend named Phoebe Berens. 'One afternoon, girl-talking with Phoebe', Pat 'bragged about how happy Roald and I were now, and what a great sex life we had. I remember Phoebe looked at me and then rolled her eyes up to the ceiling.'

Later, Felicity in turn had to have an operation, and it was at Gipsy House that she stayed to convalesce. Such intimacies come to seem merely cynical, once the falsehood underlying them has been exposed. But neither Roald nor Felicity wanted Pat to be hurt, and when she eventually learnt what was going on, they made an effort to break off. Once again, Tessa was involved. Over lunch in a Knightsbridge restaurant, Pat asked her point-blank whether her father was having an affair. Although she knew the answer, Pat went wild when she heard it. Tessa was asked to join her parents at a meeting with Felicity but, for once, stayed out. After days of increasing tension between them all, Felicity decided to go away. She wrote to Pat, saying that she was sorry to have caused such wretchedness, and was going to take a long holiday in France and Scotland. She hoped that matters would somehow resolve themselves.[22]

They didn't, of course. The Dahl family spent a tense couple of weeks in Norway. Although several more years would pass before Pat and Roald finally split up, it was their last holiday together. Roald was soon desperate to see Felicity again. He himself had to spend time in hospital, at the London Clinic, and persuaded her to visit him there. Around this time, Roald wrote Pat a long letter. He promised that he loved her and would never leave her, but told her that he still felt strongly for Liccy, and wanted to be free to spend time with her. Sex was not involved, he said – he was too tired for that: perhaps physically big men like himself tended to wear out sooner than others. But he would like both to go on living with Pat and to be close to Felicity – although this was so miserable a situation for Felicity (he said little about Pat's feelings) that he doubted she would tolerate it. In a way, Roald said, he hoped that she would not. She would probably find another man before long. But until then, the best course would be for Pat to be 'non-jealous and normal', in the certainty that 'this family will go on as long as I live.'[23]

With the possible exception of himself, no one was taken in. To his friends it was clear that the point had come where, as Dennis Pearl says, 'nothing would have persuaded Roald to give up Felicity' and that, from this point, there was no longer any hope for his marriage.

During this period, Dahl quarrelled with almost everyone he knew: family, friends, publishers. First in line was his neighbour Rayner Unwin.

Dahl was tired of Unwin's calm, courteous approach to publishing and wanted someone more dynamic. Robert Gottlieb suggested his friend Tom Maschler at Jonathan Cape. Dahl met and liked the exuberant, gossipy Maschler, and quickly began to engineer what Unwin saw as a deliberate falling-out with his old firm. He started various quarrels, turning up without warning, for example, at Allen & Unwin's production department in Hemel Hempstead, where he made a scene about the fact that people were working on a mathematical text rather than one of his own books. And when, by accident, the standard draft contract sent to him for *Danny The Champion of the World* omitted a special clause which had been inserted into his previous deals, he used the mistake as a pretext for moving on. Unwin saw no future in trying to dissuade him, and even felt a certain amount of relief. Among other sources of tension between the two partners was the fact that Dahl seemed to be going 'closer and closer to the edge' in finding ways of avoiding income tax.

Money was once again a mounting preoccupation. By the time *Danny* was published in 1975, Tessa was eighteen, Theo fifteen, Ophelia eleven, Lucy ten. The brain-damaged Theo was not flourishing at his school, and Dahl had decided to hire a private tutor for him instead. The younger girls were about to go away as boarders to Abbots Hill, a small but expensive school in Hertfordshire. As he grew older, and with Tessa's chaotic way of life in mind, Dahl was concerned to provide them with a secure financial base. Perhaps it had also occurred to him that if he were ever to break with Pat, it might be convenient if his earnings were safely tied up out of her reach. Early in 1976 he contacted the Society of Authors about the tax position on books whose copyrights are made over to people other than the author – for example, to his children.[24] The answer wasn't encouraging, but Dahl soon found another solution. He turned himself into a hard-to-trace anonymous company ('S A', meaning *société anonyme*) based in Switzerland. Unsuperstitiously, he called it Icarus.[25]

In 1977 he published *The Wonderful Story of Henry Sugar*. The title story concerns a man who learns how to see through playing cards so that he can read the hidden side. He decides to become a latter-day Robin Hood, taking money off the bookmakers in order to give it to children.[26]

Henry Sugar learns his trick from an Indian magician. Pat and Roald had been to see one like him in 1954, soon after they married.[27] In recent years, Dahl had written very little that was new (two of the seven pieces in *The Wonderful Story of Henry Sugar* first appeared in the 1940s; a third was his account of 'How I Became A Writer'). He was meanwhile also scraping the barrel by filling out his Uncle Oswald stories as a novel.

My Uncle Oswald is an extended rude joke about a fictional early twentieth-century plot to procure the semen of some of the world's great men and sell it. No one at Knopf was very enthusiastic about the book, but they were still anxious not to lose its author. Robert Gottlieb, Knopf's gifted President, had taken over as Dahl's editor, and treated the text with no less care than that of any of the more serious books he was publishing at the same time. Their correspondence about it must be one of the odder exchanges in publishing history.[28]

Gottlieb's comments fell into two categories: first, those to do with the main character and how the readers' feelings about him are controlled; second, matters of historical fact raised by the story's comic display of learning. The first category involved making the libidinous Uncle Oswald nastier, so that 'one is happier when he gets cheated in the end'. The second was trickier. Dahl's historical education was sketchy, and he anyway found anachronism intrinsically funny. In the draft, characters used the words 'queer' and 'fairy' in their modern sense, as well as contemporary phrases such as 'Boy, what a creep she was,' 'what's bugging you?'

and 'chickening out'. Gottlieb did what he could to reduce the number of these jokes. He also, and with a factuality which couldn't improve the story although it certainly made it no worse, tried to sort out various mistakes. He argued, for example, that despite Dahl's expertise in modern art, Modigliani and Léger weren't sufficiently well known in 1919 to fit Uncle Oswald's roster of famous geniuses. On the other hand, he pointed out that Balzac had died in 1850. Gottlieb suggested that there was, in 1919, 'no such animal as the "Texas millionaire" with grapefruit trees. They're a much later phenomenon' and questioned whether ping-pong and judo were known then either. And he pointed out inconsistencies other than historical ones: 'If the Sudanese beetle product is sold (even secretly) in Berlin, Amsterdam, etc., how come it's such a surprise when O. reveals it at the dinner party?' And even allowing for the nature of the story, there were certain errors of taste which the editor was particularly concerned not to let through. He was worried, for example, about references to the size of Stravinsky's penis. 'Madame S is still alive (and wonderful),' he said, 'and I feel she would be distressed.'

Dahl accepted most of Gottlieb's suggestions, but it's clear from their letters that, despite this display of evidence, he had difficulty in grasping that his editor was at least as knowledgeable as himself. Late in their exchanges, in a letter telling Gottlieb that he had decided to introduce T. E. Lawrence as a new character, Dahl still thought that he would need an explanation: 'let them [the book's readers] puzzle that one out. He's Lawrence of Arabia. A great figure in 1919.' Nor did it strike him that when the partly European-educated, Jewish Gottlieb objected to Dahl's having called Proust an anti-Semite *tout court*, his opinion might be worth considering.

These exchanges were amicable, but there was trouble in store. Emotional and physical pain (in March 1977 Dahl had a hip-replacement), heavy dependency on alcohol and analgesics, a fear that his writing might finally dry up – all of these, combined with Dahl's native vanity and argumentativeness, made him harder and harder to deal with. He was already, of course, well known to his family and friends as a maker of scenes.[29] At one dinner in New York, he tore into the elderly photo-journalist Alfred Eisenstaedt, who was telling a story about having been refused entry into a South African club of which he wasn't a member. Why the hell should he have been admitted, Dahl wanted to know? – a reasonable enough question, except that he asked it with what seemed quite disproportionate anger, and went on and on until Eisenstaedt moved to another table. On another occasion, in London, an actress dared to venture the notion that critics were a useful part of the artistic process. Dahl became so incensed that the woman's husband intervened, and soon the men had to be prised apart by other guests. After one of these turns, Dahl rang his hostess the next day – not, as she anticipated, to apologize, but to ask 'Why do you invite people who hate me?'

His reputation for such outbursts spread further at the beginning of 1979, when he made a scene at the Curzon House Club and was thrown out. He had been having dinner with Pat, Tessa and her latest boyfriend, a rich Greek. The Curzon House had been redecorated in a way which irritated him. He also took against some of his fellow-diners: Tessa says he started to complain about the number of Jews in the club. His drunken grumbles grew louder and louder, and eventually he got to his feet and began to make a speech. People at neighbouring tables told him to shut up – 'Go home if you don't like it,' one shouted. When Dahl stumbled off towards the gambling tables, he and his party were firmly deflected into the street outside. Subsequently he was deprived of his club membership.

The story was in most of the gossip columns, but by then Roald and Pat no longer bothered to conceal even from visiting interviewers that things were going badly between them. For a long time, appearances had been just about kept up. In 1978 Patricia Neal was the subject of a *This Is Your Life* programme. Dahl sat beside her throughout, eyes hooded, mouth turned down, while family and friends joined them on the platform to pay tribute. Hollywood stars appeared on video: John Wayne, Kirk Douglas (who delivered his message sitting on a horse). Eamonn Andrews jauntily urged everyone to reminisce about Roald and his 'young bride', and their early years in the sleepy village of Great Missenden. Wally Saunders made his jokes about the successive reconstructions of Gipsy House. The entire band of Pat's volunteer therapists streamed in. Pat loved it all – particularly when the fourteen-year-old Ophelia said, to her evident surprise, 'I don't think anyone realizes how lucky we all are.' The only hint of what sounded like irony came from Kenneth Haigh, an actor friend of the Dahls who was a neighbour in Great Missenden, and who referred to Roald as 'Big Daddy Survivor himself'. But for those in the know, there was an unambiguous give-away at the end, as the crowd milled around and the credits rolled. With tears of affection and gratitude in her eyes, Pat leaned over to kiss her husband's left hand. He pulled it away and stuffed it into his pocket.

In everyday life, the marriage had now deteriorated into snarls and the slamming of doors. Pat, whose emotional condition at the time Tessa moderately describes as 'dishevelled', was in the USA a great deal, and when she was in England, she for the most part lived at the house in Wandsworth. She grumbled to Angela Neustatter, an *Evening Standard* reporter, that Roald wouldn't join her on a forthcoming retreat at a US convent.[30] Dahl was cynical about this latest manifestation of her mild religious questing – a potentially strong card for Pat to have played against the Catholic Felicity, but too late.

The following year, Dahl gave a headline to another journalist, Susan Slavetin of the *Boston Globe*, by describing himself as 'an adolescent at heart'.[31] Pat had bought a house in Martha's Vineyard, and he was reluctantly and briefly staying there with her. At the end of his part of the interview, Dahl said, 'People get tired of being with each other for years – day in, day out. They need some time away from each other.' Then he wandered away. Slavetin quoted Neal as having shrugged the comment off:

'Men are such conceited asses. But I love being here on the Vineyard. Tomorrow we'll have a gorgeous party. Cagney will be here. Hellman, too.'

She smiles broadly. Somehow, the smile does not synch with what seems to be a great well of sadness in her eyes.

Dahl then returned, and delivered another scarcely-coded message: 'Our daughter Ophelia is set on becoming an actress. I find it difficult to think about. She's letting herself in for a lifetime of unhappiness, what with constant rejection and bad marriages.'

Ophelia didn't become an actress. Later, perhaps under her father's influence, her ambitions turned towards medicine. But neither she nor Lucy was to escape unhappiness as their parents' marriage disintegrated. Lucy in particular entered a phase little less wild than her elder sister's, shoplifting, setting fire to the kitchen of her school, and at sixteen becoming addicted to cocaine.[32]

Lucy says that when Dahl discovered the extent of her drug habit, 'Immediately he blamed himself. He quietly said, "Lukey, I don't know where I went wrong," and went for a long drive alone – about four hours – which was a worse punishment than screaming and shouting.' After that, he was limitlessly busy in seeking out the best help for her: so much so that her counsellor at one clinic had to fight hard to keep her when Dahl heard good word of another. 'All I had to do,' Lucy remembers, 'was to say "Help me, I need to go to a therapist," and I would have been there in an hour.' But to her father, everything he had worked so hard to make good seemed to be falling apart. It was almost as if the crises which elicited his by-now famous practicality, resourcefulness and ingenuity were somehow caused by earlier actions of his own.

Even his elaborate tax-avoidance schemes turned out to involve commitments by which he felt entrapped. In the summer of 1979, Icarus S A of rue Friesl, 1700 Freiburg, Switzerland, had entered into a contract with Knopf.[33] The Swiss company agreed to supply the publisher with four new works by Roald Dahl: *My Uncle Oswald*, two books for children, and one for either adults or juveniles, whichever 'Icarus' chose. Knopf in return would pay Icarus $750,000 when the contract was signed, and a further $115,341.34, plus simple interest at 5 per cent per annum from the date of the agreement, on delivery of each of the other stipulated works.

At first sight, the interest payments look mysterious. Why should anyone pay interest on a debt not yet incurred? But as the contract's small print makes clear, the lump sums were not in fact advances at all. They were money already owed to Dahl from his previous books. The promised new works were from the start to earn him royalties over and above these payments. Dahl's plan – which he flattered himself was 'semi-legitimate'[34] – was to avoid income tax not only on future earnings, but on the more than one and a quarter million dollars which his earlier books had already earned, and which Knopf (whose role in these arrangements was not improper) had been banking for him while he decided what to do with it.

Whatever the apparent advantages of the agreement to Dahl, it began to chafe on him almost as soon as it was signed. Random House had exacted a price for co-operating: they had made him commit himself to letting them publish not only *My Uncle Oswald*, but three further books after that. And until these were delivered, part of the money the publishers already owed him was tied up. It was, he pretended – to Bernstein, to Gottlieb, even to himself – an imposition, a monstrously unfair trick. The angry irrationality of his complaints is hard to convey without quoting the letters in full: those on the receiving end began to think he was unhinged. Surely, Dahl railed at Gottlieb in 1979, never before in literary history had an author's income from existing books been frozen until he finished new work. Did Gottlieb and Bernstein imagine that such a policy would increase his affection for them, or encourage him to stay with them when he had fulfilled his contract?[35]

Still, the effect was to make him get back to his writing. Within a year he had delivered drafts of three books for children. They were short, but were to be among his most popular: *The Twits, George's Marvellous Medicine* and a collection of comic poems, some of which were to form the nucleus of *Revolting Rhymes*.[36] Dahl was delighted to hand over the typescripts. He asked Gottlieb for written confirmation that what he called the crooked four-book agreement between Knopf and his Swiss company has now been completed. 'I have felt that fucking contract clutching at my throat like a bloodsucking vampire ever since it was written.'[37]

13

Pencils

In 1983, thirty years after their marriage and eighteen years since Patricia Neal's strokes, she and Dahl were finally divorced. He was sixty-six years old, she fifty-six. For Pat, disabled, and rejected in favour of a younger woman, the past years had been a period of almost unalleviated wretchedness, but there was worse to come. The divorce settlement was, she says, worth next to nothing: the lawyers took account of her house in Martha's Vineyard and her earnings from films and lecture-tours, as well as of Dahl's claim that most of their children were to varying degrees dependent on him. Although Tessa was now married to a successful business-man, James Kelly, Theo was living at home and working at a new incarnation of his father's antiques business, proudly renamed Dahl & Son; and Ophelia and Lucy were still in their late teens.

Most of Pat's old friends who afterwards kept up with her ex-husband (including those most critical of him) speak well of his second wife, and of the effects of the marriage on him. One or two go so far as to claim that it even benefited Pat, by finally pushing her out of her despondency and into a fully independent life. Pat's own feelings on the matter have inevitably been more complicated, and not without bitterness, but today she is often generous about Felicity and about the care she has taken of her step-children, particularly Theo.

To outsiders looking in – as millions have been invited to do by magazine features, television programmes and books – a jarring element is the thoroughness with which the new marriage is pre-sented as having supplanted everything that went before it. Felicity and Roald Dahl's book, *Memories with Food at Gipsy House*, begins with a family tree. The couple's parents are at the top: Harald and Sofie Dahl on Roald's side; Alfonso and Elizabeth d'Abreu on Felicity's.[1] Children proliferate below: Felicity's three and Roald's four. Patricia Neal and Charles Crosland aren't there. It is as if they are nothing to do with their children – not even with their having been born.

To the Dahl children themselves, the change couldn't have failed to be painful. The older ones in particular felt loyal to Pat, and worried about her disappearing to the USA in her present misery. But even more strongly, all of them sensed a threat to their relationship with their father. Ever since Pat's illness, they had felt that in some way they had had him to themselves. Lucy says of Felicity, using an American cartoon-film baby's voice for what seems, all the same, only partly a joke, 'This woman was taking away my *Deaddy*!' Until now, Felicity's role in the family, although considerable, had been limited. As Tessa remembers things, Felicity had from time to time made what seemed like promises: that she, Felicity, would never take their father away from their mother; then, that she would never move into Gipsy House; then, that if she were to move in, she wouldn't change it at all. Inevitably, such hopes were bound to be dashed. According to their friends, Felicity's strength of will was one of her main attractions for Dahl. She also possessed formidable domestic skills. Among other things, she was interested (to a degree that Pat hadn't been) in interior decoration, eventually making it her profession: in the mid-1970s she had helped set up a successful antique restoration business named Carvers and Gilders. In *Memories with Food at Gipsy House*, some emphasis is laid on the fact that Liccy's tastes reflect an inherited view of how life should be lived in a country house. Her mother's family, Catholic recusants named Throckmorton, had lived at a grand house which now belongs to the National Trust: Coughton Court in Warwickshire.[2] Again, this was an aspect of her appeal to Roald. So, soon after Roald and Felicity married at the end of 1983, Wally Saunders' sledge-hammer was at work once again. Meals, henceforward, were to be served in an elegant dining room, rather than the familiar, scruffy, crowded kitchen. In Lucy's words, 'Suddenly we had to have all these *manners* at the table. And posh wallpaper was being put up. I mean – *oh*.'

These don't seem to be the most heinous of interventions. The girls, after all, were by now for the most part no longer living at home: during the week, Lucy was in London, sharing the Wandsworth house with Ophelia while she studied cookery. And their father may have come to think that 'manners' were not such a bad thing after all. He himself was delighted to have his surroundings transformed, so long as no one touched his writing hut or tried to stop him from passing around the chocolate bars after dinner. He was old, famous and rich. He liked living in a beautiful house and eating well in it. With these tangible indications of success, happily married for perhaps the first time, he pressed ahead with what was already proving a newly productive phase of his writing. It was during the 1980s that he published some of his best books: among them *The BFG, The Witches, Matilda* and the two autobiographies, *Boy* and *Going Solo*.

If Felicity created the way of life which her husband needed for the work he did in his last years, another important relationship was also involved. Dahl had been introduced to the illustrator Quentin Blake by Tom Maschler in the late 1970s. On and off, their partnership was to last until the writer died.

In the USA and Britain alone, Dahl had already gone through more artists than he had written children's books. Most were suggested by his publishers, and had no direct contact with the author. Blake was in his mid-forties and well established in Britain, both through prize-winning children's books and as a teacher at the Royal College of Art, where in 1978, around the time of his first meeting with Dahl, he became Head of the Department of Illustration. Blake was the writer-illustrator of many children's books of his own, and Maschler had paired him with Russell Hoban in the early 1970s; one of their collaborations, *How Tom Beat Captain Najork and His Hired Sportsmen*, had won a Whitbread Prize.

Educated at Cambridge, where he read English at Downing College under F. R. Leavis, Blake is a gentle, reflective man, in many ways Dahl's antithesis. There seems to be no malice in him, and the generosity of his sense of humour made him hesitate over some of the first Dahl stories on which he worked. However, he says that *The Enormous Crocodile* became pleasant enough to draw 'once it had been toned down by its editors', although Blake didn't find it particularly striking.[3] And although he found the next book, *The Twits*, 'very black', its extreme changes of style gradually grew on him.

On Dahl's side, one obstacle was financial. He wanted the best illustrator but, as with the earlier notion of approaching Maurice Sendak, was reluctant to sacrifice more of his royalties than he had to. Bob Gottlieb wanted Blake's drawings for the US editions, but Knopf's contract with Icarus promised Dahl 15 per cent, and Dahl argued that the illustrator should be paid over and above that. From the publisher's point of view, this was outrageous, particularly for books in which illustrations and text are of almost equal importance. Eventually, a deal was agreed by which Dahl conceded to Blake roughly a third of the authorship royalties. At the same time, he demanded that sizeable new advances be paid to Icarus, in addition to the sums already agreed with Random House and to those which Cape were paying separately.[4]

It would be hard not to like *The Enormous Crocodile*, which has a simple, cumulative plot, exciting in its threat to the children whom the crocodile is determined to eat, and funny in his simple, repeatedly-thwarted stratagems for doing so. Quentin Blake's illustrations turn the crocodile into an amiably incompetent character. He says that what he had in mind was the crocodile in a Punch and Judy show, but the result is less a reptile than a mischievous, mad-eyed, long green puppy. Dahl was happy with this collaboration and with the two that followed, but kept his options open for the long-planned book (eventually, three books) of comic poems on which he was simultaneously working, and for which he now wanted someone different. He was looking, he said, for illustrations less impressionistic and more fully representational than

Blake's – preferably by a new, young artist, who might also, of course, be persuaded to accept a lower payment.[5]

For Dahl, now in his sixties and often in poor health, keeping so many new projects in the air simultaneously was complicated. This may have contributed to his mounting irritability with his US publishers, and a corresponding rise in the influence of Tom Maschler in London. Where editorial differences arose, it was natural that Dahl should enjoy Maschler's quick enthusiasm more than the probing attentions of Gottlieb. More than ever, he tended to believe his own publicity, and when Random House wanted to Americanize some usages in *The Twits* (flannel to washcloth, long knickers to long underwear, holiday to vacation), he came on very grand and subjunctival: 'I think an English book by an English author, although it be for young children, should have an English flavour to it. Do they Americanize the Christmas Carol . . . or the novels of Jane Austen?'[6] He also took exception when an article about Gottlieb in the books section of the *New York Times* failed to mention that he edited the children's books of one writer alone – Dahl himself.[7] Still, Dahl did agree to his US publishers' request that he cut from *The Twits* a gruesomely detailed passage about nose-blowing. He also rewrote the ending of *George's Marvellous Medicine* along lines they suggested, and paid attention to notes on the comic poems from Gottlieb – who was not deterred from commenting on them by Dahl's telling him that Maschler had seen each one as it came along, and that Cape were 'enormously high' on the book.

Meanwhile, a new illustrator still had to be found. He and Maschler were, he archly joked, 'trying out a young lady – if that is the right way to put it.'[8]

Despite Dahl's restlessness, it was clear to most readers that Quentin Blake's amiable drawings were an excellent complement to his writing. They helped to unify what was in the late 1970s and early 1980s a varied output, and they softened the way the books spoke to a child's worst prejudices and fears. In *The Twits*, for example, Dahl uses children's fastidiousness as an opportunity to dwell on his own obsessive physical revulsions, particularly at facial hair. The bearded Mr Twit and the ugly, one-eyed Mrs Twit live in squalor, cruelty and mutual hatred, united only by their pursuit of birds to eat. Mr Twit keeps a cage full of pet monkeys, who join forces with an exotic bird to save the ordinary birds from slaughter. In the ensuing war – in part a reworking of *The Magic Finger*, combined with Dahl's 1945 fantasy 'Smoked Cheese'[9] – the creatures invade the house of the 'foul and smelly' and now gun-toting Twits, turn it (literally) upside down, and destroy their oppressors.

In Blake's drawings the extremism of all this is calmed by the fact that he depicts ugliness much as a child would: huge nostrils and gaping teeth sketched flat on to the face, hair a mass of bristly scribbles, fingers a bunch of bananas. And where the words are at their most microscopically disgusted – for instance, in the description of the morsels of old food lodged in Mr Twit's moustache – Blake supplies a detached, comic-book diagram, with arrows marked 'cornflake' and 'tinned sardine'.

He was similarly adroit in his handling of *George's Marvellous Medicine*. Here, the earlier book's connubial malice is replaced by frank ageism, most memorably in the depiction of the grandmother, her small mouth puckered up 'like a dog's bottom'. It is on her that the restless eight-year-old George experiments with his home-made size-altering potion. Like *The Twits*, this knockabout horror story owes something to a circus act or a Punch and Judy show: George 'really *hated* that horrid old witchy woman. And all of a sudden he had a tremendous urge to *do something* about her. Something *whopping* ... A sort of explosion.' But again Blake lightens things by visually reminding the reader both how small George is and, as he wanders around the house looking for ingredients for his medicine, how lonely and innocent. His actions come across as prompted more by curiosity than cruelty.

So too with the books of rhymes on which Blake eventually worked. *Dirty Beasts* was originally given to a new illustrator, Rosemary Fawcett; the collection of reworked fairy stories, *Revolting Rhymes*, to Blake. Blake started later but for various reasons his book appeared sooner, in 1982. In keeping with their folk-tale

16 Valerie Eaton Griffith with Patricia Neal and Roald Dahl.

17 On the set of *The Night Digger*, autumn 1970, with the film's director, Alastair Reid.

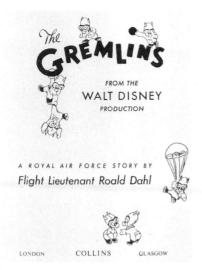

18 The title page of Dahl's never-reissued first book.

19 Black pygmy Oompa-Loompas, illustrated by Faith Jaques for the first British edition of *Charlie and the Chocolate Factory*, 1977

20 Politically corrected Oompa-Loompas, illustrated by Michael Foreman for the revised British edition, 1985

21 & 22 Two Rosemary Fawcett illustrations for the original British edition of *Dirty Beasts*, 1983. Above, 'The Porcupine'; below, 'The Tummy Beast'.

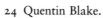

23 Preliminary drawing for *The BFG* by Quentin Blake.

24 Quentin Blake.

25 Dahl at his writing desk.

26 Tessa Dahl with her father, on the steps of the caravan at Gipsy House in 1986.

27 Theo and Ophelia Dahl with their father in 1982.

28 Felicity Dahl at Gipsy House.

29 Roald Dahl.

30 In the graveyard of the church of SS Peter and Paul, Great Missenden.

originals, the poems are as comically ruthless as anything Dahl wrote, and Blake was conscious of the artist's power with such material: when the prince, in the new version of 'Cinderella', beheads one of the Ugly Sisters (' "Try this instead!" the Prince yelled back. / He swung his trusty sword and *smack* – / Her head went crashing to the ground. / It bounced a bit and rolled around'), how much should the illustrator depict? His solution is as vivid and funny as the words, but there are no terrifying gouts of blood or splinters of bone: the head jumps up from its neck like a slice of potato, and the reader's attention is as much caught by an enormous shoe, bigger than the prince's thigh, dropping from the victim's pudgy hand. The pictures also match, but don't exaggerate, the louche, down-at-heel modernity of Dahl's rhymes – anachronistic in a way which hadn't worked in *My Uncle Oswald* but does here. There is the muddy, jerry-built market-place Blake drew for 'Jack and the Beanstalk', for example, like somewhere in Ceausescu's Romania; or Goldilocks, sprawling with her telephone and her hair-dryer; or the eager, schoolmasterly types who are Snow White's dwarves – little men with moustaches and tweed jackets, clutching at the statuesque legs of her jeans.

Blake later did a set of illustrations for the companion volume *Dirty Beasts*, to replace the ones which had been commissioned for the first edition.[10] The new version appeared in 1984, by which time he was working with Dahl directly, rather than through Tom Maschler. The results of their collaboration – a rare experience for Dahl – are to be seen in *The BFG*. But this is to jump ahead. Both *The BFG* and *Dirty Beasts* were to appear in the USA under the imprint of a new publisher, Farrar Straus Giroux. First, Dahl had to disengage himself from Knopf, a process which coincided with the final breakup of his marriage.

Quite apart from the stresses of his private life, his illnesses and his acrimonious business dealings, Dahl was contending at this time with the often burdensome intimacies prompted by being a world-renowned author. He never took his telephone number out of *Who's Who*, and at four o'clock one winter's morning, when he was about to leave for a holiday in Morocco, a man with a Brooklyn accent rang and said 'At last I have found you.'[11] Dahl was furious, but his caller apologized and explained that his eight-year-old son had died the day before. The boy had loved Dahl's books – would the author write a few words for the funeral? He agreed, and dictated something that night over the phone from Marrakesh. It was a typical response to personal tragedy. No less typically, he made sure that his friends knew about it.

One winter's morning in that same year, 1980, in her office on the twenty-first floor at 201 East 50th Street, Manhattan, Karen Latuchie, assistant to the President and Editor-in-Chief of Alfred A. Knopf Inc., opened a letter from Great Missenden. Roald Dahl wished to announce that he was running out of pencils. He said that he never failed to use Dixon Ticonderoga, and stipulated the precise type: 1388 – 2–5/10 (Medium). Would Robert Gottlieb please oblige him by instructing someone 'competent and ravishing' to buy him a packet of six dozen and send them airmail?[12]

The two men had barely resolved the latest of their quarrels concerning the Icarus contract, and Gottlieb decided that this was meant as some kind of a joke.[13] He didn't bother to reply. Three months later, Dahl wrote again.[14] Had his request for pencils reached Gottlieb? This time, after a delay of two weeks, Latuchie responded on Gottlieb's behalf. None of the local stores seemed to stock Dixon Ticonderoga, but she enclosed samples of the nearest alternative she had been able to find.

Dahl was dissatisfied. The pencils she had sent were, he said, inordinately expensive yet useless. They had no built-in erasers, weren't soft enough, and were not the right colour. He asked her to continue her efforts on his behalf by telephoning the Joseph Dixon Crucible Company in Jersey City, New Jersey, and getting hold of their sales staff. 'This surely,' he added, 'will solve our problem.'[15]

To judge from the addresses and telephone numbers of stationery firms scribbled all over this letter, some hapless office junior spent the best part of a day on the search – presumably with success, since there was no further correspondence about it. But pencils were far from the end of Dahl's demands. Apart from his continuing grievance about what he described as the grotesquely unjust four-book deal which, he said, had been forced on him by Knopf,[16] he was now dissatisfied with the royalty payable to him from a long-standing US paperback agreement negotiated on his behalf by Knopf.[17] These financial complaints brought with them a host of other irritations. In January 1981 he was enraged by the US cover design for *The Twits*, because his name was smaller than the title and 'a good deal more unobstrusive [sic]'.[18] In February he wrote to Gottlieb, comparing him unfavourably with Tom Maschler in his attention to such matters, and claiming too that Gottlieb didn't use his position in the company to 'protect' Dahl.[19] There was yet another grumble. Random House, Dahl now wildly alleged, had tricked him by arranging a life-insurance policy for which he said that he had discovered he had to make hundreds of thousands of dollars' worth of top-up payments. The firm's legal department was making difficulties, he also claimed, and he had decided that if such sources of dissatisfaction continued, he would offer his next book to another house.

Gottlieb had had enough. As a publisher, he has always operated on what he calls the 'Fuck You' Principle – under which he will take 'almost any amount of shit from any given writer', with the unspoken proviso that when he can take no more, he is free 'to turn around and say "Fuck You" '.[20] He now activated the principle in a letter to Dahl:

Dear Roald,

This is not in response to the specifics of your last several letters to me and my colleagues, but a general response to everything we've heard from you in the past year or two.

In brief, and as unemotionally as I can state it: since the time when you decided that Bob Bernstein, I and the rest of us had dealt badly with you over your contract, you have behaved to us in a way I can honestly say is unmatched in my experience for overbearingness and utter lack of civility. Lately you've begun addressing others here – who are less well placed to answer you back – with the same degree of abusiveness. For a while I put your behavior down to the physical pain you were in and so managed to excuse it. Now I've come to believe that you're just enjoying a prolonged tantrum and are bullying us.

Your threat to leave Knopf after this current contract is fulfilled leaves us far from intimidated. Harrison, Bernstein and I will be sorry to see you depart, for business reasons, but these are not strong enough to make us put up with your manner to us any longer. I've worked hard for you editorially but had already decided to stop doing so; indeed, you've managed to make the entire experience of publishing you unappealing for all of us – counter-productive behavior, I would have thought.

To be perfectly clear, let me reverse your threat: unless you start acting civilly to us, there is no possibility of our agreeing to continue to publish you. Nor will I – or any of us – answer any future letter that we consider to be as rude as those we've been receiving.

Regretfully,
BG.

According to Gottlieb, when his letter went off, everyone at Knopf who had lately been dealing with Dahl 'stood on their desks and cheered'.

Perhaps publishing, as much as marriage, represents the triumph of hope over experience. When Tom Maschler steered the typescripts of *Dirty Beasts* and *The BFG* downtown to Farrar Straus Giroux on Union Square, Dahl's next US publishers were delighted: none more so than a young editor, Stephen Roxburgh. In his previous career both in a children's library and as an academic specialist in children's literature, Roxburgh had seen the extraordinary hold his new author exerted over child readers – readers who, in the prosperous and indulgent post-Spock middle-class families of the 1980s, had a good deal more say than previous generations of children over which books were bought for them.

As always, Dahl was keen to start the relationship on a footing of complicity. He wrote to Roxburgh, inviting his comments on *The BFG* while making it clear that he didn't want to have to do any major new work on the book. In the course of the letter, he took the opportunity to disparage both Gottlieb ('too much arrogance there and that is not easy to stomach') and his former publishers in general. He promised that on a future occasion, he would reveal to Roxburgh what he described as the 'astonishing financial evils perpetrated by the Random House gang'.[21]

A serious, precise, tweed-jacket-and-grey-flannel-trousers anglophile, Roxburgh was flattered. He admired and liked Dahl personally, and quickly became a proxy son, with whom the older man could trade opinions about books and wine. In a way, it was the relationship with Alfred Knopf with the seniority – and the power – reversed.

Their first dealings were straightforwardly professional. Farrar Straus decided to delay publication of *Dirty Beasts*, partly to avoid a clash when Knopf brought out *Revolting Rhymes*, but principally because they wanted to begin their association with Dahl on a more substantial book. It was already clear – not least to its author[22] – that *The BFG* had the makings of a commercial success comparable at the very least with that of *James* or *Charlie*.

In imaginative terms, the draft was already superior to both of the earlier books. As in most of Dahl's children's stories, the essential plot is like a folk-tale: a giant and a small girl together bring about the defeat of a cannibalistic tribe of monsters.[23] Both the relationship and the bullying which threatens it were situations of a kind that had always brought out Dahl's strongest feelings, but there are several other elements. The Big Friendly Giant is a resonant fictional character, with his funny and in a way beautiful confusions of speech (learnt from Pat), and his skill as a dream-maker. And out of the familiar child's-story premises of reversal and changes of scale, Dahl had invented some memorable comic episodes: the downward-acting lemonade which makes the BFG fart (he calls it whizzpopping) rather than burp; his breakfast in the ballroom at Buckingham Palace, off a ping-pong table resting on four grandfather clocks. There was plenty here for Quentin Blake to work on.

The draft had already been seen by an editor at Cape, Valerie

Buckingham, who made a number of comments which, if 'politically correct', were more importantly motivated by narrative plausibility.[24] For example, she suggested to Dahl that the BFG's original list of the international victims of the Bonecruncher would impress Sophie more if they weren't all men. 'Agree,' Dahl cheerily replied. 'It takes a woman to spot this!' Similarly, he agreed to her idea that when the BFG says that boys despise girls' dreams, it would be natural for Sophie to show some reaction.[25] His concessions, though, were based on character and plot: he was persuaded by what made sense in relation to Sophie, not by any appeal to the tastes of his audience. When his editor's caution extended to a religious-cum-dietary anxiety about the BFG's demands for sausages and bacon at breakfast in Buckingham Palace, Dahl was unmoved.

All of Valerie Buckingham's comments were passed on to Farrar Straus, but the ambitious Stephen Roxburgh preferred to do his own editing, and approached the typescript afresh as if all the responsibility were his own. He took the book home and read it several times, working in the evenings and at weekends. He even read it aloud. Then he spent a couple of days drafting a letter to Dahl: ten typed pages in single line-spacing, commenting minutely on inconsistencies, superfluities, repetitions, clichés and matters of taste.[26] He also entirely rewrote two short passages of dialogue,[27] and made a number of other substantive comments, one of which was to prompt Dahl to write the famous episode in which the BFG whizzpops for the Queen. All this was more, of course, than had been asked for. Roxburgh diplomatically dressed his comments up with compliments to the author on his 'unusual' and 'wonderfully refreshing' attention 'to the minutest aspects of the manuscript'. Nothing he had picked on was of any great significance, he said. The book 'could be published as it is and be quite successful.'

Quite successful? In US English the adverb means 'very', but in Britain its usual implication is 'moderately'. Perhaps half-jokingly, Dahl seized on it in his reply, saying that he believed he had never written a book which was only averagely successful. But for the rest, he fell into the BFG's own boisterous idiom and said that he was 'absolutely swishboggled and sloshbunkled' by the trouble Roxburgh had taken, assuring him – as he had previously assured Robert Gottlieb, and before him Fabio Coen – that no editor had ever treated his work so meticulously. Dahl now incorporated word for word Roxburgh's new passages of dialogue.[28] He even accepted without demur that there was too much danger of causing offence with his original description of the Bloodbottling Giant, a dark-skinned, flat-nosed monster with 'thick rubbery lips . . . like two gigantic purple frankfurters lying one on top of the other'. This was a 'derisive stereotype', Roxburgh had told him plainly. At the end of his reply, Dahl scrawled, 'The negro lips thing is taken care of.'[29]

In their exchanges, Roxburgh often referred to classic authors such as Walter Scott or Robert Louis Stevenson, and phrased his comments on Dahl in the critical language he might have used of them. The author repaid the compliment in a way that reflected still further glory on himself, by nicknaming Roxburgh 'Max Perkins' after the famous editor of Scott Fitzgerald and Hemingway. In one letter, Dahl also compared himself with Flannery O'Connor, who had said that after the first draft, she took all the advice she could get.[30] Meanwhile, he and Roxburgh began to correspond regularly about other writers: Steinbeck, Golding, Graham Greene. Dahl resisted the younger man's recommendation of Isaac Bashevis Singer, but shared his enthusiasm for thriller writers, particularly Robert B. Parker and Elmore Leonard. Soon, Roxburgh was invited to stay with Roald and Felicity at Gipsy House where, in the course of many subsequent visits, he gradually came to meet most of the family. When Ophelia visited New York in her late teens, she was encouraged to spend time with him, and they became good friends. Dahl also asked him to look out for one of Felicity's daughters, Charlotte, when she visited New York on the rebound from a love-affair.

It was a far cry from Rayner Unwin's view of the proper relationship between publisher and author. Unwin says he saw himself, like his father before him with the third Earl Russell, as an Edwardian tradesman: each party kept his distance. Roxburgh's intimacy with his author was likely to end badly, not only because most of Dahl's professional friendships did, but because as the younger man's editing became more and more thorough – a matter of wholesale reconstruction, rather than simply of adjustment – so it became obvious to Dahl that his protégé was in danger of seeing himself as someone important. In terms of Dahl's writing, he soon was important.

For a year or two all continued smoothly. That Roxburgh's reverence for Dahl had limits was obvious both to himself and to his boss, Roger Straus, as early as February 1983, when Roxburgh wrote an internal memo on a selection of classic ghost stories which Dahl had put together twenty-five years earlier for Alfred Knopf's movie-producer half-brother Edwin, and which Cape were now planning to publish.[31] Roxburgh thought the selection not only outdated and excessively British, but uninteresting even on its own terms. The introduction, he said, was 'hopeless – a long ramble involving women in the arts, children's books, personal reminiscence and, it seems, anything else that came to mind while he was at his desk'. But a typescript with more potential was about to arrive at Farrar Straus. It was the first draft of what was to become one of Dahl's most popular books, *The Witches*.[32]

Dahl was now writing steadily and fast. *The BFG*, published in 1982, *The Witches* (1983), *Boy* (1984), *Going Solo* (1986) and *Matilda* (1988), are all full-length narratives, and he also turned out another picture book for young children, *The Giraffe and the Pelly and Me* (1985), dedicated to his stepdaughters Neisha, Charlotte and Lorina. One factor in his productivity, as well as in the books' fast-increasing success, was, as we have seen, the relationship with Quentin Blake. At first Maschler wanted only a few pictures for *The BFG*. Blake roughed out sketches of the main characters and scenes and showed them to Dahl, but he was disappointed that there were not more, and they discussed how to develop them.[33] Both men were prepared to work hard on the minutest details. The BFG originally wore boots, but when Dahl saw the drawings, he decided that a change was needed. Together, he and Blake considered other forms of footwear, until the author produced a Norwegian type of sandal which he himself wore, and which Blake copied. Similarly, an apron which the BFG was described as wearing in the original draft 'got in the way' in the pictures, so Dahl removed it. These harmonious dealings, and Dahl's with Roxburgh, formed a basis for the fuller collaborations which were to follow.

In the case of *The BFG*, Dahl was also rewarded by one of those coincidences in which life imitates fiction. The story takes the giant to Buckingham Palace, where he blows a dream through the Queen's bedroom window warning her of the bad giants' attacks on children. When she wakes, Sophie is sitting on the window-sill while the BFG prowls in the garden outside. One night in July 1982, between the book's completion and its publication, the real Queen Elizabeth II woke up in Buckingham Palace to find a man called Michael Fagan in her bedroom. Dahl delighted in the story and, long after it had died down in the newspapers, he would fantasize ribaldly that Fagan had 'actually done it' with the Queen, and had been got rid of by the security services.[34]

The most likeable of all Dahl's books, *The BFG* was an instant success. In Britain, it was reviewed in almost every newspaper and magazine, by other children's writers, novelists, academics.[35] A report by the Book Marketing Council showed that of the ten books bought in largest numbers at the time for children, four were by Roald Dahl: *The BFG*, *George's Marvellous Medicine*, *Revolting Rhymes* and *The Twits*. The new story became Dahl's most popular children's title in Germany.[36] In France, where he is better known than any French writer for children, it is second only to *Charlie and the Chocolate Factory*.[37] It was translated into Afrikaans, Basque and Slovene, and appeared in a bilingual edition in Japan. Dahl rewarded himself by taking Felicity for a winter holiday in Barbados.

The first edition of *Dirty Beasts*, with Rosemary Fawcett's illustrations, had a less smooth passage. To one British critic, Russell Davies, 'the buzz of misanthropy from Roald Dahl grows stronger'.[38] Candida Lycett Green rightly said that there was nothing new about this mood: she saw the first poem, in which a pig forestalls its destiny by turning on the farmer and eating him, as a version of the macabre, much earlier story 'Pig', in which a boy brought up as a vegetarian ends up in an abattoir.[39] She thought that Dahl's imagination was well illustrated by Rosemary Fawcett: 'the nastiness of her pictures is exceptional'.

This was meant as a compliment, but not everyone saw things this way. There couldn't be a bigger contrast than between Quentin Blake's benignly funny sketches and the giddying, lurid, surrealistic images Rosemary Fawcett produced. Her cover picture sets the tone: a child in bed with a teddy bear, both of them bug-eyed with terror at the sight of something positioned above and behind the viewer's head. It is the perspective that is often most violent in these images – that and the colours. For 'The Tummy Beast', Fawcett threw the greedy child over so that he is somehow flying upside down, all chubby knees and protruding eyeballs, beneath a gaudy table full of purple and mauve blancmanges and ice-creams. And in 'The Porcupine', the reader is made to peer as if through a keyhole on to a murky scene lit by a single lamp, in which a goggling dentist waves his gigantic pointed pincers over the little girl's much-spiked rump.

Fawcett does more than justice to Dahl's ferocity, but not to his humour or his underlying traditionalism. Dahl himself hated the drawings. He said he couldn't face giving the book to any of his relations, and offered to incinerate all the unsold copies and dance around the bonfire.[40] Many of the British reviews warned that Fawcett's pictures would give children nightmares, and this was the general opinion in the USA, where the children's librarians were in full, squeamish cry: 'sadistic, predictable and unfunny'[41]; 'From stem to stern this is a gross, course [sic] unpleasant book.'[42] The edition didn't sell badly in Britain, but although, according to Murray Pollinger, Tom Maschler swore by Fawcett's work,[43] the illustrations were unpopular with Continental publishers.[44] *Revolting Rhymes*, meanwhile, had sold over 100,000 copies in Britain alone. So Fawcett's *Dirty Beasts* was eventually allowed to go out of print, and Quentin Blake was brought back in for the new edition.

Stephen Roxburgh was not surprised by the response to *Dirty Beasts*, and was keen to educate Dahl about other aspects of the new climate in which his books were appearing. This was not 'censorship'. Like any good editor, including Robert Gottlieb before him, Roxburgh saw it as part of his job to point out where an elderly, conservative, distinctly bloody-minded Englishman might, in the modern USA, cause offence of kinds or degrees which he perhaps hadn't intended, or which, even if intentional, seemed gratuitous. Dahl was free to reject these suggestions, but was not always as inflexible about them as might have been anticipated.

In the case of *The BFG*, as we have seen, some of the softening up had already been done by Valerie Buckingham, the editor who first worked on the typescript at Cape.[45] For *The Witches* Roxburgh was in sole charge, and because Dahl had been so impressed by his work on the earlier book, he let him see the new manuscript in what, to the editor's eyes, was a much less finished state. This time, the first discussions took place in England, and in an atmosphere of some tension.[46] Dahl dropped the book off at the house in London where Roxburgh was staying. Almost immediately, the author's agent was on the phone. Dahl, he said, was anxiously waiting for a response.

Unintimidated but not without apprehension, the methodical Roxburgh read the typescript through twice. The following morning, he travelled by train from Marylebone to Great Missenden. Dahl met him at the station, took him home to Gipsy House, organized coffee and cigarettes, and asked for his reactions.

The draft contained the embryo of the final version: a plot by the Grand High Witch and her fellow hags to turn all the children of the world into mice. As in the published book, the plan is accidentally discovered by a little boy and his grandmother. But in the manuscript, they otherwise took little part in the action. Their function was to give Dahl an opportunity to include long passages of autobiographical material about Norway and his school-days.

In another narrative strand, a different boy, the gluttonous Bruno Jenkins, single-handedly outwits and defeats the Witches.

Roxburgh wrote to a friend soon afterwards, describing his reaction to the draft, and his solution:

A thoroughly disagreeable character, other than the first person narrator, gets all the good parts, while the narrator, the barely displaced Dahl/boy, was merely an observer . . . somehow the narrator had to become the hero. My suggestion . . . was that Dahl have the witches turn the narrator into a mouse and then he could do everything that Bruno did. It took quite a while for me to nerve myself up to making this suggestion, because [those I made] for THE BFG, while extensive, were hardly radical – i.e. entailing a complete revision of the manuscript. Frankly, I wasn't at all sure how he would take to what I had to say. Well . . . he immediately saw what I was about, and began imagining the consequences of such a development. We toyed with it for an hour or two, came up with some terrific possibilities, and broke off for a walk after about two and a half hours. He was going to proceed according to what we had discussed and send me a revised ms.[47]

Roxburgh also suggested that, in revising the book, Dahl should set aside most of the autobiographical material.

A second version reached Farrar Straus in March. Once again, Dahl's agent telephoned immediately, spelling out to Roxburgh that he had better be 'both gentle and quick'.[48] Once again, the editor wrote his author a long letter.

Dahl had taken all Roxburgh's advice, but several weaknesses remained, and others had been introduced with the new material. The Grandmother was now a strong character – perhaps too strong, if the little boy was to be the book's hero. He needed more initiative and more autonomy, and Roxburgh cautiously proposed some new turns in the plot:

Our hero, for instance, could remember that the Witch's room is under their own. He could, perhaps, remembering his experiments with William and Mary [his pet mice] suggest some kind of rope trick that he could perform. In other words, he could initiate some of the action and proceed, if you will, through the maze of the plot, finding his way around obstacles as he does in the new scenes you've created.

There were other suggestions, to do with the characterization of the Grand High Witch and the tone of the ending. All these new details were finally incorporated by Dahl, as well as Roxburgh's idea that the witches might find it harder to smell dirty children than clean ones, and dozens of other minor points about consistency, repetition and probability.

Meanwhile, with a fair amount of apology for the 'pseudo-liberal librarian mentality', Roxburgh drew Dahl's attention to occasions in the story when women took 'a lot of abuse'. The author dismissed all this as brusquely as his editor's concern for wig-wearers (who, Roxburgh seems to have feared, might be upset by the Grandmother's assertion that all witches are bald). 'No,' Dahl replied, 'I am not as frightened of offending women as you are.'

Besides, as he pointed out, the nicest character in *The Witches* is a woman: the Grandmother. And one of the story's points lies in her encouragement of unorthodoxy. For example, she is a heavy smoker, and offers her grandson a puff of her cigar.[49] With Roxburgh's help, Dahl had developed the relationship into an unexpectedly benign parable of toleration. In the first draft, the child was turned back into a human being. In the new version, he remains a mouse, and the moral is explicit: 'It doesn't matter who you are or what you look like so long as somebody loves you.' This is like the lesson the BFG learns, when his fear that he speaks 'the most terrible wigglish' is allayed by Sophie's telling him she thinks he talks beautifully.[50] Later, there was to be a similar appeal on behalf of outsiders in the characterization of Matilda – an outcast at home because she is clever, likes reading and is a girl. Under the combined influences of Stephen Roxburgh and of marital happiness, Dahl's books were changing, and had something more durable to offer to readers than current social orthodoxy.

Both in Britain and in the USA, however, literary criticism was at the time turning into a kind of secular Inquisition, bent on rooting out heresy. From a historical perspective, there was something depressingly circular about a response to *The Witches* published in the *Times Educational Supplement*, where the feminist cultural commentator Catherine Itzin compared the book with fifteenth-century witch-hunting tracts, without noticing that she was talking like something of a witch-hunter herself. Itzin described Dahl's story as 'part of the process' of both pornography and the physical abuse of women.[51] It didn't matter that Dahl's much seized-upon words, 'A witch is always a woman', are followed in the book by 'a ghoul is always a male. So indeed is a barghest.' Nor did it change anything to argue that the idea 'witches are always women' isn't the same as 'women are always witches'. Despite all this, and despite the character of Grandmamma, *The Witches*, Itzin asserts, is an example of 'how boys learn to become men who hate and harm women'.

A difficulty in answering such criticism is that when Itzin says 'Womanhatred is at the core of Dahl's writing', some of his earlier fiction seems to bear her out. Stories like 'Nunc Dimittis' and 'The Last Act' could easily be thought to hate women. But even in them, Dahl's misogyny is arguably just one side of his misanthropy. In other stories, such as 'The Way Up To Heaven' and 'William and Mary', the gender-sympathies are reversed, women taking enjoyably savage revenges on men who have ill-treated them. Similarly, *The Witches* is *The BFG* after a series of sex-changes. An old woman and a little boy collaborate in overthrowing the forces of evil, represented by (female) witches. In *The BFG*, the characters are an old man, a little girl, and (male) giants.

For this kind of argument, though, it was enough to have found a few examples of unpleasant women in his children's books: the aunts who are disposed of at the beginning of *James and the Giant Peach*; the grandmother in *George's Marvellous Medicine* who doesn't want George to grow, and who is therefore obviously a castrator. According to one critic, 'Almost every one of [Dahl's] numerous books re-hashes the same tired plot: a meek small boy finally turns on his adult female tormentors and kills them.' This was Michèle Landsberg, in a reference guide to children's literature published (to Dahl's fury) by Penguin in 1986.[52] To make her theory work, one has to improvise a fair amount. Perhaps Danny (whom Landsberg doesn't mention) has bumped off his own mother before his story begins. Both Sophie and the bad giants in *The BFG* (also omitted) are, say, transvestites. And in *Fantastic Mr Fox* (again, not referred to), the husband and children must be secretly planning to turn Mrs Fox over to the gunmen outside. But if such dogma takes on an imaginative life of its own, its results couldn't be more comical than Landsberg's own reading of the moment in *George's Marvellous Medicine* when the grandmother feels the first effects of George's powerful potion: 'There's squigglers in my belly!' she cries, 'There's bangers in my bottom!' This, Landsberg says, is 'a parody of a rape'.[53] It's hard to imagine what she might have made of the BFG's whizzpopping in front of the Queen.

Dahl won support in all this from an unexpected quarter. One of the best reviews of *The Witches* was written by Erica Jong for the *New York Times* Book Review.[54] Jong, the author of a book about witches, praised Dahl for seeing that 'children love the macabre, the terrifying, the mythic'. His witches have to be horrifying, she says, in order for the tale to convey not only its heroism, but its deeper meaning, which is 'about the fear of death as separation and a child's mourning for the loss of his parents':

> Mr Dahl's hero is happy when he is turned into a mouse – not only because of his speed and dexterity (and because he doesn't have to go to school), but also because his short life span now means that he will never have to be parted from his beloved grandmother as he has been from his parents. Already well into her 80's, she has only a few years to live, and he as a mouse-person is granted the same few years . . .
>
> 'The Witches' is finally a love story . . . It is a curious sort of tale but an honest one, which deals with matters of crucial importance to children: smallness, the existence of evil in the world, mourning, separation, death.

Jong's short review, which also conveys the fun of the book, helps to bring into focus how Dahl – here as in *The BFG* – was drawing together and fantasizing upon his deepest relationships: with his dead mother and father, and with his own children and his grand-daughter, Tessa's child Sophie – after whom the heroine is named. In the case of *The Witches*, it was his editor who had shown him how to link these preoccupations to the narrative which, originally, was simply superimposed on them. Dahl told Roxburgh, 'I am overwhelmed by the help you have been giving me.'[55] Not long afterwards, he wrote saying that he was horrified that someone like himself, who had once been quite a good writer of short stories, skilled at paring his work down to the minimum, was now 'having to be taught this art all over again – by you'.[56]

He was by then at work on a new project which Roxburgh had put to him. Why, he had asked, didn't Dahl take some of the autobiographical material he had finally left out of *The Witches* and put it towards a separate memoir, written for child readers?[57] Dahl answered that he found the notion 'rather intriguing', and agreed that perhaps he could collect some anecdotes. But he disapproved of straight autobiography: 'I regard that as the height of egotism.'[58]

14

Three Cheers for Stephen Roxburgh

While Dahl was becoming increasingly dependent on Stephen Roxburgh's input into his writing, he also got on very well with
Roxburgh's boss, the shrewd and tough Roger Straus. All the more
so after the income tax inspectors found out about Icarus, and
demanded almost a million dollars in overdue taxes.[1] Searching for
ways to help Dahl raise funds, Straus discovered a loophole in the
US paperback contract on his earlier children's books – one of
the agreements with whose supposed iniquities Dahl had become
so obsessed. There was a clause, Straus discovered, which allowed
the author to free himself in the event of Random House's coming
under new ownership – as had recently occurred with the take-
over by 'Si' Newhouse. After lengthy negotiations, and despite the
increasingly frantic pleas of Random House (who were themselves
planning a new juvenile paperback imprint[2]), Dahl triumphantly
carried off the paperback rights in six of his best-known titles,
among them *James and the Giant Peach* and *Charlie and the Chocolate Factory*, to Peter Mayer, chief of Viking Penguin, who was
expanding his children's list, Puffin, in the USA. The advance payment on the deal was $1.3 million, although Dahl grumbled to
Straus that after slices had been taken by the Inland Revenue,
Random House and his agent, his share would only come to
$50,000 a year.[3] Still, Dahl described it as 'a victory over the forces
of evil'. What a monster his former Random House publisher Bob
Bernstein now seemed! He had just appeared on British television.
'My God, how ugly he is,' Dahl wrote of his old friend, before

launching into a minute, repulsive verbal caricature of his appearance.[4]

By now, 1987, Penguin had in print more or less everything Dahl had ever published except *The Gremlins*, which is owned by Walt Disney, *Sometime Never*, which he had decided to forget about, and a couple of autobiographical pieces which he now intended to rework in his memoir. For some time already, paperback readers had been able to buy not only all of Dahl's original short story collections, including *Over To You* and *Someone Like You*, but also, or instead, many of the same stories reshuffled under new titles: *Tales of the Unexpected* (1979) and *More Tales of the Unexpected* (1980). After 1986 they could buy them yet again, as *Completely Unexpected Tales*. All of these volumes were kept in print simultaneously. The packaging of Roald Dahl had begun.

Part of the process involved his being presented as not only an extremely good writer of children's books and a bestseller, but a Great Writer. From his earliest Washington days, Dahl had not only imagined being, but had behaved as if he were Great, and saw no inconsistency between this and his willingness to tailor his writing to the market. After his return to England, he had been irritated by the fact that he wasn't always being mentioned – indeed, perhaps hadn't even been heard of – by leading British critics of the time such as Cyril Connolly, V. S. Pritchett and Peter Quennell.[5] In the eyes of Martha Gellhorn, his literary ambition was one of the things that differentiated him from Ian Fleming. According to her, Fleming's writing was 'so embarrassing it was never *mentioned*. But Ian didn't have any notion of anything else. I think Roald thought he was really writing very good stuff [for adults]. He thought he was a serious and good writer, and I don't think he was very pleased that nobody serious *took* him seriously.'

As we have seen, the reasons why Dahl had offered his first children's books to Alfred Knopf were that adult stories were no longer coming to him and that, when they did, he found it hard to get them published in the kinds of magazine that were respected.[6] In more recent times, though, he had increasingly come not only to accept but to insist that he was a classic children's author. On the vexed issue of Americanization, he argued to Stephen Roxburgh much as he had to Robert Gottlieb, that to change *The Witches* for US readers would be as absurd as to rewrite *Alice* for them.[7] Beyond the question of his personal standing, if there was one thing he and the literary critics could agree on, it was that children's books were a last bastion of cultural values against the inroads of television. And if writing for children was therefore more important than writing for adults, it was also, he now claimed, much harder. The fact that so few famous adult authors tried to do it was in his view clear proof that he was right. He had seen Iris Murdoch on television talking about the value of children's books, and told people he had wanted to ask the 'silly old hag' why she didn't produce some herself.

One of the reasons for his vociferousness about this was that, in his own country, Dahl's popularity was not matched by any kind of official recognition. Just as at school he wasn't a prefect, and during the war he had won no medals, so it was not until 1983 that he was awarded a British literary prize: the Whitbread Prize, for *The Witches*. He was delighted, but it wasn't enough.[8] He was beginning to expect a knighthood.

His first move in this direction was a new campaign of self-publicity. Dahl took pride in what he called his 'Child Power'.[9] Without much exaggeration, he said that he could walk into any house in Europe or the USA and if there were children living there, he would be recognized and made welcome. It would have been all the more pity, then, if what they knew about him as a person had been presented in an unfavourable light. One of the ways in which Roxburgh made a memoir seem a good idea was to remind Dahl of a forthcoming biographical book about him which was being written for children by Chris Powling,[10] and to hint that what the kids really wanted was Dahl's own version: 'I think it would be so much better for young children to have your account written as only you can write it of whatever part of your life you choose to make open to them.'[11]

The suggestion was attractive now, coming as it did only a

couple of years after the embarrassingly-timed transmission of a television film, *The Patricia Neal Story*, based on Barry Farrell's *Pat and Roald*. Directed by Anthony Page and Anthony Harvey, the drama-documentary about Patricia Neal's stroke and recovery was completed at around the time that the couple were splitting up. Dahl himself, played by Dirk Bogarde, is favourably treated in the film (and has a great deal more hair than in real life), but although his behaviour is seen as crucial to Neal's rehabilitation, there is no fudging of its toughness – early on, in the hospital, he is shown slapping her face hard – or of the moody aggressiveness of his temperament in general. To Dahl, another unwelcome surprise may have been that the main character in the script, unlike in the book, was not himself but Neal. According to Anthony Page, Dahl telephoned Dirk Bogarde at the Connaught Hotel during the shooting and said he wanted to rewrite the whole thing. If there was any resistance, Bogarde and Glenda Jackson would have to leave the project. 'He was just trying it on. But he wasn't at all pleased with the result.'[12]

Other, more compliant accounts of Dahl's life appeared in the 1980s. As it turned out, Chris Powling's *Roald Dahl*, first published in 1983, proved as satisfactory as Barry Farrell's book. Here, once again, was the Dahl who had been 'shot down and crippled in an air-battle',[13] who invented the RAF myth of the Gremlins,[14] and was the first to expose the USA's dastardly plan 'to take over Europe's commercial airlines after the war' – a discovery which Dahl now made all the more dramatic by redating it so that it came before Pearl Harbor.[15] There were new elements to the myth. In 1965 Dahl had ditched the then little-known Robert Altman from an ultimately unrealized film project which had been Altman's own idea.[16] In Powling's book the episode is presented as a battle fought on Altman's behalf, but lost to the mighty producers, who 'couldn't recognize talent when they saw it staring them in the face'.[17]

Meanwhile, the autobiography encouraged by Stephen Roxburgh enabled Dahl to put his legend in a longer perspective, and to record too some colourful stories of his early life with which he had entertained his own children. In compiling them, he used

Roxburgh as a research assistant, sending to New York boxes full of childhood letters to Sofie Dahl, school essays and photographs. Roxburgh put them in order, sifted them, and cannibalized them for information which he then returned to Dahl for the narrative. Or narratives – for it soon became clear that there was enough material for more than one book, and that episodes which Dahl had drafted about Shell, East Africa and the war in Greece could be saved for a subsequent volume, leaving the first focused on his school-days.[18]

The draft still consisted of little more than a number of scrappy and unlinked anecdotes. Roxburgh suggested various ways in which Dahl could develop, expand and pull them together, for example by repositioning a section about holidays in Norway, adding to the material about Repton, and particularly by giving shape to the relationship with his mother, whose full importance Roxburgh had gleaned from the childhood letters. 'You are not the only ... major character', Roxburgh boldly told Dahl. 'From before your birth until 1936, your mother dominated your life.' For this reason, he thought that *Boy* (for which the first title suggested by Dahl was 'I Want to Grow Up'[19]) should end with the family's seeing the young man off at the docks, bound for Africa. The eventual climax of the second volume could be his return from the war, 'straight into the arms of the waiting mother.'

In effect, Roxburgh was explaining Dahl to himself, turning a collection of noisy but unassimilated memories into a more coherent and reflective story. It may not be a coincidence that during the couple of years in which they worked together, reconstructing his childhood, Dahl's tendency to slip back into the idiom of a rather stagy English schoolboy became increasingly marked. His letters were strewn with 'By golly' and 'Absolutely spiffing'. 'Three cheers for Stephen Roxburgh,' he wrote to Roger Straus about *Boy*.[20]

If Roxburgh helped Dahl to interpret himself, he also confirmed his sense of Greatness. He sees Dahl as 'a truly great writer', and told him at the time that the childhood papers he had sent to Farrar Straus were 'an extraordinary archive of a life, a period in history, and a society.' Dahl repaid the compliment by inviting Roxburgh to be his official biographer. It was understood that progress would be slow. The book was not intended for publication during its subject's life, and Roxburgh had domestic commitments as well as a full-time job. But by May 1985 he had cleared his desk of other work, and was beginning to plan his research.

Although Roxburgh didn't notice, things were already beginning to show signs of going wrong. Dahl had become very keen on his paperback publisher Peter Mayer, Chief Executive of Penguin and a charming, gifted and energetic man. His author always liked to deal direct with the top. Roxburgh was still only a relatively junior figure at Farrar Straus – although, partly as a result of Dahl's encouragement, he was gaining confidence and prestige to a degree that the older man did not always welcome. When, in the summer of 1984, Dahl delivered *The Giraffe and the Pelly and Me*, Roxburgh didn't send one of his diplomatic letters, full of cautiously-presented suggestions, but simply annotated the typescript.[21] Dahl wrote thanking him but – somewhat ominously to anyone who knew the history of his dealings with publishers – enclosed a copy of an enthusiastic letter about the book from Tom Maschler: 'Vintage Dahl. And with new aspects as well. What more could one ask?'[22] Socially too it seemed to Dahl that Roxburgh was becoming bumptious. Roxburgh thinks, with hindsight, that he may have angered the old man by finishing an anecdote for him in front of other people, and by arguing with him on a question of wine.[23] Dahl began to complain about such solecisms to Maschler, telling him 'I can't stand that pedantic, prissy Roxburgh any more.'[24]

There was no opportunity yet for a major row. Roxburgh was doing more of what Dahl called his super-editing on 'Boy 2', the draft of *Going Solo*, while the author was very busy elsewhere. *Sophiechen und der Riese (The BFG)* won the major German prize for children's books, the Deutscher Jugendliteraturpreis, in 1984. Dahl was in continual demand all over the world for lectures, book-signings and other appearances, at which he drew unprecedented crowds. Although he had forsworn any direct involvement in movies, he spent some time discussing the possibility of turning a Grimm story into a film-script, and sold the film rights in *The BFG, Danny* and *The Witches*.[25] After Icarus was rumbled, Dahl had dissolved the family trusts. All his business was now conducted, under the name Dahl & Dahl, from an office behind Gipsy House. Here, clerical staff dealt with his sacks of correspondence while, dressed in a loose cardigan and an old pair of trousers, he sat at the dining table smoking, making decisions, telephoning his bookies and dictating replies to fan letters: 'Dear lovely, gorgeous Sheila and all the clever children in your class . . . '.[26]

At weekends, it was rare if he was not surrounded by at least some of his large family – wife, children, stepchildren, grandchildren, sisters and their broods. He enjoyed knowing that their cars, many of which he had paid for, were drawn up like a circle of wagons at the back of the house, next to his BMW, Liccy's Ford and Theo's Vauxhall.[27] On Friday nights, a random assortment of friends would come for the ritual snooker game: Wally, who now acted as the Dahls' chauffeur; the local plumber; a surgeon from the Chiltern Hospital; and whoever else happened to be around. Visitors noticed how happy Felicity had made her husband. 'All the years that I first knew Roald I never saw him peaceful,' one neighbour says. 'If there's such a thing as inner peace, that came with Liccy.'

Both he and Felicity were hospitable, and knowledgeable about food and wine. Roald had always bought wine cleverly, sometimes at country house auctions. Often, now, he went straight to the source – he 'went banco' on the excellent clarets of 1982, of which he invested in 'a thousand cases'.[28] Felicity employed and trained a succession of gifted cooks. *Memories with Food at Gipsy House* is a panegyric to the subtleties of this variety of onion or that ham, and the right places to buy butter or pick mushrooms. To a modern version of feudal clan values also. The recipes were provided by relatives, friends and retainers, including Felicity's grandfather's ex-batman. Posed pictures of napery and fresh vegetables vie for space with family snapshots: picnics, cricket on the lawn. In the all-inclusive but unmistakably hierarchical scheme of things, near the end of the book there is a page about dogs – just before the section on suppliers, whose addresses hover somewhere between the photo credits of a glossy magazine feature and an older, more cap-in-hand form of advertising. You half expect Candle Makers Suppliers ('Food-Grade Wax for Jam Jars') of 28 Blythe Road, London W14, to have a badge over the door: By Appointment to the Late Roald Dahl, Esq., Purveyors of Culinary Sealants.

Some of Felicity's stepchildren missed the days when everyone used to sit around the untidy kitchen table, Pat often still in her dressing-gown, Roald with a Bloody Mary, listening to *The World At One*.[29] But a stand-off had been reached, partly as a result of firmness on Roald's part. One day, when Lucy was being particularly intractable, her father called her into his bedroom and told her that she had to give Felicity a chance, 'and if you can't be nice to her, you're not welcome here any more.' She says they are the worst words she can remember his ever having spoken to her. After that, she kept her distance, and her father never mentioned the matter again.

For all Dahl's new happiness, life was still often difficult. One or other of his daughters always seemed to be in trouble. His health continued to be worryingly unreliable. And he hadn't lost his appetite for quarrels.

In the summer of 1983 he was asked if he would review a polemical picture-book about the recent Israeli invasion of Lebanon, with text by a *Newsweek* journalist, Tony Clifton. The request came from the *Literary Review* – and not from the magazine's editor, but from its new owner, Naim Attallah, a wealthy Palestinian businessman, one of whose other enterprises-cum-hobbies is Quartet, a publishing house he himself founded.

Attallah had two strong reasons for wanting the book, *God Cried*, to be favourably reviewed. Like many people, he was disgusted by the savage bombardment of West Beirut. And he was the book's publisher. Such was his eagerness to get it a good press that he did some of the promotional work in person. He would invite a literary editor to lunch and spend the meal haranguing him about the importance of *God Cried* and the crucial responsibility involved in his choice of reviewer.[30] Attallah had met Dahl, and had heard his stories about his own time in Palestine.[31] He may also have known something of his views about the State of Israel. But Dahl was more than anti-Zionist. As we have seen, despite his friendship with several individual Jews – among them his current publishers Tom Maschler, Roger Straus and Peter Mayer – he was, like many Englishmen of his age and background, fairly consistently and by no means secretly anti-Semitic. His old Washington acquaintance Sir Isaiah Berlin excuses this on the ground that Dahl's opinions were essentially fanciful.[32] 'I thought he might say anything,' Berlin says. 'Could have been pro-Arab or pro-Jew. There was no consistent line. He was a man who followed whims, which meant he would blow up in one direction, so to speak. No doubt his imagination went into his works.' It is true that his whims usually went no further than jokes. 'The best part of those two guys was thrown away when they were circumcised',[33] he once wrote to Charles Marsh about a couple of Jews. But they could have a violent tinge (as in the fantasy about Charles Marsh and the Jewish waiter)[34], and Dahl had a weakness for fictional stereotypes like the rapacious and cowardly Meatbein in *Sometime Never*,[35] or the 'filthy old Syrian Jewess' Madame Rosette in the story named after her.[36] According to Robert Gottlieb, the tendency grew worse after Dahl's falling out with him and Robert Bernstein: 'that's where the later anti-Semitic spewings began'.[37] He began to identify all Jews with Israelis, telling Jewish people in London, 'You want to watch what your chaps are doing out there, they're getting your country a bad name.'[38] As Dahl explained to a journalist in 1983, 'there is a trait in the Jewish character that does provoke animosity . . . I mean there's always a reason why anti-anything crops up anywhere; even a stinker like Hitler didn't just pick on them for no reason.'[39]

The review Dahl wrote of *God Cried* claimed that in June 1982, when the Israeli attack on Lebanon was launched, 'we all started hating the Jews'. And he assured prospective readers of the book that, whatever their present opinions, it would make them 'violently anti-Jewish'. The then editor of the *Literary Review*, Gillian

Greenwood, changed 'Jews' to 'Israel', 'Jewish' to 'Israeli',[40] allowing Dahl to claim later, 'I am not anti-Semitic. I am anti-Israel.'[41] But throughout the article, even as it was finally published, he associated actions of the Israeli government (roundly condemned by many other commentators) with the behaviour and beliefs of Jews everywhere. On this occasion, his habit of lumping people together was made all the more inflammatory by his claim to be representing the views of everyone else, the 'we all' who hate the Jews and know that most of the troubles in the Middle East have been caused by Israel and its American Jewish supporters. 'General opinion', Dahl threatened, is that the Arab countries will 'annihilate the State of Israel . . . within the next fifty years', unless prime minister Menachem Begin and defence minister Ariel Sharon – in Dahl's overheated opinion, 'almost exact copies in miniature of Mr Hitler and Mr Goering' – learned to behave better.

In all this, he quoted the opinions of 'the shrewdest Arabs in the Middle East', and referred to factual information from 'my own sources' about Israeli–US agreements. What these sources were, he didn't say, but Dahl had been a critic of Zionism since 1946[42] and was a generous benefactor of Medical Aid for Palestinians (MAP), a charity which is also a powerful pressure group.[43] Many of the views expressed in Dahl's piece – for example, that the invasion served no other purpose than to distract attention from Israel's annexation of the West Bank – chimed with those of the pro-Palestinian lobby.[44]

Dahl's essential charge against Israeli cruelties was just, but his extremist tone didn't help the Palestinian cause. In the *Spectator*, the pro-Israeli commentator Paul Johnson rightly called the article reckless and crude.[45] Some contributors began to boycott the *Literary Review*, in response to Johnson's (itself not especially moderate) call 'for reputable writers to refuse to be associated with a journal which publishes such filth'. Dahl, meanwhile, poured oil on the flames by claiming that Jews were cowards, and that they passively submitted to the Nazi Final Solution. On the Allied side in the Second World War, he said, 'we saw almost none of them in the armed services':[46] a claim which enraged representatives and kin of the 60,000 Jews who served in the British forces between 1939 and 1945, many of them winning decorations (including the Victoria Cross) for their courage.[47] It was in this same interview that Dahl said Hitler hadn't picked on the Jews for no reason.

The row was widely reported in the by no means universally pro-Zionist British press, and soon travelled. In Israel, a British TV drama series called *Tales of the Unexpected* was boycotted because Dahl was wrongly believed to be its author. (He had contributed some episodes to an earlier series with the same title, but was not associated with the sequel.) In the USA, an article in the *New Republic* added its own touch of hysteria by interpreting Dahl's unmistakably ironic story 'Genesis and Catastrophe' as 'a tale that has the reader rooting for the health of a baby who turns out to be Adolf Hitler'.[48] American Jewish readers began to return Dahl's books to his publishers, and some booksellers announced that they would no longer stock them.[49] In reply, Roger Straus – himself Jewish – argued that his author's views were not reflected in his books. Dahl himself tried to make amends with an episode in *Going Solo* sympathetic to German Jewish refugees in wartime Palestine.[50] But the damage was done, to both Jews and Palestinians as well as to Dahl's reputation in the USA. Years after the original fracas, he was still getting letters about it. In April 1990, for example, an entire school class of small children in San Francisco wrote to him. One letter said:

Dear Mr Dahl,
 We love your books, but we have a problem . . . we are Jews!! We love your books but you don't like us because we are jews. That offends us. Can you please change your mind about what you said about jews! . . .
Love,
Aliza and Tamar[51]

Dahl replied to their teacher, insisting that it was injustice he was against, not Jews. He was less conciliatory when he was telephoned by the *Jewish Chronicle*. 'I'm an old hand at dealing with you buggers', he said. 'No comment.'[52]

*

As was sometimes the case when Dahl caused a row, he turned out to have been falling ill. In 1985, when he was almost seventy, he went into the Chiltern Hospital for surgery for cancer of the bowel. The first operation was not successful, and according to one of Dahl's nurses, he 'began to sink'.[53] Ophelia, who based herself at Gipsy House, came in every day to massage her father's back. Tessa flew in and out with histrionically large pots of flowers.

There was another operation, and Dahl slowly recovered. But he was left very weak, hobbling the hundred yards to his hut with the aid of two sticks, and writing in a shaky hand to the many people who had sent him messages. He was particularly proud of a letter from Graham Greene, congratulating him on *Boy*.[54]

Perhaps to make up to Tessa for having given her a scare, her father soon afterwards did a piece of writing on her behalf which reads like a throwback to his practical jokes with Charles Marsh. Tessa had a new baby, was about to hire an Australian nanny-housekeeper, and had asked for help in finding the plane fare. Dahl was more cautious these days about doling out money to his children, and suggested that a magazine might be persuaded to pay, if the nanny offered an interview with him in exchange. Better still, he would write the interview himself. Sitting in his shed with a blanket over his knees, he scrawled a 5,000-word eulogy of himself and his household and sent it to the publicity department of Penguin.[55]

Dahl, his article said, was without doubt the most popular of living writers for children, yet he spent 'half his life performing dotty and unusual acts and going out of his way to make someone happy.' Exceptionally warm and attentive to the needs of others, he was rarely without some philanthropic task to occupy him. His hospitality was described at length, and praise was lavished on his family, particularly his wife – 'a lovely lady'. Then the piece turned to the garden, and the row of pleached limes leading to Mr Dahl's writing hut. Here, the great man recounted his history to the imaginary interviewer – how he had been shot down in the war, and so forth – before going on to talk about the importance of writing good children's books: a much more difficult task than adult fiction, he said. He described his approach to writing: the solitary agony of thinking up a plot, which must be lively, imaginative and utterly original; the lonely labour of endless revision. In his covering letter to Penguin, Dahl conceded that there was something a little odd about this exercise in autobiography, but 'My own opinion is that it's quite a good little essay'. In more usual circumstances he said he would expect it to earn a fee of about £5,000.

The struggles of authorship were a frequent theme of Dahl's in these years.[56] He tried making a comeback as an adult writer with two sketchy and mildly pornographic fairy-tales, 'Princess Mammalia' and 'The Princess and the Poacher', which were printed in a little hardback to celebrate his seventieth birthday in 1986. (They were discreetly omitted from the *Collected Short Stories* published after his death.) 'The Bookseller', Dahl's plagiarism of James Gould Cozzens, appeared in *Playboy* in 1987.[57] *Playboy* also published 'The Surgeon', about some jewels hidden in an icebox which turn up in the stomach of a burglar who has helped himself to a cold drink.[58] But most of his effort went into his last substantial book, *Matilda*. Once again, Stephen Roxburgh was closely involved. Despite, or perhaps partly because of, all his efforts, Roxburgh was to lose the book for Farrar Straus Giroux and Roald Dahl with it.

Millions of readers know the story of *Matilda* as it was eventually published. A precocious little girl, extremely well-read and good at maths, suffers both at home, because of her philistine parents, and at her school, which is run by a sadistic and reactionary headmistress, Miss Trunchbull. With a new alertness to the climate of the times, Dahl emphasizes how unfairly Matilda's father discriminates in favour of her talentless brother. A liberal teacher at school, the mysteriously impoverished Miss Honey, tries to educate the parents about their daughter's gifts, but it transpires that she is herself in the headmistress's thrall: an orphan, Miss Honey is the niece of the hideous Trunchbull, who has tricked her out of her inheritance. Meanwhile, Matilda develops magical powers which she uses to expose the villainess, restoring Miss Honey's little fortune and her happiness.

As Dahl would sometimes relate, the original version was not at all like this. He didn't say that the main changes were prompted by his editor, or that after the work was done, Dahl picked a fight with him, took the book away from Farrar Straus and left them for good.

In the first draft of *Matilda*, a copy of which is still in the Dahl files at Farrar Straus, the heroine, not unlike Hilaire Belloc's Matilda, was 'born wicked'. She spends the first part of the book inflicting various tortures on her harmless and baffled parents. Only later does she turn out to be clever. The headmistress, Miss Trunchbull, is characterized much as in the final version of the book, although some details, such as her 'shadow of a jet-black moustache' and her dressing in men's clothes of a military type, were eventually dropped. (Dahl was to base her new appearance on that of the principal of a horticultural school near Thame, where he and his sisters bought plants.[59])

In the second half, nothing in the draft corresponds with the final story as Roxburgh suggested it to Dahl, except that both versions are in the style of Victorian sentimental melodrama, and in both, Matilda is brought face to face with her teacher's poverty. In the original version, when Matilda's teacher – called Miss Hayes – learns of her pupil's secret powers, she makes a confession of her own. A bookie's daughter, Miss Hayes is a compulsive gambler, and has run up debts of £20,000 on the horses. Keen to help, the fascinated Matilda has the idea of using her powerful eyes to nobble a race. She practices energetically by knocking over nearby cows and ponies. Meanwhile, Miss Hayes pawns an old ring of her mother's for £2,000. The two go off to Newmarket and put the money on a fifty to one outsider. It wins. Miss Hayes pockets £100,000, takes them both home in a taxi and renounces gambling for ever. By now, the beginning of the book has been forgotten. Matilda has long ago stopped being naughty, and Miss Trunchbull has disappeared from view altogether.

The structural problems with this enjoyable nonsense must have been easier to identify than their solutions, but Roxburgh saw various new possibilities, both in Matilda's cleverness and in the clash between Miss Trunchbull and Miss Hayes over educational methods. He realized, too, that the book would have more shape, and Matilda more identity, if Miss Hayes' values (nature, poetry, etc.) were contrasted with those of her pupil's parents. It was clear that in some way the young teacher's predicament should arise out of the situation already established in the early chapters. Within what was usable, there would need to be some cuts, particularly in the Trunchbull scenes, and in the duplication between Matilda's naughtiness and that of her friends Hortensia and Lavender.

Roxburgh put all these points to Dahl. If they proceeded as before, Dahl would incorporate his suggestions into a new draft, on which the editor would offer further comments, having polished and cut as much as his author would tolerate.

The first stage went well. Dahl saw the advantages of emphasizing Matilda's intelligence and enthusiasm for books. Following Roxburgh's suggestions, he developed a contrastingly boorish home background for her, and reduced the episodes of her bad behaviour, turning them into acts of revenge on her illiterate, sexist and semi-criminal father. The aptly renamed Miss Honey was built up, meanwhile, into an attractive, sweet-natured and liberally-inclined teacher, a much stronger foil to Miss Trunchbull. All of this took up considerably more of the book – almost a hundred pages of typescript, to the first draft's fifty – allowing Miss Honey's new revelations about the financial and domestic villainy of Miss Trunchbull to come closer to the climax. Here, Matilda's powers now play a positive, much briefer and more dramatic role: the exposure of Miss Trunchbull through magical writing on the blackboard.

All this was in Dahl's next draft. Inevitably, there were still various roughnesses. There was too much both of Miss Trunchbull and now of Matilda's parents. The antique school-story idiom ('New scum', 'We've seen her at prayers', ' "Steady on," the boy said. "I mean, dash it all, Headmistress" '), however reassuring to middle-class British parents, was incongruous in the setting of a contemporary day school, and wouldn't make much sense to American kids. But Roxburgh could put all this to Dahl in person at Gipsy House, when they discussed what was needed in the final draft.

Except that, as it turned out, this was the final draft. Perhaps because he was increasingly busy at Farrar Straus, perhaps (as Dahl complained) because of complications in his private life, but perhaps also because he had been irked to hear that Dahl had been complaining about him at dinner parties with other publishers, Roxburgh's letter about the new manuscript was not fulsome. 'The story holds together and moves along briskly', he wrote, early in October 1987.[60] 'I had hoped to read the manuscript one more time before returning it, but Frankfurt [the Book Fair] looms.' He suggested that he might come to Great Missenden on his return in two weeks' time, to review the draft, 'or whatever'.

Dahl was tired of being put to so much work. And when financial negotiations began, it became clear that there was a way out. In all the editorial discussions about *Matilda*, Roxburgh had omitted to make sure that Farrar Straus had a contract with Dahl for the book. They didn't, and Dahl was now quick to demand, through his agent, a full 15 per cent royalty over and above whatever was paid to Quentin Blake. Roxburgh was left with little choice except to agree, but instead of capitulating graciously, he made the mistake of warning Pollinger that he wouldn't be able to offer such good terms if Farrar Straus were the originating publishers of any future Dahl book.[61]

Pollinger showed Roxburgh's letter to Dahl, who flared up at this hint not only of reduced earnings but, as he chose to take it, of a desire to charge him for editorial help.[62] Not even the redoubtable Max Perkins, he said, had dared to expect such a thing. There were disagreements too over paperback royalties. But most of all Dahl resented the fact that in conversation, his US editor had implied that the book was not yet ready to publish: this despite the fact that his British publishers, Cape, said that they were delighted with it, and were already announcing it for the spring of 1988.

From a purely literary point of view, Roxburgh was right. But Dahl was again falling ill, and may have felt that he would never be able to satisfy his perfectionist editor. He discussed the matter with Felicity and Ophelia, and sent Roxburgh a self-extenuating letter. His family were very sad about the decision, he said, but agreed that he 'must not allow sentiment to prevent me from getting the best terms I can for my works.'[63] They believed that it was best at this juncture for Dahl to make a move. Despite all that Roxburgh had done with the book, Dahl also pretended that the younger man was too busy these days for 'the kind of super-editing that you did for me in the past.'

Dahl now made some changes to the last chapter of *Matilda*. Cape's editors corrected a few spelling mistakes (arithmatic, repell-ant, and so on[64]) and added some punctuation. Otherwise the printed book exactly followed the second draft, incorporating all of Roxburgh's suggestions. In the USA, its publisher was Viking, the hardback wing of Peter Mayer's Penguin. Their confidence in the story as it stood was amply justified. No book of Dahl's ever sold so fast. In Britain alone, half a million paperback copies went across the counter within six months. Stephen Roxburgh's role, of course, was never acknowledged.

15

You're Absolutely Wrong and I Am Right

The public side of Dahl's life now often wearied him as much as his dealings with his publishers. Book fairs made him particularly irritable. At Frankfurt in 1986, when his foreign publishers lined up to pay their respects on his seventieth birthday, he was as difficult as a spoilt child.[1] At Gothenburg the following summer, he harangued an audience of '500 idiotic Swedes' for what seemed to him an hour and a half, and remembered Alfred Knopf's remark that the Swedes were Germans in human shape: too generous a verdict, in Dahl's view.[2] As if what he saw as the audience's dull complacency weren't enough, he then had to sit at 'the so-called Banquet' between Iris Murdoch and Margaret Drabble ('not many laughs') and opposite John Updike.

Not the least disadvantage of book fairs is that they make a writer aware of other writers, and how highly some of them are regarded. If illness and pain were principal causes of Dahl's cantankerousness, envy was another. *Going Solo* had been an inspired title for the second volume of his autobiography; he could never be a mere member of a group. According to one friend, 'A committee, to Roald, would be twelve men and women who had to be dominated. His view was the only view. If black is white today, then that is it, and until I've persuaded you dolts that that is the case, we are going to have to have a confrontation.'[3] This was the Dahl encountered by the journalist Lynn Barber, who disagreed with something he said in the course of an interview. 'You're wrong!' he shouted. 'You're absolutely wrong and I am right. Do you understand now? I am right and you are *wrong*.'[4]

A BBC radio interviewer, Brian Sibley, was almost routed in a similar exchange, but saved the occasion by quoting verbatim the last words of *George's Marvellous Medicine*, about making contact with a magic world.[5] Was that what Dahl wanted to do in his books, Sibley appeasingly asked? Dahl paused, calmed down, then said, 'Do you drink?' According to Sibley, it was ten in the morning, but two large scotches were poured and the conversation continued until and through lunch. The mollified author signed Sibley's first edition of *The Gremlins* for him, dating the autograph 1943 'so as to cause your executors hell when they come to sort your affairs out' (an unsigned copy at that time was already worth several hundred pounds).

Such quirks made loyal allies as well as enemies. Many people – Lynn Barber among them – liked the elderly Dahl for what they saw as admirable plain-speaking. Others simply found him enjoyable as a turn. He could be depended on to enliven public events in Great Missenden. Once, taking part in a local charity show based on *Going for A Song* – the TV programme in which panellists, supposedly talking impromptu, identify and value antiques and bric-à-brac put in front of them – he threatened to walk out when he learned that the professional auctioneers appearing with him had been allowed to examine the objects in advance. Though he was persuaded to stay, he vented his feelings by dismissing everything shown to him as 'total crap' which he 'wouldn't have in the house'.[6] To some of the audience, it was Dahl himself who should be kept out of the house. He was 'insufferable', according to one. 'He could be a very nasty piece of work if he wanted to, yet he expected to be greatly admired and deferred to, like a very successful movie director. He had to show off.' This was certainly the impression he gave at a charity performance given by the actors Michael Denison and Dulcie Gray at their home in Amersham, in aid of a naturalist trust. Dahl introduced the evening but, having done so, sat disgruntledly in a prominent seat, swigging from a hip flask, banging his stick on the floor and growling that the whole thing was bloody boring. Eventually, he stalked out, taking Felicity with him.[7]

The knighthood he craved was still proving elusive. He was offered an OBE, but turned it down.[8] Nothing less than a knight-hood would do: he wanted his wife to be Lady Dahl, and was busy doing the things people said you had to do to secure this ambition. Much consisted of philanthropy, of the kind he enjoyed and was good at, particularly dealing with troubles similar to those which his own family had experienced. He gave the £3000 proceeds of the Whitbread prize to an Oxford hospice for terminally ill children.[9] He bought equipment for disabled children and for research programmes into neurological disorders, supported hospi-tal fund-raising schemes (on behalf of the Great Ormond Street Hospital, for example). He gave time and money to organizations concerned with learning difficulties, particularly the Dyslexia Insti-tute, and backed anyone he heard of who was doing anything to encourage children to read. Dahl involved himself personally in all these projects, ringing up the organizers to find out exactly what they were doing, and making personal visits to sick and injured children.

In 1988 the then Education Minister, Kenneth Baker, invited Dahl to join the most recent of the Conservative Party's ever-chan-ging working parties on English teaching. This was his best chance of making a mark with the medal-givers, but he was so alienated by the slow, collective procedures of the specialist committee that after the first meeting he never returned, and was finally persuaded to resign. He told the chairman, Professor Brian Cox – perhaps with more wisdom than he realized – that circumstances had changed since he was at school in the 1920s.[10] Later he publicly disagreed with the panel about Enid Blyton, whose books the majority wanted to exclude from a list of approved texts, but which he backed because children liked them.[11]

Dahl was beginning to think that his chances of becoming Sir Roald had been blown by the *God Cried* scandal.[12] But even in the English-teaching debate, he wasn't unequivocally on the same side as the Conservative powers-that-were. True, Dahl told the *Daily*

Mail that he was a firm believer in the necessity of teaching 'proper parsing and proper grammar'.[13] Yet *Matilda*, which was published in the same year as Dahl's resignation from the Baker–Cox Committee, is among other things an onslaught on Gradgrindian teaching methods. Soon afterwards, the cultural commentator Bryan Appleyard suggested that in his authoritarian guise, Dahl 'should disapprove of his own books' because they were subversive. The author admitted to Appleyard that he had no answer to this. 'It's a tightrope act and you've got me in a bit of a corner.'[14]

It is such ambiguities, of course, which make the books both distinctive and underlyingly true to life. There was nothing uncertain, on the other hand, about his opinions when Salman Rushdie was forced into hiding, early in 1989, by the fundamentalist Islamic *fatwa* condemning him to death for the supposed blasphemy of *The Satanic Verses*. Many writers probably experienced a twinge of the envy Gore Vidal admitted to, that anyone could have written a book about which people cared so much. Dahl's lack of sympathy for Rushdie's plight may also have been prompted by personal dislike. Rushdie remembers their meeting one night, long before he wrote *The Satanic Verses*, at the home of a mutual acquaintance. Rushdie was lodging there at the time, but Dahl seemed bent on making him feel *de trop*, telling the Indian-born novelist how much he admired the anti-immigrant politician Enoch Powell.

Now that Rushdie had written something that had given offence, and was being bullied, Dahl might have been expected to support him. But in the London literary circles by which Dahl still felt himself excluded, everyone seemed to be on the younger author's side. Dahl wrote to *The Times* saying he had not heard any non-Muslim voice raised in criticism of Rushdie, and accusing him of being a 'dangerous opportunist' who had brought his fate upon himself by a calculated pursuit of notoriety, prompted by greed for sales.[15] Freedom of speech was 'a very proper principle', Dahl accepted; but all artists should censor themselves. As some readers pointed out, it was an odd line to be taken by the inventor of the Oompa-Loompas and the reviewer of *God Cried*.

Somewhat to his surprise, Dahl found himself opposed on the issue by much of the Conservative political establishment. Despite the mutual dislike between it and the vociferously anti-Thatcherite Rushdie, the government defended not only Rushdie's freedom of speech but his life, and with noticeably less hesitation than the Labour hierarchy. Dahl found some satisfaction, however, in being opposed by the overwhelming majority of his fellow writers, whom he derided for treating the novelist as 'some sort of a hero'. A few members of the Society of Authors demanded that he be expelled from the society for his comments, but were reminded by wiser heads that this would have had bad connotations in an argument about freedom of speech.[16] Dahl revelled in it all. Martin Amis, invited to Gipsy House one night for a game of snooker, argued about the case with his host, and mentioned that he was about to have dinner with the hapless Rushdie, who was by now moving from house to house with an armed bodyguard of secret service men. 'Tell him he's a shit', Dahl said amicably.[17]

Among the things which grated about Rushdie was the fact that as long ago as 1981, his *Midnight's Children* had won the Booker Prize. The prize (launched in 1969) is restricted to novels, so Dahl's only chance of winning – two years before Rushdie's success – had been with *My Uncle Oswald*, which was panned by critics otherwise rarely found in agreement, from Peter Kemp to Auberon Waugh. Dahl later regretted having published the novel.[18] But he took a swipe at the Booker Prize when, in 1989, he was chairman of a rival but less prestigious contest, the *Sunday Express* Book of the Year Prize. In a widely publicized speech, he said – not entirely unjustly – that the Booker judges tend to choose what they call a beautifully crafted book, 'which is often beautifully boring'. A great writer, Dahl went on, was one who pleased the marketplace: the only purpose of the novel was to entertain. 'Balls', shouted another popular writer present, Laurie Lee. More soberly, *Publishers Weekly* pointed out that if the Booker Prize judges were so misguided, it was strange that they had short-listed the very book which Dahl's panel had chosen to win, Rose Tremain's *Restoration*.[19]

*

There were many such flare-ups in his last years. His familiar din-ner-party tetchiness, the private outbursts of a volatile, impatient man with a few drinks inside him, had moved into a larger arena. Even his public attempts to defend people who needed defending (like the Palestinians) were liable to backfire. This quixotic trait was particularly evident to Dahl's friend Peter Mayer, who was one of the publishers of Rushdie's *The Satanic Verses* and as a result, along with his colleagues at Viking Penguin, subjected to repeated death threats and bomb scares after the *fatwa*. Having, in the view of many at Viking Penguin, contributed to their problems – especially the controversy over paperback publication of the book – Dahl busied himself making numerous suggestions to Mayer about how the issue might be resolved.

An earlier episode produced similarly confused results. One spring day in 1988, Roald and Felicity were driving through Hyde Park when they saw several policemen fighting with a black man.[20] Shocked by the violence of the scene, and perhaps also aware that this was a chance to counteract the charges of racism which were now often made against him, Dahl told his friends that he had seen an unmotivated assault by six police on a victim whose face they had left 'covered in blood'. The story was widely reported, but a taxi driver who had seen the fight and heard Dahl's description of it on the radio came forward with a different version. The 'six police' were in fact, the driver rightly said, three policemen and one police-woman, who were having difficulty in arresting an extremely aggressive man much larger than any of them. The man did not seem to have been much hurt. This version was supported by another bystander. While Felicity and two other witnesses agreed with her husband that the police had acted roughly, only Dahl alleged that the man's face was bleeding. These discrepancies, com-bined with the fact that the victim had been wanted for non-pay-ment of a fine, made it easy for the Police Complaints Authority to dismiss a case which, if it had been put more moderately, might, on the balance of the rest of the evidence, have been upheld.

Dahl was now more or less permanently in pain from his joints and his back, and it soon became clear that he was suffering from a form of leukaemia. He took a robust, practical view of the situation, wanting to know exactly what was involved and saying that as he had battled his way through so much, he would manage to do so again. Nothing kept him from his enjoyments. Whatever his doctors advised, he regarded Cartier cigarettes, gin and sweets as indispensable. During one of his spells in hospital, he successfully bid at auction for a small Van Gogh drawing of a peasant woman, a study for *The Potato Pickers*, with which he was so pleased that when he went to the Isle of Wight to convalesce, he took it with him and hung it in his hotel room.[21]

On occasions, he showed signs of having become a touch chastened. He spoke often about his difficulties with some of his grown-up daughters: only one of them had a nice boy-friend, he grumbled; the others, you didn't know who they were with. When he was young, you had to take a girl out to dinner for six months before you got a kiss.[22] He also spoke of making efforts to become a better person.[23] He said he regretted that he couldn't fully believe in Christianity. He thought that the pre-eminent value was kindness and, headline-seeking to the last, told an interviewer from the *Guardian* that this was a good argument for ordaining women as priests: if they want to be ordained, he said, it would be unkind not to let them be.[24] He mentioned dying: the sad thought that he wouldn't see his family any more, but against this, the fact that the world didn't seem to be becoming a better place, and that 'the human is not a very nice animal'. No, fear did not come into his feelings about death. When Olivia died, almost thirty years previously, he had decided, 'If she can do it, I can do it.'[25]

He continued to write, and to involve himself in every detail of what happened to his books. They were selling stupendously well: in Britain alone, in paperback, over two million copies a year. There was a proliferation of tape-recordings, dramatizations, cartoon strips, a *Roald Dahl Newsletter*. Films, too, of course. There was one of *Danny* which he didn't mind much, although he thought Jeremy Irons a little too well-manicured as the father. And Anjelica Huston, daughter of his old acquaintance John Huston, starred in *The Witches*, which he called a 'stupid horror film' and urged everyone to boycott.[26] It was, he thought, too 'adult' in treatment (by which he may in part have meant too contemporary: the bald witches look like a convention of punks). He was also furious that it reverted to the original ending, which Stephen Roxburgh had persuaded him to change, where the hero is turned back from a mouse into a boy.

And there were still more books, with a new kindly tone: *Esio Trot*, a romance in which a lonely old man wins the heart of an old woman by a trick which convinces her that he can control the growth of her pet tortoise; and *The Vicar of Nibbleswicke*, about a back-to-front young clergyman who gets into trouble by saying 'dog' for 'God', 'pis' for 'sip', 'krap' for 'park'. (At Dahl's request, the rights to the book were auctioned in aid of the Dyslexia Institute.) In *The Minpins*, which, like *The Vicar of Nibbleswicke*, would not be published until after Dahl's death, a boy escapes from his over-protective mother into a region threatened by a fire-breathing monster. The dwarfish inhabitants have learnt to fly – they travel about on birds – and in his successful attempt to conquer their enemy, the boy makes his own first flight on the neck of a swan, which takes him through smoke and flames to victory, and safely home again.

The Minpins worried some readers because of its apparent indebtedness to Carol Kendall's *The Minnipins* (1959). But apart from the title and the midget world which both stories share with many others for children, Dahl's book is essentially his own, and recapitulates the myth of himself which he had written several times in different forms. In an earlier published version of the story, 'The Swan', two bullies take an air-gun to a bird sanctuary, the favourite retreat of Peter, a solitary boy who loves wildlife. (For no reason necessary to the narrative, the reader is twice told that the sanctuary's owner is a Mr Douglas Highton – the name of Dahl's closest friend at prep school.[27]) Finding him there, the other boys torture Peter in various ways before finally tying his arms to the wings of a swan they have killed. Then they force him to climb a tree and launch himself from it. 'Some people', the narrative says, when they have taken too much and have been driven beyond the point of endurance, simply crumble and give up. There are others, though they are not many, who will for some reason always be unconquerable. You meet them in time of war and also in time of peace. They have an indomitable spirit, and nothing . . . will cause them to give up.

Dahl himself, of course, had half a century previously flown through flames against an enemy, and had returned to his mother.

Early in 1990 he and Felicity received a letter from Pat, proposing a reconciliation. They eagerly agreed, and invited her to come to a party for Theo's thirtieth birthday. It was the last time she saw Roald alive. That summer, he and Felicity made an exhausting promotional trip to Australia and, on their return, went to dinner with their neighbour Elizabeth Stewart-Liberty. Dahl was full of complaints about Australian journalists who knew nothing about his books, but the old contemptuous energy was missing. Although his hostess served two of his favourite dishes, oysters and lobster, he had little appetite, and left early.[28] By the autumn, he was in hospital in Oxford, in unremitting pain.

Felicity was not unhopeful. She had seen him rally before, and according to Tessa, persuaded him against taking morphine, which would have weakened him further.[29] Tessa disagreed with her. She says it was obvious that her father was going to die, and since pain-killing drugs were anyway among his pleasures, he should have been allowed them. Both of his Hesselberg aunts had become morphine addicts in old age, she says, and Dahl himself 'loved oblivion', and used to glamorize anaesthetics when any of his children needed hospital treatment. 'They'll put the needle in,' he would say in his seductive, cooing growl, 'and you'll count 10, 9, 8 . . . ' According to Tessa, he was now in such agony that some nights when she was alone with him, although he had always repulsed physical contact with his children, he told her, 'Squeeze me, hold on to me.' More than once, he asked desperately, 'What am I going to do?'

*

Dahl died on 23 November 1990. He is buried, not in Olivia's large plot with its alpine garden at Little Missenden, which had been intended for both him and Pat, but on the hillside opposite Gipsy House. Immediately above his grave is that of Felicity's daughter Lorina, who had died from a brain tumour eight months earlier, aged twenty-seven: for Dahl, a last crushing family tragedy.

His estate was valued at almost three million pounds. The figure is no more than the annual income now generated by his work, under the adroit management of Dahl & Dahl (in his will, simply described as 'the Business'). Perhaps because he had been fearful of the effect of big inheritances on the already untidy lives of some of his children, he left everything, including the future royalties from his books, to Felicity for her lifetime. In the hospital, immediately after he died, she gave her stepchildren some small memorabilia – Dahl's watch to Ophelia, his folding walking stick to Tessa. From now on, whatever they couldn't earn for themselves, they would have to seek from her.

By most accounts, Felicity Dahl uses her wealth both scrupulously and generously. She divides half the income from 'the Business' between her four stepchildren. From the remaining half, she helps to fund a charity which she set up in her husband's name.[30] The idea was not Dahl's but, appropriately enough, came to Felicity from an old letter to her husband about Charles Marsh's Public Welfare Foundation, which she found in the writing hut after his death. The Roald Dahl Foundation makes grants to projects in areas with which he was himself concerned – haematology, neurology and literacy – and concentrates each year on a particular problem. In 1992, the chosen field was epilepsy, and the Foundation helped to build a library for an epileptics' centre in Cheshire and provided a minibus for a school for epileptic children. The organization has also launched a series of musical events, commissioning composers to write settings of work by Dahl. The first of these schemes – a concert performance of his comic-rhyme version of 'Little Red Riding Hood', with music by the young composer Paul Patterson – was given by the London Philharmonic at the Royal Festival Hall in November 1992, the second anniversary of his death. Other commissions have followed. The aim is to bring children into the world of serious modern music, and to provide their teachers with back-up material for use in the classroom. The Foundation owns the copyrights in the works it commissions, which will provide another major source of revenue for future projects.

Some of Dahl's daughters have reservations, not that these aren't valuable and appropriate ways for their father's money to be spent, but about the degree of control held by Felicity in what Tessa describes as 'this step-matriarchal society'. But in explaining their feelings, Lucy Dahl for one puts a brave face on what is clearly a difficult situation. This is what her father chose, she says, and 'he didn't want anything to do with anyone who sat around and moaned.' Besides, as she points out, money is the least of their difficulties. Both Lucy and Tessa volunteer that a harder problem – not least in their and Ophelia's relationships with other men – is for them to take Roald Dahl 'off his pedestal'. Even Tessa, who is less inclined to reverence than most of the family, says simply, 'He was a Great Man.'

The funeral was traditional.[31] Scores of family and old friends gathered in the parish church at Great Missenden, among them Patricia Neal, and had the wry pleasure of hearing the Great Man counted among the blessed who have not walked in the counsel of the ungodly, nor sat in the seat of the scornful. Another of the readings was from Dahl's favourite poet, Dylan Thomas:

> And you, my father, there on the sad height,
> Curse, bless, me now with your fierce tears, I pray.
> Do not go gentle into that good night.
> Rage, rage against the dying of the light.[32]

The lines spoke for Dahl's children, and also reminded everyone, especially his sisters, of the father Roald himself had missed for seventy of his seventy-four years. But the most moving words, because the most personal and frank, were Peter Mayer's about his differences with his friend. Dahl's 'unsubtle and perhaps idiosyncratic distinctions between the general and the particular, the objective and the subjective' had caused awkwardness between them, Mayer said. But 'in the passing and crossing over, just as my people say on our Day of Atonement, we are all children united with our parents.'[33]

I visited Dahl's grave when I began to write this book. On it were a few small, rather dilapidated toys – a plastic parrot, a teddy bear, a broken jack-in-the-box in the form of an egg. And, instead of the chrysanthemums and gladioli on neighbouring plots, his favourite vegetable: a large, handsome, tough-skinned, many-layered onion.

Further Acknowledgements

Apart from those mentioned at the beginning of this book, I am grateful to many individuals who assisted in various ways, not least by answering letters, responding to advertisements or simply getting in touch with information about Roald Dahl. I can't mention them all individually. For example, large numbers of Reptonians and former member of 80 Squadron RAF replied to circular letters from me, apologizing for the fact that they had no memories of Dahl; and I had scores of answers (the first of them from Francis Wyndham) to a published enquiry about the original publication of Curt Siodmak's 'Donovan's Brain'.

Others, however, were too helpful to go unnamed.

Kaare Hesselberg kindly corresponded with me about the family of his kinswoman Sofie Dahl, Roald's mother.

The Secretary of the Old Reptonian society, J. F. M. Walker, helped in various ways, particularly by putting me in touch with the following contemporaries of Dahl's at the school (other than those named on page xi) who wrote to me or talked to me about their memories: R. R. Acheson, John F. Barclay, J. T. J. Dobie, T. B. Ellis, Jim Furse, I. B. Mackay, J. F. Mendl, A. P. D. Montgomery, B. L. L. Reuss. I must also thank Michael Stones, currently House-master of Priory House; J. C. Knapp, Headmaster of The Cathedral School, Llandaff; and Col. W. J. Hotblack, whose grandfather founded St Peter's School, Weston-super-Mare.

The following people associated with 80 Squadron RAF provided useful information: Alex Angus, Roy Ballantyne, Squadron Leader C. J. Bartle, Gregory F. Graham, Air Marshal Sir Edward Gordon Jones, Wing Commander G. V. W. Kettlewell.

Many others who knew Dahl or came into contact with him gave assistance, other than those mentioned in the Preface. I am especially grateful to: Jane Adams, Martin Amis, Roger Angell, Maarten Asscher, Lynn Barber, Patrick Benson, Solveig Bøhle, Mrs Butler (of Great Missenden), Michael de Capua, Peter Carson, Emma Chichester Clark, Fabio Coen, Brian Cox, Carl Djerassi, Hon. R. T. Fisher, Michael Foreman, Brendan Gill, Charles Gray, Richard Hough, Stephen Koch, William Koshland, Hermione Lee, Mark Lefanu, Penelope Lively, Helen Lillie, Anne Lømo, Koukla MacLehose, Susan Mayes, Arthur Miller, Peggy Miller, Caroline Moorehead, John Mortimer, Anthony Page, Murray Pollinger, Michael Rosen, Salman Rushdie, Caroline Seebohm, Gita Sereny, Brian Sibley, Elizabeth Stewart-Liberty, Bing Taylor, Judy Taylor, Ann Thwaite, Alice K. Turner, Claudia Warner, David Wolton and Sebastian Yorke.

For making suggestions or answering enquires of various kinds I must also thank the following: Erik Arthur, Margaret Baxter, Graham Binns, Nick Collins, Saul Cooper, Mrs Ferris (of Llandaff), Colin Greenland, Sir Stuart Hampshire, Hans Georg Heepe, Carolyn Hemmings, Katherine Nouri Hughes, Angela Huth, Marjut Karasmaa, Daniel J. Kevles, Eric Korn, William Koshland, John Lawrence, Blake Morrison, J. R. Prawer, Tony Ross, Ben Sonnenberg, Jean Stein, Dinah Stroe, Vavi Toran, Jessica Warner, Marina Warner, Auberon Waugh, Tony Wilmot.

I had invaluable help from the staff of various libraries and institutional archives, particularly the BBC Written Archives in Reading; the TV Archives of the Canadian Broadcasting Corporation; the Glamorgan Archive Service and South Glamorgan County Library, Cardiff; the Harry Ransom Humanities Research Center at the University of Texas at Austin; the Margaret Herrick Library of the Academy of Motion Picture Arts and Sciences, Los Angeles; the Ministry of Defence RAF Personnel Management Centre; the Osborne Collection of Early Children's Books, Toronto Public Library; the Police Complaints Authority; the Public Record Office; the publishers' archives collection in the Reading University Library; the library of the Royal Air Force Museum, Hendon; the archives of Shell Centre, London; the Principal Registry of the Family Division, Somerset House; the Department of Special Collections, University of California, Los Angeles; the Walt Disney Archives, Burbank; the Welsh Industrial and Maritime Museum, Cardiff; and Woodspring Central Library, Weston-super-Mare.

In the course of researching the book, I enjoyed the hospitality of Keith Brown and of Peter Christophersen in Norway, of John Sutherland in Pasadena, of Mimi Summerskill and her family in New Jersey, and of Mrs Charles Marsh in Washington, DC.

The authorship of copyright materials from which extracts have been quoted is made clear either in the text or in the notes, or both. The claims in copyright of the authors of those materials or their heirs and assigns are acknowledged by the author and publishers of this book. The process of deciding what I might and might not quote has been facilitated by some copyright-holders who simply gave me outright permission, either in advance, or after reading relevant sections of the book in draft. I am particularly grateful to the following: Mrs Charles Marsh; Alfred A. Knopf, Inc.; Farrar Straus Giroux; The Disney Publishing Group; The British Broadcasting Corporation; The Public Record Office.

Abbreviations

Sources frequently referred to in the notes are abbreviated as follows:

AK   Archives of Alfred A. Knopf, Inc., in the Harry Ransom Humanities Research Center at the University of Texas at Austin.
BBC   BBC Written Archives, Reading.
CM   Correspondence of Charles Marsh, in the possession of his widow.
FSG   Archives of Farrar Straus Giroux.
MS   Letters to Matthew Smith, in the possession of Alice Keene.
NY   *The New Yorker* card file for RD.
PRO   Public Record Office files.
WD   Walt Disney Archives, used by permission of © The Walt Disney Company.

Abbreviated titles:

As I Am	Patricia Neal, *As I Am: An Autobiography*, 1988.
ASML	*Ah, Sweet Mystery of Life: The Country Stories of Roald Dahl*, 1989.
CCF	*Charlie and the Chocolate Factory*, 1964, Puffin, 1973.
Danny	*Danny The Champion of the World*, 1975, Puffin, 1977.
JGP	*James and the Giant Peach*, 1961, Puffin, 1990.
KK	*Kiss Kiss*, 1959, Penguin edition, 1962.
'Lucky Break'	'Lucky Break: How I became a writer', in *WSHS* (below), p. 187f.
Memories with Food	Felicity and Roald Dahl, *Memories with Food at Gipsy House*, 1991.
OTY	*Over To You*, 1946, Penguin, 1973.
Pat and Roald	Barry Farrell, *Pat and Roald*, 1969.
'A Piece of Cake'	'A Piece of Cake: My first story – 1942', in *WSHS* (below), p. 224f. (revised version of 'Shot Down Over Libya', below).
Powling	Chris Powling, *Roald Dahl*, 1983.
'Shot Down Over Libya'	'Shot Down Over Libya ... factual report on Libyan air fighting', *Saturday Evening Post*, August 1942 (first version of 'A Piece of Cake', above).
SLY	*Someone Like You*, 1954, Penguin, 1970.
WSHS	*The Wonderful Story of Henry Sugar*, 1977, Penguin, 1988.

References to other Dahl titles are to the Penguin or Puffin editions where they exist, otherwise to the first UK hardback edition.

Notes

PREFACE

1. See below, p. 241f.
2. Information from Amanda Conquy.

CHAPTER 1

MAIN SOURCES:

CM.

Interviews with Creekmore Fath, Antoinette Haskell, Claudia Marsh, David Ogilvy.

Caro, Robert A., *The Years of Lyndon Johnson*, vol. 1 *The Path to Power*, 1982.

Nicholas, H. G., ed., *Washington Despatches 1941–45. Weekly Reports from the British Embassy*, 1981.

NOTES:

1. Correspondence of Charles Marsh (hereafter 'CM').
2. See Nicholas, H. G., ed., *Washington Despatches 1941–45. Weekly Reports from the British Embassy*, p. 345f.
3. Ibid.
4. See below, p. 12.
5. Caro, Robert A., *The Years of Lyndon Johnson*, vol. 1 *The Path to Power*, pp. xiii, 477 and *passim*.
6. Sir Isaiah Berlin says that Marsh 'was obviously very vain, spoke in staccato, disjointed sentences, gave the impression of

being powerful, not to say sinister . . . [He was] not exactly abnormal, but [I thought] that there was a screw faintly loose somewhere – and I felt rather frightened of him, as if in the presence of someone slightly unbalanced.'

7. CM 27 June 1943.
8. CM 1943, no date.
9. Interview with Colin Fox.
10. Interview with Claudia Warner
11. *The Gremlins*, see pp. 56f.
12. British sales figures given are for children's paperbacks published by Puffin. According to Puffin's Publishing Director, Elizabeth Attenborough, 11,326,700 copies were sold in 1980–90. The figure for 1989 was 2,383,518. The birth rate rose in 1980–90 from about 700,000 to just under 800,000 per annum: a total for the decade of about 7.5 million.
13. Eleanor Roosevelt, *This I Remember*.
14. Bing Taylor in *The Good Book Guide*, Spring 1980, p. 4.
15. See below, Chapters 11–14.
16. Payn, Graham, and Morley, Sheridan, eds., *The Noël Coward Diaries*, 1982, p. 231, 14 February 1954.
17. Compare, for example, *Danny the Champion of the World* with its earlier, adult version, 'The Champion of the World', *George's Marvellous Medicine* with *My Uncle Oswald*, *Esio Trot* with 'Mr Botibol', and *The Twits* with Dahl's adult tales of domestic cruelty, particularly 'William and Mary' or 'The Way Up to Heaven'.

CHAPTER 2

MAIN SOURCES:

FSG.

Interviews and correspondence with Tessa Dahl, Kaare Hesselberg, Douglas Highton, J. F. M. Walker, and with Old Reptonians

listed in individual notes and in the Further Acknowledgements.

Boy; Memories with Food; The Dahl Diary, 1992.

Thomas, Bernard, ed., *Repton, 1557–1957,* 1957. Contemporary
volumes of the Repton school magazine, *The Reptonian.*

NOTES:

1. Information about the Hesselberg family: letters from Kaare
   Hesselberg; *Memories with Food.*
2. But Patricia Neal says that, later, Sofie 'was not at all beautiful'.
3. Chappell, Edgar L., *History of the Port of Cardiff,* 1939,
   p. 121.
4. *Boy,* p. 17. Ty Mynydd was a big house, but the turrets are
   surely those of Castell Coch.
5. In a letter to the Marshes many years later, Sofie said that she was
   worried that Roald might take after his father, who 'was difficult if the babies made a noise to disturb his work and I think
   Roald is just as bad. I feel sorry for Pat.' CM 16 January 1956.
6. *Boy,* pp. 18–19.
7. Cutting from an unidentified Cardiff paper, sent by Kaare Hesselberg. In conversation, Roald Dahl later rounded the figure
   up to a quarter of a million (*Pat and Roald,* p. 74).
8. *Working for Love,* 1988, pp. 30, 51.
9. BBC 'Bookmark', 1985.
10. *Memories with Food,* pp. 65–6.
11. Wintle, Justin and Fisher, Emma, *The Pied Pipers: interviews
    with the influential creators of children's literature,* 1974,
    p. 111.
12. Bierce, Ambrose, ed., *Can Such Things Be,* 1926 edn,
    pp. 14–15.
13. Interview with Douglas Highton.
14. *A History of Elm Tree House School,* privately printed,
    [1984].
15. *The Dahl Diary,* 1992.

16. *Boy*, p. 33.
17. Interview with Mrs Ferris.
18. Interview with Brough Girling.
19. RD to his mother, FSG.
20. Material from St Peter's school magazine, supplied by Woodspring Central Library, Weston-super-Mare.
21. See note 19.
22. Letter from B. L. L. Reuss.
23. Interview with Douglas Highton.
24. Telephone interview with Sir Stuart Hampshire.
25. *Boy*, p. 147f.
26. *Boy*, p. 144f.
27. Dahl's friend was subsequently expelled, and the issue was made public in the school. Several people who were at the top of Priory House at the time have discussed it with me, particularly B. L. L. Reuss and John Bradburn.
28. Letter from John F. Barclay. B. L. L. Reuss has written to me that Fisher 'very rarely beat anyone'. And even Denton Welch ended up being favourably impressed by the future archbishop (*Maiden Voyage*, second printing, 1945, pp. 77–8).
29. Interview with Sir David Sells. Meeting Sells much later, the archbishop asked him whether they had overlapped at the school. Only by a term, Sells told him. 'You're lucky,' Fisher said. 'I was pretty crisp.'
30. Telephone interview with Sir Stuart Hampshire.
31. Review of *J. T. Christie: A Great Teacher* (a selection of his writings, with introductory memoirs by Donald Lindsay, Roger Young and Hugh Lloyd-Jones), *London Review of Books*, 3 October 1985.
32. Interview with Sir David Sells.
33. Letter from J. T. J. Dobie.
34. Letter from B. L. L. Reuss.
35. Telephone interview with John Bradburn.
36. *The Dahl Diary*, 1992.
37. 'Galloping Foxley' appeared in *Town and Country* in 1953, and first collected in *Someone Like You* in the same year.

38. For example, pp. 96–7 of 'Galloping Foxley' (*Someone Like You*, Penguin, 1970) became pp. 155–7 of *Boy* (Penguin, 1984).

39. David Atkins in *The Author*, Spring 1992, p. 24. Atkins tells various other stories about his friendship with Dahl, but his memory isn't faultless. He thinks Dahl had a Norwegian accent, and that they both arrived at Repton 'on the same day in September 1930', along with Welch and Geoffrey Lumsden. Dahl had in fact joined the school in January, Welch the previous September, and Lumsden in May 1928.

40. Interview with Dennis Pearl.

41. Thomas, Bernard, ed., *Repton, 1557 to 1957*, 1957, pp. 104–5; Dudley Edwards, Ruth, *Victor Gollancz: A Biography*, 1987, pp. 95–125.

42. The Roman statesman Cato the Elder was so impressed by the power of Carthage that he famously ended every speech by saying that the rival city must be destroyed: *Delenda est Carthago*.

43. Debates recorded in *The Reptonian*, 1931–32, p. 31; 1933–34, pp. 11, 13.

44. *The Dahl Diary*, 1992.

45. Interview with Ian Rankin.

46. Letter from B. L. L. Reuss.

47. *The Dahl Diary*, 1992.

CHAPTER 3

MAIN SOURCES:

FSG.

80 Squadron's Operations Record Book in the Public Record Office (PRO Air 27, 669).

Typescript volumes of the official RAF Narrative of the Second World War, held by the library of the RAF Museum, Hendon.

Interviews and correspondence with Tessa Dahl, Dennis Pearl, Antony Pegg, and with survivors of 80 Squadron named in the notes or in the Further Acknowledgements.

Boy; *The Dahl Diary, 1992*; *Going Solo*; *Memories with Food*; *Over To You*; 'A Piece of Cake'; 'Shot Down Over Libya'.

Clarke, Dennis, *Public Schools Explorers in Newfoundland*, [1935].
The Shell Magazine, 1936–37.
Shell pamphlets: 'The Shell Company of East Africa Limited' and 'East Africa Tanganyika: History of Shell-B.P.'
Shores, Christopher, *Strike True: The Story of No. 80 Squadron Royal Air Force*, 1986.
Terraine, John, *The Right of the Line: The Royal Air Force in the European War 1939–45*, 1985.

NOTES:

1. FSG.
2. Interview with Dennis Pearl.
3. The organization continues today as the British Schools Exploring Society.
4. Clarke, Dennis, *Public Schools Explorers in Newfoundland* [1935].
5. Ibid.
6. *Boy*, p. 170.
7. Interview with Antony Pegg.
8. *The Shell Magazine*, 1936–37.
9. Interview with Dennis Pearl; Roald Dahl, 'A Book That Changed Me', *Independent on Sunday*, 15 July 1990.
10. *Memories with Food*, p. 20.
11. *The Dahl Diary, 1992*.
12. Shell pamphlets: 'The Shell Company of East Africa Limited' and 'East Africa Tanganyika: History of Shell-B.P.'
13. *Going Solo*, p. 20f; *Memories with Food*, p. 34.
14. FSG.
15. *Going Solo*, p. 8.

16. ABC radio interview with Terry Lane, 1990.
17. See below, p. 186f.
18. CM 30 April 1950.
19. *Someone Like You*, Penguin, pp. 117–28.
20. *Collier's*, 3 June 1950.
21. FSG.
22. Interview with Dennis Pearl.
23. FSG.
24. Letter from Roy Ballantyne.
25. For detailed information in this section, I have relied princi-
    pally on 80 Squadron's Operations Record Book in the Public
    Record Office (PRO Air 27, 669), and the relevant volumes in
    the typescript official RAF Narrative held in the library of the
    RAF Museum at Hendon.
26. *Going Solo*, pp. 97–121.
27. See p. 53, below.
28. PRO Air 27, 669.
29. RD to Sofie Dahl, 20 November 1940, FSG.
30. *Going Solo*, p. 132. Dahl attributes the criticism to his friend
    David Coke, also a relative newcomer to the squadron. Jones
    had in fact been wounded in action soon after his arrival in
    Greece in November 1940, when his Gladiator was shot to
    pieces. As usual, what Dahl says has to be treated with at least
    a double amount of caution. He glamorizes Coke as heir to the
    Earl of Leicester, 'although anyone acting less like a future Earl
    I have never met'. But the future Earl was his elder brother.
31. Letter from Air Marshal Sir Edward Gordon Jones.
32. *Going Solo*, pp. 121, 117.
33. Telephone interview with G. E. Wilson.
34. Dahl doesn't mention Coke's brother in *Going Solo*, although
    he was impressed by the aristocratic connection: see note 30.
35. The squadron history [Shores, op. cit., p. 22] attributes no
    claims to Dahl before 20 April. In his own version (*Going
    Solo*, pp. 122–45), he was credited with one Junker 88 on his
    first day, 15 April, and another on 16 April.
36. *Going Solo*, p. 146.

37. Dahl's Flight-Sergeant 'Rivelon', for example, whose death he records on 17 April, is Rivalant, who two days later was officially credited with having shot down a dive-bomber.
38. RAF Narrative, vol. cit., p. 70.
39. 80 Squadron Operations Record Book summary for April 1941; Shores, p. 22; RAF Narrative, vol. cit., p. 70.
40. See the later comment of his his squadron leader, below, p. 44.
41. *Ladies' Home Journal*, March 1944.
42. *Going Solo*, p. 174f.
43. *Going Solo*, p. 184.
44. *The Dahl Diary*, 1992.
45. *Going Solo*, pp. 194–200. Dahl seems not to have heard, either, of the Balfour Declaration, by which in 1917 Lloyd George's Foreign Secretary promised the Jews a national home in Palestine.
46. 80 Squadron Operations Record Book, PRO Air 27, 669, 9 June 1941.
47. Ibid., 16 June.
48. See above, note 30.
49. Letter from Sir Edward Gordon Jones.
50. Letter from Creekmore Fath.
51. Interview with Robin Hogg.
52. *Over To You*, Penguin, 1973, p. 23.
53. FSG.

CHAPTER 4

MAIN SOURCES:

AK; CM; WD.

Interviews with Annabella, Sir Isaiah Berlin, Tessa Dahl, Creekmore Fath, Martha Gellhorn, Antoinette Haskell, Alice Keene (Matthew Smith's executrix), Stephen Koch, Helen Lillie, Claudia Marsh, David Ogilvy, Claudia Warner.

Going Solo; 'Lucky Break'; 'Searching for Mr Smith', 1979, reprinted in *Matthew Smith*, catalogue of the Barbican Art Gallery exhibition of 1983, pp. 54–5.

Brinkley, David, *Washington Goes to War: The Extraordinary Story of the Transformation of a City*, 1988.

Caro, Robert A., *The Years of Lyndon Johnson*, vol. 1 *The Path to Power*, 1982.

Cave Brown, Anthony, *The Secret Servant: The life of Sir Stewart Menzies, Churchill's Spymaster*, 1988.

Hyde, H. Montgomery, *The Quiet Canadian: The Secret Service Story of Sir William Stephenson*, 1962.

Nicholas, H. G., ed., *Washington Despatches 1941–45. Weekly Reports from the British Embassy*, 1981.

Shale, Richard, *Donald Duck Joins Up: The Walt Disney Studio During World War II*, 1982.

For Dahl's own version of his career in British Security Co-ordination I have used his accounts to Chris Powling in *Roald Dahl* (1983), to Terry Lane for ABC, and on a CBC TV programme about Sir William Stephenson, *A Man Called Intrepid*, 1974. Dahl also talked about all this to Professor Stephen Koch, in connection with his forthcoming book on literary spies.

NOTES:

1. *Matthew Smith*, catalogue of the Barbican Art Gallery exhibition of 1983, p. 42.
2. See Dahl's article 'Searching for Mr Smith', 1979, reprinted in the catalogue of the Matthew Smith exhibition (see note 1), pp. 54–5.
3. *Matthew Smith*, p. 50.
4. See Justin Wintle, *The Pied Pipers: interviews with the influential creators of children's literature*, 1974.
5. ABC interview with Terry Lane.
6. See below, p. 56f.

7. Interview with Sir Isaiah Berlin.
8. Berlin added, 'Captain Hornblower was a kind, generous, sweet, second-rate imitator and admirer of Somerset Maugham (who in turn was an imitator of Maupassant).'
9. *Going Solo*, p. 97.
10. The revised text appeared as 'A Piece of Cake' in *OTY*, first published in 1946, and again in *WSHS*, 1977, where it is subtitled 'My first story – 1942'.
11. Interview with Martha Gellhorn.
12. Brinkley, David, *Washington Goes to War: The Extraordinary Story of the Transformation of a City*, 1988, Chapter VI, 'Parties for a Purpose'.
13. Brinkley, op. cit., p. 152.
14. Brinkley, op.cit., p. 160.
15. Interview with Tessa Dahl.
16. *As I Am*, p. 157.
17. Page, Graham, and Morley, Sheridan, eds., *The Noël Coward Diaries*, 1982, p. 69, 22 May 1951.
18. Isaiah Berlin, for example, recalls Dahl's dramatic response to being offered a house for rent after its occupier, a woman official of OSS, had been shot dead by her lover. 'He went along and sat in the twilight to see if ghosts would occur – which as a creative writer he would find disturbing to cope with. The ghosts duly appeared, and he did not take the house.' Berlin was also house-hunting at the time, and when Dahl told him about the place and the reason for his decision, Berlin unsuperstitiously rented it. He lived there with a friend for two or three years, undisturbed by ghosts.
19. *Switch Bitch*, p 38.
20. Information in this section comes from correspondence in the Walt Disney archives (hereafter WD), used by permission of © The Walt Disney Company.
21. Shale, Richard, *Donald Duck Joins Up: The Walt Disney Studio During World War II*, 1982.
22. WD 13 July 1942.
23. *Cosmopolitan*, December 1942.

24. WD 19 May 1943.
25. WD 14 October 1942.
26. WD 30 November 1942.
27. WD 1 February 1943.
28. WD 8 November 1942.
29. Minutes of story meeting, WD 20 August 1943.
30. WD 8 October 1942.
31. WD 22 May 1943.
32. Wynn, Kenneth G., *Men of the Battle of Britain*, 1989, pp. 40–41.
33. WD 20 September 1942.
34. WD 18 September 1942.
35. WD 7 October 1942.
36. In his autobiographical piece, 'Lucky Break: How I Became A Writer', he says 'I also had a go at a story for children. It was called "The Gremlins", and this I believe was the first time the word had been used' (*WSHS* p. 216). In an interview with him on Australian radio in 1989, Terry Lane tried to suggest that the gremlins had already been widely current in RAF lore, but Dahl insisted that it was he who had put them there.
37. They appeared in the *Ladies' Home Journal* in March and September 1945.
38. Interview with Creekmore Fath.
39. Hyde, op. cit., p. 190.
40. Powling, p. 44.
41. Interviews with Sir Isaiah Berlin, Creekmore Fath and David Ogilvy.
42. Correspondence with Helen Lillie, according to whom Stephenson gave a military rank and a uniform to anyone working with agents.
43. Letter from Ministry of Defence RAF Personnel Management Centre: 'After a thorough search of the above officer's records, I can find no indication that he served either in the substantive or acting rank of Wing Commander.'
44. Correspondence with Helen Lillie.
45. Powling, op. cit., p. 43; CBC TV's *A Man Called Intrepid*; Terry Lane interview.

46. The pamphlet's title was *Our Job in the Pacific*. One of the authors was the controversial sinologist Owen Lattimore. See Cave Brown, *The Secret Servant*, pp. 482–3.

47. See *Washington Despatches 1941–45*, 4 March 1942 and *passim*. Indian independence was another of Clare Boothe Luce's hobby-horses. Noël Coward wrote in his diary on 20 February 1943, that he had just seen her and 'she became rather shrill over the Indian question' (Payn, Graham, and Morley, Sheridan, eds, *The Noël Coward Diaries*, 1982).

48. *Washington Despatches 1941–45*, 21 February 1943.

49. See Chisholm, Anne and Davie, Michael, *Beaverbrook*, 1992, p. 447.

50. CM 31 March 1943.

51. CM 5 April 1943.

52. Letter from Helen Lillie. She adds, 'I think it was in character that he should predominantly write for children, where his superiority was assured.'

53. Interview with Annabella.

54. *Ladies' Home Journal*, May 1949.

55. 'My Lady Love, My Dove', *SLY*, pp. 57–72.

56. Ibid., p 61.

57. Interview with David Ogilvy.

58. Interview with David Ogilvy.

59. AK 30 July 1943.

60. AK 10 August 1943.

61. AK 23 August, 1943.

CHAPTER 5

MAIN SOURCES:

AK; BBC; CM.

Interviews with Tessa Dahl, Martha Gellhorn, Antoinette Haskell, Claudia Marsh, Dennis Pearl, Claudia Warner.

ASML (Preface); *OTY*; *Sometime Never.*

Brians, Paul, *Nuclear Holocausts: Atomic War in Fiction 1895–1984*, 1987.

NOTES:

1. To her grandchildren and others in the family, she became 'Mormor', the Norwegian word for grandmother (literally, 'mother's mother').
2. CM 28 February 1946.
3. CM 9 March 1948.
4. CM 5 September 1946.
5. Preface to *ASML*.
6. Told by Dahl to Stephen Roxburgh.
7. RD interview with Brian Sibley, 'Meridian', BBC World Service, November 1988.
8. 'The Ratcatcher', 'Ah, Sweet Mystery of Life', 'Mr Hoddy' and 'Rummins' respectively. Some of these, along with the dog-race story 'Mr Feasey', appeared in the 'Claud's Dog' section of *Someone Like You* (first published in the USA in 1953). They were all collected, with 'Parson's Pleasure' and 'The Champion of the World', as *Ah, Sweet Mystery of Life* (1989).
9. Preface to *ASML*, p. vii.
10. CM 19 and 22 December 1946.
11. *OTY*, pp. 152–3.
12. See above, p. 74.
13. Payn, Graham, and Morley, Sheridan, eds., *The Noël Coward Diaries*, 1982, p. 50, 29 January 1946.
14. *TLS*, 18 January 1947.
15. *Saturday Review of Literature*, 9 March 1946.
16. BBC 23 August 1948.
17. CM 22 July and 12 October 1947.
18. CM 19 July 1946.
19. CM 28 September 1946.
20. Brians, Paul, *Nuclear Holocausts: Atomic War in Fiction 1895–1984*, 1987.

21. See Mayo, Marlene J., 'Literary Representation in Occupied Japan: Incidents of Civil Censorship', in *Legacies and Ambiguities: Postwar Fiction and Culture in West Germany and Japan*, edited by Schlant, Ernestine, and Rimer, J. Thomas, 1991, p. 150.
22. *Sometime Never*, p. 53.
23. Ibid., p. 100.
24. Ibid., p. 112.
25. Ibid., p. 236.
26. As published, *Sometime Never* reads as if no one at Scribner's more than glanced at it before sending it to the printer. On one page, the idea that the pilots look as if they have been poured into their chairs is repeated three times (p. 33). On another, Dahl doodles: 'All day the flying men were up there in the sky, always moving; moving, moving, moving, so that movement became a function of their lives . . . Movement swirled around them . . . Movement followed them', etc. (p. 40).
27. Ibid., p. 143.
28. CM (copy of letter to Stuart Rose), November 1946.
29. BBC 7 July 1948.
30. BBC 23 August and 9 September 1948.
31. BBC 14 September 1948.
32. BBC 28 November 1948.
33. BBC 10 January 1949.
34. BBC 8 and 17 March, 1 August and 13 September 1949.
35. BBC 5 September 1951.
36. In the first half of 1949, the pound was worth more than $4. (By 1950 it had dropped to $2.80.) *Whitaker's Almanac* says that the purchasing power of sterling at the time was roughly fourteen times what it is today.
37. CM 5 May 1949.
38. On 29 October 1949, he wrote to Marsh that he had suffered two months of imaginative constipation.
39. CM 5 May 1949.
40. *Saturday Evening Post*, 20 September 1947. The story was collected in *WSHS*, pp. 52–81.

41. CM 22 July 1947.
42. CM 11 October 1945.
43. CM 22 July 1946.
44. CM 26 July 1946.
45. CM 1 August 1947. The 'reply' to Sydney Rothman is dated 30 July. The Settlement remains active, and several survivors of the 1940s are involved. Since none of them has any recollection of Dahl's letter, it seems safe to assume that he neither sent it, nor intended to. I am grateful to the Settlement's former director, Nick Collins, for his help.
46. CM 14 September 1946.
47. Interviews with Claudia Warner and Antoinette Haskell.
48. BBC 5 September 1951.
49. CM 28 May and June 11 1946.
50. CM 2 April and 19 July 1946.
51. CM 22 May 1950.
52. MS, no date, and interview with Alice Keene.
53. CM 23 October 1950.
54. CM 14 October 1950.
55. CM 10 September [1953]. (Year supplied by Patricia Neal.)
56. CM 11 May 1947, 6 April and 29 October 1948, 4 June 1949.
57. Interviews with Alice Keene and Antoinette Haskell.
58. CM 17 August 1950.
59. CM 3 September 1950.
60. CM 6 April 1948.
61. CM 10 September 1951.
62. Interview with Martha Gellhorn.
63. CM 10 September 1951.

CHAPTER 6

MAIN SOURCES:

AK; BBC; CM.

Interviews with Betsy Drake, Colin Fox, Brendan Gill, Edmund and Marian Goodman, Antoinette Haskell, Alice Keene, Patricia Neal, David Ogilvy.

As I Am.

Johnson, Diane, *Dashiell Hammett: A Life*, 1983.

NOTES:

1. Johnson, Diane, *Dashiell Hammett: A Life*, 1983, p. 211.
2. Interview with Brendan Gill.
3. Quoted by Diane Johnson, op. cit., p. 229.
4. *As I Am*, pp. 110–11.
5. Ibid., p. 131.
6. Ibid., p. 133.
7. Ibid., p. 139.
8. CM 10 February 1952
9. Interview with Antoinette Haskell.
10. See above, pp. 85–6.
11. *Memories with Food*, p. 225
12. BBC 13 September 1951.
13. *SLY*, p. 10.
14. Interview with Brough Girling.
15. Interview with Angela Hogg.
16. *As I Am*, p. 155.
17. Ibid., p. 160.
18. Interview with Colin Fox.
19. Patricia Neal, who is still friendly with Fox, says, 'Colin was not an orphan. He was a Cockney reared at home with two parents and a sister.'
20. *As I Am*, p. 166.
21. Diane Johnson, op. cit., p. 275.
22. CM 25 April 1952
23. *As I Am*, p. 158.
24. Ibid., p. 158. Interviews with Patricia Neal and Dennis Pearl.
25. CM 17 February 1953.

26. CM February 1952.
27. Dahl's dealings with Knopf are recorded in the firm's archives (hereafter AK) in the Harry Ransom Humanities Research Center at the University of Texas at Austin.
28. AK 24 March 1952.
29. AK 17 June 1952.
30. See above, p. 73.
31. *New Yorker*, 17 May 1952.
32. *New Yorker*, 19 January 1952.
33. 'The Ratcatcher', 'Rummins' and 'Mr Hoddy'.
34. See above, p. 65.
35. AK 10 March 1952.
36. *Harper's*, September 1953.
37. 'Galloping Foxley', *Town and Country*, October 1953.
38. *Collier's*, September 1953.
39. *SLY*, p. 168.
40. *SLY*, p. 177.
41. *SLY*, p. 186.
42. Interview with Alice Keene.
43. *SLY*, pp. 179, 169, 171.
44. *As I Am*, p 170.
45. MS 14 May 1953.
46. CM 20 June 1953.
47. CM 1 October 1953.
48. CM 20 June 1953.
49. Diane Johnson, op. cit., p. 275.
50. Interview with Maria Tucci Gottlieb, who was told this by Mildred Dunnock.
51. CM 1954, no date.
52. See, for example, the petrol station in *Danny*.
53. This came out in the 1978 TV programme, *This Is Your Life*, devoted to Neal.
54. CM January 1954.
55. Interview with Claudia Marsh; *As I Am*, p 156.
56. Interview with Claudia Marsh.
57. CM 19 January 1954.

58. *As I Am*, p. 182.
59. Information from Claudia Warner.

CHAPTER 7

MAIN SOURCES:

AK; CM; MS.

Interviews with Annabella, Betsy Drake, Alice Keene, Patricia Neal, Charles Pick, Marina Warner.

As I Am; *The Dahl Diary, 1992.*

Bryce, Ivar, *You only live once: Memories of Ian Fleming*, 1975.

NOTES:

1. *New York Times*, 8 November 1953.
2. Charles A. Brady in the *Buffalo News*, AK cuttings file.
3. AK January 1954, no date.
4. *Post*, Houston, Texas, 10 January 1954.
5. *TLS*, 11 June 1954.
6. CM [summer] 1954, no date.
7. *KK*, p. 46.
8. AK 3 January 1955.
9. CM February 1955, no date.
10. *As I Am*, p. 190.
11. *As I Am*, p. 191.
12. *As I Am*, p. 191.
13. CM 20 May 1955
14. CM 31 August 1955.
15. 'Some Notes on Keeping a Diary', in *The Dahl Diary, 1992.*
16. These details come from *The Dahl Diary, 1992.*
17. BBC *Bookmark*.
18. 'Parson's Pleasure', 'Royal Jelly', 'Mrs Bixby and the Colonel's Coat', 'William and Mary' (again), 'Genesis and Catastrophe', 'Mrs Mulligan' and 'Pig'.

19. Interview with Alice Keene.
20. Interview with Marina Warner.
21. Bryce, Ivar, *You only live once: Memories of Ian Fleming*, 1975.
22. Interview with Marina Warner.
23. Dahl postcard to Matthew Smith, March 1958.
24. Quoted in *As I Am*, p. 206.
25. *New Yorker*, 9 September 1958.
26. CM no date: received 11 July [1954].
27. *As I Am*, p. 210.
28. Interview with David Ogilvy.
29. *As I Am*, p. 213.
30. Interview with Charles Pick.
31. It appeared in the *Sunday Times* on 5 June 1960.
32. *Times Literary Supplement*, 28 October 1960.
33. *New York Times*, 7 February 1960.
34. Robert Phelps, unattributed review in Knopf file on *KK*.
35. *Harvard Crimson*, 19 March 1960.
36. *Peterborough Examiner* (Ontario), 18 June 1960.
37. AK 13 April 1960.
38. Letter from Hans Georg Heepe of Rowohlt Verlag.
39. AK 2 May 1960.
40. AK 11 July 1960.
41. *JGP*, p 133.
42. AK 5 July 1960.
43. AK 26 August 1960.

CHAPTER 8

MAIN SOURCES:

AK.

Interviews with Amanda Conquy, Annabella, Camilla Corbin, Tessa Dahl, Betsy Drake, Virginie Fowler Elbert, Edmund and

Marian Goodman, Angela Kirwan Hogg, Alice Keene, Gerald Savory, Kenneth Till, Patricia Neal.

As I Am; *Pat and Roald*.

For medical details in this chapter I am particularly indebted to my conversation with Kenneth Till, and to two articles by him published in *Lancet*, 25 January 1964, p. 202: 'A valve for the treatment of hydrocephalus' and 'Introducer for intraventricular catheter used in treatment of hydrocephalus'.

NOTES:

1. Interview with Edmund and Marian Goodman.
2. Letter from Patricia Neal.
3. Interview with Patricia Neal.
4. Interview with Angela Kirwan Hogg.
5. *As I Am*, p. 216.
6. Interview with Edmund and Marian Goodman.
7. Interview with Kenneth Till, and his notes in *Lancet*, 25 January 1964, p. 202, see above.
8. *As I Am*, p. 219.
9. AK 28 January 1961.
10. AK undated cutting.
11. AK 17 April 1961.
12. *As I Am*, p. 245.
13. *This Is Your Life*, 1978.
14. CM 4 June 1949; interview with Angela Kirwan Hogg.
15. Interview with Kenneth Till.
16. AK 9 June 1962.
17. Interviews with Camilla Corbin and Amanda Conquy.
18. Interviews with Patricia Neal and Alice Keene.
19. AK 3 October 1962.
20. *As I Am*, p. 230.
21. Dahl, quoted by Barry Farrell in *Life* magazine, 22 October 1966.
22. AK 4 February 1963.
23. *As I Am*, p. 238.

24. AK 19 April 1963.

25. *As I Am*, p. 239. One Christmas several years afterwards, their third daughter Ophelia (then herself aged seven) asked him why God had allowed Olivia to die. Dahl said, 'Have you ever thought that there might not be a God after all?' ('What I told Ophelia and Lucy about God', *Redbook: The Magazine for Young Women*, December 1971.) Dahl was as contrary in his disbelief as in other matters. On holiday in France in 1967, he put the case for faith to a depressed Patricia Neal, and said that whenever he was in church he tried to commune with Olivia. (*Pat and Roald*, pp. 207–8.)

26. Interview with Gerald Savory. Savory had first met them when he directed a brief British run of Dahl's play, *The Honeys*.

27. Interview with Annabella.

28. Interviews with Tessa and Lucy Dahl, and Patricia Neal.

29. AK 16 April 1963

30. *Library Journal*, 15 November 1961.

31. *Boston Herald*, 19 November 1961.

32. AK 4 February 1963; telephone interview with Michael de Capua.

33. AK 30 January and 7 February 1963

34. AK 4 February and 19 April 1963.

35. Interview with Virginie Fowler Elbert.

36. AK 26 April 1963

37. AK 21 May 1963.

38. See below, p. 186f.

39. *CCF*, p. 74.

40. *CCF*, p. 160.

41. ABC interview with Terry Lane; *As I Am*, p. 251.

42. Interview with Patricia Neal. Dahl himself told different versions of the story, the blandest of them to Barry Farrell: 'He had sold his first original screenplay . . . in the month after Pat's stroke, but in his urgency had settled for half the money agreed upon, and the unpleasantness of that experience only confirmed his aversion to any dealings involving producers and directors.' (*Pat and Roald*, p. 151).

43. *As I Am*, p. 245.
44. AK 17 June 1964. The eventual film was *Thirty-Six Hours*, directed by George Seaton.
45. See above, p. 56.
46. *Library Journal*, 15 December 1964.

CHAPTER 9

MAIN SOURCES:

AK.

Interviews with Annabella, Betsy Drake, Edmund and Marian Goodman, Valerie Eaton Griffith, Angela Kirwan Hogg, Patricia Neal, Dennis Pearl, Judy Taylor, Kenneth Till.

As I Am; *Pat and Roald*.

Eaton Griffith, Valerie, *A Stroke in the Family*, 1975, and *'So they tell me': an encounter with stroke*, 1989.

NOTES:

1. *As I Am*, p. 238.
2. Barry Farrell, *Life* magazine, 22 October 1965.
3. Interviews with Angela Kirwan Hogg, Dennis Pearl and others.
4. AK 12 May 1964.
5. AK 9 October 1964.
6. The history of Dahl's early dealings with British publishers over his children's books is set out in a letter asking for advice from Alfred Knopf's wife Blanche: AK 27 November 1964.
7. AK 24 November 1964.
8. AK 4 December 1964
9. Interview with Judy Taylor. She found Richard Adams, whose *Watership Down* she was also to reject, similarly imperious.
10. *Daily News* 24 August 1964.
11. When he got into *Who's Who* in 1976, he listed his recreations

as 'gaming, cultivating orchids (phalaenopsids only), drinking fine wine, collecting paintings, furniture and antique objects of all kinds.' The list changed in subsequent years, and the orchid house gave way to a guest wing.

12. Interview with Angela Kirwan Hogg.
13. *As I Am*, pp. 250–2.
14. 'The Last Act', *Switch Bitch*, pp. 103–111.
15. NY 21 April 1965.
16. *Switch Bitch*, pp. 105–6.
17. Interview with Dennis Pearl.
18. 'The Bookseller', *Playboy*, January 1987.
19. Information from Alice K. Turner, Fiction Editor of *Playboy*.
20. Cozzens, James Gould, 'Foot in It', *Redbook*, lxv, August 1935; anthologized as 'Clerical Error' in Ellery Queen, ed., *The Literature of Crime*, 1950. Information supplied by Alice K. Turner, Fiction Editor of *Playboy*.
21. *As I Am*, p. 252.
22. *Pat and Roald*, p. 8.
23. For this section I have depended on an article in the 'Medicine' section of *Time* magazine, 26 March 1965, as well as Patricia Neal's own account in *As I Am* and Barry Farrell's in *Pat and Roald*. Some details are owed to interviews with Angela Kirwan Hogg and Kenneth Till.
24. *Working for Love*, p. 49.
25. *As I Am*, p. 261. Interviews with Patricia Neal and Valerie Eaton Griffith.
26. *As I Am*, p. 263.
27. Interview with Angela Kirwan Hogg.
28. Interviews with Betsy Drake and Angela Kirwan Hogg.
29. Foreword to Eaton Griffith, Valerie, *A Stroke in the Family*, p. 9.
30. Interview with Valerie Eaton Griffith.
31. *Pat and Roald*, p. 125.
32. Article by Barry Farrell in *TV Guide*, 5 December 1981.
33. *Pat and Roald*, p. 65.
34. AK 5 April 1965.

35. Interview with Virginie Fowler Elbert.
36. AK 5 April 1965.
37. AK 7 April 1965.
38. *Pat and Roald*, p. 85.
39. *Life*, 22 October 1965. The article was reprinted as part of the printed programme for 'An Evening with Patricia Neal', on behalf of the New York Association for Brain-Injured Children, 12 March 1967.

CHAPTER 10

MAIN SOURCES:

AK.

Interviews with Harold Jack Bloom, Amanda Conquy, Camilla Corbin, Tessa Dahl, Lewis Gilbert, Valerie Eaton Griffith, Ken Hughes, Patricia Neal, Alastair Reid, Mel Stuart.

As I Am; *Pat and Roald*; Powling.

Hibbin, Sally, *The Official James Bond Movie Book*, 1987.
Rubin, Steven Jay, *The James Bond Films*, 1981.

This chapter also draws on the cuttings files at the Margaret Herrick Library, Los Angeles, and on information in Leslie Halliwell's reference books, *Halliwell's Film Guide* (7th edition, 1989) and *The Filmgoer's Companion* (9th edition, 1988).

NOTES:

1. *As I Am*, p. 291.
2. AK 9 February 1966.
3. *Life* magazine, 22 October 1965; AK 14 December 1967.
4. AK 24 April 1967.
5. Pearson, John, *The Life of Ian Fleming, Creator of James Bond*, 1966, 1989 edn, pp. 312, 323.

6. See Rubin, Steven Jay, *The James Bond Films*, 1981, and Hibbin, Sally, *The Official James Bond Movie Book*, 1987.
7. For example in *Playboy*, June 1967, p. 86, and in Powling, p. 55.
8. See note 6, above.
9. Telephone interview with Lewis Gilbert.
10. Telephone interview with Harold Jack Bloom.
11. *Variety Weekly*, 14 June 1967.
12. *New Yorker*, 24 June 1967.
13. Interview with Patricia Neal.
14. AK 2 May 1966: in-house report on the television programme transmitted on 25 April.
15. Eaton Griffith, Valerie, *A Stroke In The Family*, p. 12.
16. Eaton Griffith, Valerie, 'So They Tell Me', p. 4.
17. Interview with Colin Fox.
18. Conversation with Caroline Seebohm.
19. *As I Am*, p. 277.
20. AK 14 December 1967; *Pat and Roald*, pp. 202f, 212f.
21. Interview with Tessa Dahl. Nicholas Logsdail is now an art dealer.
22. Interview with Valerie Eaton Griffith; *Pat and Roald*, p. 214.
23. *Pat and Roald*, p. 209.
24. Telephone interview with Ken Hughes.
25. *New York Times*, 22 October 1967.
26. *New Yorker*, 4 January 1969.
27. For example to Powling, p. 58.
28. Margaret Herrick Library folder on *Chitty Chitty Bang Bang*.
29. His copy of the screenplay, which is in the Richard Maibaum collection at the Margaret Herrick Library in Los Angeles, gives visible evidence of the 'retreading': at least five different typewriters were used.
30. *Pat and Roald*, p. 181.
31. AK 2 April 1968.
32. Interview with Valerie Eaton Griffith.
33. Interview with Alastair Reid.
34. *Hollywood Reporter*, 12 January 1971.
35. *Variety*, 12 January 1971.

36. Dennis Pearl strongly defends Dahl's behaviour. 'He was absolutely certain that the only way to restore anything like normality was to compel Pat to make unceasing efforts herself. This was not easy . . . But he knew it was absolutely vital and that he simply must not let up. Some people . . . have been critical, but they knew nothing whatever about the subject.'
37. Interview with Mel Stuart.
38. Interview with Mel Stuart.

CHAPTER 11

MAIN SOURCES:

AK.

Interviews with Lucy Dahl, Tessa Dahl, Robert and Maria Gottlieb, Valerie Eaton Griffith, Patricia Neal, Rayner Unwin.

As I Am.

Crosscurrents of Criticism: Horn Book Essays, 1968–1977, selected and edited by Paul Heins, 1977.

NOTES:

1. AK 31 March 1968.
2. AK 5 November 1968.
3. Interview with Rayner Unwin.
4. For example in *The Times*, 25 November 1967.
5. *Bookseller*, 2 December 1967.
6. AK 9 February 1966.
7. AK 22 March 1968.
8. AK 16 July 1968.
9. AK 6 April 1968.
10. AK 11 August 1968.
11. AK 17 July 1968.
12. AK 31 October 1968.
13. AK 20 November 1968.

14. AK 21 July 1968.
15. AK 25 November 1968.
16. Interview with Tessa Dahl.
17. Interview with Lucy Dahl.
18. Interviews with Rayner Unwin and Tony Lacey.
19. See above, p. 119.
20. See above, p. 56.
21. *The Horn Book*, October 1972, pp. 433–40. Reprinted in *Crosscurrents of Criticism: Horn Book Essays, 1968–1977*, selected and edited by Paul Heins, 1977.
22. Ibid., p. 437.
23. *The Horn Book*, February 1973. Also reprinted in Paul Heins's selection, referred to above in note 21.
24. Ibid.

CHAPTER 12

MAIN SOURCES:

AK.

Interviews with Annabella, Robert and Helen Bernstein, Lucy Dahl, Tessa Dahl, Colin Fox, Robert Gottlieb, Valerie Eaton Griffith, Patricia Neal, Dennis Pearl, Ian Rankin, Rayner Unwin.

As I Am.

NOTES:

1. Interviews with Rayner Unwin and Ian Rankin.
2. Interview with Ian Rankin.
3. Interview with Valerie Eaton Griffith.
4. The Volunteer Stroke Scheme is part of the Stroke Association (formerly the Chest, Heart and Stroke Association), CHSA House, Whitecross Street, London EC1Y 8JJ.
5. *Danny*, p. 8.

6. *Danny*, p. 26.
7. Interviews with Betsy Drake and Patricia Neal.
8. Interviews with Tessa Dahl and Patricia Neal.
9. Interview with Annabella.
10. Quoted in an article by Barry Farrell in *TV Guide*, 5 December 1981.
11. Angela Levin in *You* magazine, 6 October 1991.
12. Information from Valerie Finnis.
13. *Memories with Food*, p. 48.
14. Interview with Ian Rankin.
15. Interviews with Alastair Reid and Brough Girling; conversation with Martin Amis.
16. Conversation with Gitta Sereny.
17. Interviews with Robert and Helen Bernstein.
18. Some years later, the literary critic Hermione Lee visited Gipsy House to interview Dahl for a television programme. He spoke aggressively against literary criticism and academia, and the pointlessness of writing books about people like Virginia Woolf and Elizabeth Bowen – as Lee herself had done.
19. Hyde, H. Montgomery, *The Quiet Canadian: The Secret Service Story of Sir William Stephenson*, 1962.
20. Interview with Colin Fox.
21. *As I Am*, p. 325f.
22. *As I Am*, p. 337.
23. The letter is quoted verbatim in *As I Am*, p. 339.
24. Correspondence with the Society of Authors, 1 and 5 February 1976.
25. See below, p. 229.
26. *WSHS*, p. 174.
27. Patricia Neal to Charles and Claudia Marsh, CM [1954].
28. AK 24 April; 4, 18 and 25 May 1979.
29. Interviews with Edmund and Marian Goodman; conversations with Richard Hough, John Mortimer, Kaye Webb and others.
30. *Evening Standard*, 25 October 1979.
31. AK cuttings file, autumn 1980.

32. Interview with Lucy Dahl.
33. AK 4 June 1979.
34. AK 11 May 1987.
35. AK 4 December 1979.
36. At this stage, Dahl called these poems *Dirty Beasts*. Both the title and some of the rhymes he originally submitted to Knopf were in the event saved for his next book of verses, which was published in the USA by Farrar Straus Giroux. (See below, pp. 217f.).
37. AK 22 September 1980.

CHAPTER 13

MAIN SOURCES:

AK; FSG; Cape production files at Reading University Library.

Interviews with Quentin Blake, Robert Gottlieb, Tom Maschler, Stephen Roxburgh, Roger Straus.

NOTES:

1. Alfonso's first name is given there as Alphonsus, Sofie's as Sophie.
2. *Memories with Food*, pp. 32, 48.
3. For this section I have drawn on interviews with Quentin Blake and Tom Maschler, and correspondence with several of Dahl's other illustrators and publishers: see Further Acknowledgements.
4. These terms were negotiated for the Dahl/Blake books which followed *The Enormous Crocodile*, in a series of letters between Dahl and Gottlieb between January and May 1980.
5. AK 6 August 1980.
6. AK 4 December 1979.
7. AK 4 March 1980.
8. AK 22 September 1980.

9. See above, p. 81.
10. See below, p. 221f.
11. AK 12 February 1980.
12. AK 4 March 1980.
13. Interview with Robert Gottlieb.
14. AK 8 June 1980
15. AK 1 July 1980.
16. AK 10 February 1981.
17. The paperback deal (with Bantam) was made in July 1977.
18. AK 26 January 1981.
19. AK 10 February 1981.
20. AK 5 March 1981, and interview with Robert Gottlieb.
21. FSG 29 December 1981.
22. Ibid.
23. Ørnulf Hodne's *The Types of the Norwegian Fairytale* is full of stories which in outline resemble Dahl's: encounters like those in *The BFG* between children, ogres and royal personages are particularly common. Another type involves several different creatures on a voyage, in the course of which, as in *James and the Giant Peach*, each expresses its fear in a characteristic way. Many of the tales are set in magical underworlds like that in *Charlie and the Chocolate Factory*, or concern children with magical powers, or encounters between children and witches. Fox fables are also common, of course, as they are in all western European folk cultures. So are elixirs and other transforming potions. Hans Andersen has a story about miraculous flight on a swan's back (cf. p. 253, below); Grimm has several involving the pursuit of fabulous wealth in which, as in *Charlie and the Chocolate Factory*, the pursuer is required to achieve the correct balance between being greedy and being too greedy.
24. Valerie Buckingham's notes on *The BFG* and Dahl's comments on them, in the FSG file on the book.
25. *The BFG*, p. 104. Dahl added the words, ' "Boys would," Sophie said.'
26. FSG 14 February 1982.

27. The Bloodbottler's words about Chileans which appear on p. 61 of the Puffin edition, and the conversation between the Queen of England and the King of Sweden, p. 173.
28. See note 26.
29. FSG 1 March 1982.
30. FSG 25 October 1984.
31. *Roald Dahl's Book of Ghost Stories*, 1983.
32. FSG 26 March 1983.
33. Interview with Quentin Blake.
34. Interview with Tom Maschler.
35. For example, Anne Pasternak Slater in *Harper's and Queen*.
36. Letter from Hans Georg Heepe, of Rowohlt.
37. Letter from Koukla MacLehose.
38. Russell Davies, *Sunday Times*, 28 August 1983.
39. *TLS*, 22 July 1983.
40. FSG 16 May 1983.
41. Maria Salvadore, District of Columbia Public Library, in FSG cuttings file.
42. Omaha Public Schools review sheet in FSG cuttings file.
43. Murray Pollinger to Roger Straus, FSG 17 November 1981.
44. According to Cape's production records, in the archives at the Reading University Library, the first printing of 25,000 sold out, and Cape printed a further 10,000 copies. But correspondence from foreign publishers, including Gyldendal in Norway, indicates an overwhelming preference for the later Quentin Blake edition.
45. See above, pp. 217–18.
46. Interview with Stephen Roxburgh.
47. Letter from Stephen Roxburgh.
48. Interview with Stephen Roxburgh.
49. *The Witches*, p. 21.
50. *The BFG*, p. 53.
51. *TES*, 27 December 1985.
52. Michèle Landsberg's *Guide to Children's Books*, 1986.
53. Ibid., p. 72.
54. *New York Times Book Review*, 13 November 1983.

55. FSG 20 May 1983.
56. FSG 25 October 1984.
57. FSG 28 April 1983.
58. FSG 16 May 1983.

CHAPTER 14

MAIN SOURCES:

FSG; files of the *Literary Review*.

Interviews with Elizabeth Attenborough, Lucy Dahl, Tessa Dahl, Valerie Eaton Griffith, Tom Maschler, Peter Mayer, Anthony Page, Stephen Roxburgh, Roger Straus.

NOTES:

1. Interview with Roger Straus.
2. FSG 15 May 1987.
3. FSG 23 August 1987.
4. FSG 22 June 1987.
5. Interview with Martha Gellhorn.
6. Dahl no longer wanted it to be publicized that he wrote for *Playboy*, and when the magazine bought parts of *My Uncle Oswald*, insisted on a contract which did not require him to acknowledge the fact in the eventual book. (AK 15 November 1979.)
7. FSG 20 May 1983.
8. Interviews with Tom Maschler and Stephen Roxburgh.
9. Interview with Brough Girling.
10. Chris Powling, *Roald Dahl*, 1983.
11. FSG 28 April 1983.
12. Interview with Anthony Page.
13. Powling, p. 11.
14. Powling, p. 42.
15. Powling, p. 43.

16. See above, pp. 143–4.
17. Powling, pp. 58–9.
18. FSG 14 February 1984.
19. FSG 15 May 1984.
20. FSG 17 August 1984.
21. FSG 26 September 1984.
22. FSG 26 September 1984.
23. Interviews with Stephen Roxburgh and Tom Maschler.
24. Interview with Tom Maschler.
25. FSG 11 and 14 September 1984
26. Powling, p. 66. Dahl had a variety of standard replies, comical and charming, many of them in doggerel. One – addressed to 'Dear gorgeous [name of teacher] and all the clever people at [name of school]' – began, 'Oh, wondrous children miles away, / Your letters brightened up my day'. Another ended by saying that Dahl was glad to know that he had made 'You children, and occasionally the staff / Stop work, and have instead a little laugh.' (Information supplied by Liz Attenborough and Carolyn Hemmings.)
27. 'A Visit to Roald Dahl', by 'Karen Coad', see below, pp. 240–41.
28. *Memories with Food*, p. 227.
29. Interviews with Lucy Dahl and Tessa Dahl.
30. Personal experience of the author. The *Times Literary Supplement*'s reviewer, Malcolm Yapp, was moved by the book's pictures but found the text tendentious and sensationalist. (*TLS*, 26 August 1983.)
31. *New Statesman*, 26 August 1983.
32. Interview with Sir Isaiah Berlin.
33. CM 26 July 1946.
34. See above, pp. 88–9.
35. See above, p. 82.
36. OTY, p 74.
37. Interview with Robert Gottlieb.
38. Interview with Brough Girling.

39. Quoted by Mike Coren in the *New Statesman*, 26 August 1983.
40. Article by Sebastian Faulks in the *Daily Telegraph*, 18 September 1983; files of the *Literary Review*.
41. For example in a letter to *The Times*, 19 September 1983.
42. See above, p. 89.
43. Conversation with David Wolton. Dahl was a guest at the 1989 MAP dinner where Mona Bauwens, the daughter of a PLO leader, first met the Conservative minister David Mellor, a relationship that was later to force his resignation.
44. See Malcolm Yapp's review in the *TLS*, 26 August 1983, where he argues with David Gilmour for saying this.
45. *Spectator*, 3 September 1983.
46. *New Statesman*, 26 August 1983.
47. Letters to the *New Statesman* from Marion Woolfson, and from Sidney Goldwater of the Association of Jewish Ex-Servicemen and Women, 2 and 16 September 1983.
48. *New Republic*, 31 October 1983.
49. One was Mort Levin, President of the Regent Book Company, New Jersey: FSG 19 December 1983.
50. See above, p. 44.
51. The letter was part of a project organized by Dinah Stroe, a teacher at Brandeis Hillel Day School, San Francisco, to whom, and to Vavi Toran, I am grateful for sending me copies of all the relevant material.
52. Quoted in *The Northern California Jewish Bulletin*, 3 March 1990.
53. Interview with Camilla Corbin.
54. FSG 29 May 1985
55. Puffin file, RD to Barry Cunningham at Penguin, 17 June 1985.
56. For example, in Puffin's promotional video for *Matilda* (Puffin file).
57. See above, p. 153.
58. *Playboy*, January 1988.
59. Interview with Valerie Finnis. Dahl had been friendly with the

principal of the Waterperry Gardening School, Miss Beatrix Havergal, who was now dead. Miss Havergal was a large woman, whose unchanging costume consisted of a green linen smock beneath a dark green blazer with brass buttons, green breeches, green woollen stockings, brown tie and brown felt hat. Dahl used her as a model for Miss Trunchbull's clothes and physique (but not her personality), and asked her colleague Valerie Finnis (Lady Scott) to send him a photograph of her, so that Quentin Blake would get her exactly right. He did, Lady Scott says, except that he mistakenly drew her shoes with large protruding tongues.

60. FSG 5 October 1987
61. FSG 23 December 1987.
62. FSG 15 January 1988.
63. FSG 15 January 1988.
64. Matilda, second FSG draft, pp. 24, 90. Dahl also often wrote 'your's' and 'it's' for 'yours' and 'its'.

CHAPTER 15

MAIN SOURCES:

FSG.

Interviews with Elizabeth Attenborough, Amanda Conquy, Brian Cox, Lucy Dahl, Tessa Dahl, Peter Mayer, Peggy Miller, Patricia Neal, Stephen Roxburgh, Elizabeth Stewart-Liberty.

Report of the Police Complaints Authority, 3 July 1989.

NOTES:

1. Interviews with Peter Carson and Peggy Miller.
2. FSG 23 August 1987.
3. Interview with Robin Hogg.
4. Lynn Barber, *Mostly Men*, revised edn, 1992, p. 97.
5. Telephone interview with Brian Sibley.

6. Interview with Elizabeth Stewart-Liberty.
7. Conversations with John Mortimer and Susan Mayes.
8. Interviews with Stephen Roxburgh and Tessa Dahl.
9. Letter from RD to Valerie Finnis.
10. Letters to Kenneth Baker and Brian Cox, 27 July 1988.
11. *Daily Mail*, 16 November 1988.
12. When the journalist Angela Levin raised the issue with Felicity Dahl, 'Tears welled into her eyes again. "The reaction ... meant that he lost any form of knighthood. Not that he wanted one, but he would have liked a little recognition from his country for whom he wrote great literature and fought bravely ... during the war." ' (*You* magazine, 6 October 1991.)
13. *Daily Mail*, 16 November 1988.
14. *Independent*, 21 March 1990.
15. *The Times*, 28 February 1989.
16. Conversation with Penelope Lively.
17. Conversation with Martin Amis.
18. Interview with Stephen Roxburgh.
19. *Publishers Weekly*, 15 December 1989.
20. Report of the Police Complaints Authority, 3 July 1989, and press reports, eg *Daily Telegraph* 14 July 1989.
21. Obituary note by Spiv and Marius Barran in the *Independent*, 28 November 1990. Further information from Elizabeth Attenborough and Amanda Conquy.
22. Dutch TV interview with Ivo Niehe.
23. For example to Terry Lane on ABC Radio.
24. *Guardian*, 12 August 1989.
25. Article by Christopher Sykes, *The Times*, 30 November 1990.
26. Article by Martin Kettle, *Guardian*, May 19 1990.
27. *WSHS*, pp. 84, 97.
28. Interview with Elizabeth Stewart-Liberty.
29. Interview with Tessa Dahl.
30. Interview with Amanda Conquy.
31. Interview with Patricia Neal, who lent me a recording of the service.

32. 'Do not go gentle into that good night.' Thomas, Dylan, *Collected Poems 1934–52*, 1952, p. 116.

33. Peter Mayer, 'A Tribute to Roald Dahl', privately printed, 1990.

Index

Index

Index

Index

'Parson's Pleasure', 121
Pat and Roald, 158, 188, 232
Patricia Neal Story, The, 232
Patterson, Cissy, 55
Patterson, Paul, 255–6
Pattle, Thomas, 41, 42
Pearce, Perce, 60–61
Pearl, Dennis, x, 32, 33–4, 80, 152,
    198–9
Pearson, Drew, 52
Pearson, John, 162
Peel, Major & Mrs, 43
Pegg, Antony, 30, 33
Pell, Senator Claiborne, 100
Penguin (Viking Penguin), 186, 229,
    230, 234, 240–41, 245, 251
'People Nowadays', 79, 85
Pepper, Senator Claude, 75
Phelps, Robert, 122
Phillips, Bunny and Gena, 100
Pick, Charles, 120–21, 147
'Picture for Drioli, A', 85
'Piece of Cake, A', 39
'Pig', 13, 117, 222
Pinter, Harold: *The Homecoming*, 79
Playboy, 144, 151–3, 241
Pleasence, Donald, 155
'Poison', 35–6, 93
Police Complaints Authority, 251
Pollinger, Laurence, 148, 244
Pollinger, Murray, 222
'Porcupine, The', 222
Post of Houston Texas, 111
Powell, Enoch, 249
Power, Tyrone, 71, 72, 99–100
Powling, Chris: *Roald Dahl*, 231, 232
Preminger, Hope, 155
Preminger, Otto, 136
'Princess Mammalia', 241
'Princess and the Poacher, The', 241
Priory House (Repton), 19–28
Prokosch, Frederic, 81
Psyche 59, 136
Public Schools Exploring Society, 29
Public Welfare Foundation, 87–8, 92,
    100, 116, 130, 156
Publishers Weekly, 250
Pudney, John, 64
Pumpkin Eater, The, 149, 155

Quartet, 236

Random House, 179–82, 186, 210, 211,
    215, 217, 229

Rankin, Ian, 189, 194
'Ratcatcher, The', 97, 103
Reagan, Nancy, 113
Reagan, Ronald, 94–5
Reid, Alastair, 173, 174–5
Repton, 19–28
Revolting Rhymes, 205, 212–13, 217,
    221, 222
Reynal & Hitchcock, 78
Ritt, Martin, 150
Roald Dahl Foundation, 255–6
Roald Dahl Newsletter, 252
Robinson, Sir Robert, 190
Rodgers, Richard, 95
Rogers, Millicent, 54
Roomful of Roses, A, 116
Roosevelt, Eleanor, 7, 64
Roosevelt, Franklin D., 2, 5, 55, 68,
    69–70
Rose, Stuart, 84–5
Rothman, Sydney, 88
Roxburgh, Stephen, ix, 216–20, 223–5,
    228, 231, 232–4, 241–5
Royal Air Force (RAF), 38–45, 48, 49,
    52–3, 67; gremlins, 50, 56–63, 65,
    66
Royal Family of Broadway, The, 118
'Royal Jelly', 117
Rubin, Steven Jay, 164
'Rummins', 97, 103
Runyon, Damon, 32
Rushdie, Salman: *The Satanic Verses*,
    249–50, 251

St Peter's Preparatory School, 15, 16–19
Saltzman, Harry, 162
Saturday Evening Post, 52–3, 63, 64,
    84–5, 86
Saturday Review of Literature, 78
Saunders, Wally, 129–30, 203, 208, 235
Savory, Gerald, 135
Schindelman, Joseph, 140
Scribner's, 80, 86
Secker & Warburg, 110, 112
Second World War, 37–74
Sellers, Peter, 194
Sells, (Sir) David, 25–6
Seltzer, David, 175–6
Selznick, David, 95
Sendak, Maurice, 138, 140–41
Sereny, Gitta, 196
Seven Women, 150, 153, 155
Shakespeare, William: *The Merchant of
    Venice*, 86

Index

Warner, Claudia, 6
Washington, DC, 1–6, 14, 35, 51–74
Watkins, Ann, 63, 102
Waugh, Auberon, 80
Wavell, General A., 40, 44
Way Out (television series), 128
'Way Up to Heaven, The', 112, 121, 226
Wayne, John, 100, 136, 149, 202
Weidenfeld, George (Lord Weidenfeld), 148
Welch, Denton, 20, 24; *Maiden Voyage*, 20–21
Wells, H.G.: *The World Set Free*, 81
Welty, Eudora, 81
Werfel, Franz: *Jacobowsky and the Colonel*, 71, 72
Westminster (school), 22
Whitbread Prize, 231, 248
White, Katharine S., 114
Who's Who, 213

Wilder, Thornton: *The Bridge of San Luis Rey*, 32
'William and Mary', 112–14, 121, 128, 226
Williams, Tennessee: *Cat on a Hot Tin Roof*, 116; *Suddenly Last Summer*, 119
Willkie, Wendell, 2
Willy Wonka and the Chocolate Factory (film), 174–6, 177
'Wish, The', 103
Witchball, The, 192, 195
Witches, The, 13, 220, 223–8, 231, 235; film of, 252–3
Wollheim, Richard, 22–3
Wonderful Story of Henry Sugar, The, 186, 200
Wright, Michael, 51

You Only Live Twice, 161–5
Young, Freddie, 163